TOYOTA
by TOYOTA

Reflections from the Inside Leaders
on the Techniques That
Revolutionized the Industry

Edited by
Samuel Obara and Darril Wilburn

CRC Press
Taylor & Francis Group
Boca Raton   London   New York

CRC Press is an imprint of the
Taylor & Francis Group, an **informa** business
A PRODUCTIVITY PRESS BOOK

CRC Press
Taylor & Francis Group
6000 Broken Sound Parkway NW, Suite 300
Boca Raton, FL 33487-2742

Printed in the United States of America on acid-free paper
Version Date: 20120411

International Standard Book Number: 978-1-4398-8075-3 (Hardback)

Visit the Taylor & Francis Web site at
http://www.taylorandfrancis.com

and the CRC Press Web site at
http://www.crcpress.com

Contents

Foreword ix
Introduction xi
About the Authors xiii

Chapter 1 Courage, Humility, Kaizen 1
Darril Wilburn
The Toyota Way 2001 2
Courage, Humility, Kaizen at the Heart 4
Teaching Others 14

Chapter 2 Stability and Standardized Work 21
Gerson Valentim Damiani
Importance of Standard Work 27
Why Work Using Standards? 28
Operational Procedures, Work Instructions, and Work
and Labor Procedures 29
How the Work Was Done at Toyota: Standard Work
before Technology 31
How Standard Work Was Done at Toyota after the
Introduction of Technology 32
    Factory Layout 35
    Objectives of the Layout 37
    Human Factor 38
Problems in the Implementation of Standard Work 39
Where to Place Standard Work Instructions 40

Chapter 3 Jidoka 43
Renato Eiji Kitazuka, with Carlos Moretti
Origins 43
Jidoka as a Pillar of the Toyota Production System 44
So, What Is the Purpose of Using Jidoka? 48
    Using Jidoka 49
    Implementation Stages of Jidoka 51

It Was Too Early...53
Conclusion... 54

Chapter 4 Just-In-Time and Kanban 55

Carlos Yukio Fukamizu

Just-In-Time 56
  Introduction 56
Introduction of Jidoka and Just-In-Time as the Pillars
of TPS 56
  Jidoka.. 56
  Just-In-Time Manufacturing...57
Just-In-Time (JIT)...58
  Concept 58
  Total Customer Satisfaction 59
  More Evident Waste in the Manufacturing..................... 60
  Continuous Flow Process (One-Piece Flow) and
  Pull System 62
  Lean Methodologies for Waste Elimination...................63
    Examples 63
  Kaizen (Continuous Improvement) 63
Kanban as a Technique of JIT... 64
Conclusion...69

Chapter 5 Problem-Solving PDCA 71

Sammy Obara

Definition...71
Why Problem Solving Is So Important along a Lean
Transformation...71
What Is PDCA?...74
Do You Really Need a Method?...74
How and Where to Find Problems 75
The Mosquitoes Case 76
How Well Do You Understand the Problem?.......................76
Genchi Genbutsu: The Point of Cause................................77
How Well Can You State the Problem? 78
How Well Do You Understand the Causes? 81
  Doing Well What Does Not Need to Be Done 84
Project Management 85

A Quick Note on Deadlines 85

Standardization 86

Recognition 87

A Higher Level of Recognition 88

Yokoten: Spreading the Learning Laterally 90

What Is Next? 91

Chapter 6 Toyota Kaizen Methods 93

Art Smalley

Step 1: Discover Improvement Potential 100

Step 2: Analyze the Current Method 102

Step 3: Generate Original Ideas 105

Step 4: Make a Kaizen Plan 107

Step 5: Implement the Plan 108

Step 6: Verify the Results 109

Summary 109

Chapter 7 Kaizen Culture:

The Continuous Improvement Engine 111

Stephen J. Ansuini

The Key Elements of a Kaizen Culture 112

  Visible Sponsorship and Support by Management 112

    Leadership Support 113

  Clear Purpose and Aligned Goals 115

  Evolving Continuous Improvement System 117

    Phase 1: Introduction—Participation Emphasis 117

    Phase 2: Transition—Participant Development 120

    Phase 3: Process Maturation 122

  Summary 124

Chapter 8 Elimination of Waste in Product Design..................... 127

Patrick Muller

Value Engineering/Value Analysis 127

  Waste in Process Design 127

  Waste in Product Design 128

  Toyota's Purchasing Philosophy 129

    Fair Competition Based on an Open-Door Policy....130

Mutual Prosperity Based on Mutual Trust 130
Abide by the Law...131
Toyota's Purchasing Practices 131
Cost Breakdown...131
Target Costing, VE/VA, Kaizen.....................................132
Value Engineering/Value Analysis.................................... 134
History... 134
At Toyota, Suppliers Challenges 134
VE/VA and FMEA..135
VE/VA and Marketing 135
Practical Example 136

Chapter 9 Adapting Lean for Made-to-Order/High-Mix,
Low-Volume Organizations.. 137
Greg Lane
OSKKK to Learn and Transform 139
Learning the Processes before Managing Them.................140
Constraints Require More than Quick Fixes 141
Process Focused, Not Product Focused 143
Segregating Parts to Manage Differently 146
Managing in Real-Time Necessitates Other Lean
Principles 149
Proportionally More Indirect Costs Necessitate
Lean Accounting 152
Failures..155
Summary 156

Chapter 10 Lean Logistics... 159
Robert Martichenko
Part 1: Purpose + People 159
Introduction 159
Purpose 160
Customer and 3PL Collaboration................................. 161
People and Planning...162
Part 2: Process..163
Logistics Route Design...163
Pull Replenishment 164

Velocity and Understanding the Importance
of Lead-Time Reduction 165
Driving Velocity..168
Manufacturing Plant Integration 169
Leveled Flow 170
Trailer Yard Layout and Visual Management 172
Quality at the Source and Discipline of Process 173
Lessons Learned and Conclusion...174

Chapter 11 Leading a Kaizen Culture.. 177
Bob Plummer
A TPS Symphony...178
Discovering the Kaizen Culture.......................................179
Creating and Sustaining the Kaizen Culture
in American Factories...182
Implementing TPS Methods..185
Back to the Beginning..187
Leaving GM..188

Chapter 12 Hoshin Kanri... 189
Alistair Norval, with Darril Wilburn
What Is Hoshin Kanri?... 190
Why We Need a Strategic Planning System 191
What Does This Result In?...192
Countermeasure to Strategic Planning Problems.............192
Hoshin Kanri Enables Organizations to Develop
Strategic Plans That Are 192
True North...193
Tree of Focused Activity..194
Plan, Do, Check, Act (PDCA)...196
Management Process 199
Catchball.. 200
Key Thinker...201
A3...201
The Power of Hoshin... 203
Summary 205

Index...207

Foreword

Aim therefore at great things.

—Epictetus

Why another book about the Toyota Production System (TPS or *Lean*)? Because we haven't locked in the basics, and failing to do so will have consequences.

TPS has proven effective at reducing human misery, while enhancing human potential, in manufacturing and related endeavors. The past decade, Lean thinking has spread into fields as diverse as health care, business services, and construction. We need to help the good people in these areas.

Sammy Obara and the Honsha team are well suited to this task. We have been friends and colleagues for over a decade now. The opening chapter in this volume—"Courage, Humility, Kaizen"—reflects the character and purpose of the Honsha group.

We must begin with *Purpose*, as Epictetus reminds us. Tools are secondary, yet many self-styled Lean "experts" focus on them entirely. I suppose it's easier, but it does Lean learners a great disservice.

What is our Purpose? Addressed honestly, this hard question triggers the necessary reflection on shortcomings and weaknesses that are the fuel for improvement. It is a recurring theme in this volume. My Senseis at Toyota taught me, "No need, no activity!"—excellent advice. So define your Purpose, and pull in the elegant tools of Lean as needed.

Hansei, the Japanese word meaning humble and frank reflection, is another important concept in this book. Reflection, often glossed over, is fundamental to TPS and the PDCA cycle. This book records the reflections of several Toyota veterans—reflections on how they learned TPS and how they've applied the learning in companies around the world.

My study of Aikido prepared me for the Toyota "way." I understand it as *Do* or path—one that I will walk the rest of my life. I've no doubt that the Honsha team will be there walking with me.

Pascal Dennis

President, Lean Pathways Inc. (www.leansystems.org)
Author of The Remedy, Andy & Me, *and other books.*

Introduction

Why should you buy another book on *Lean*? The number of Lean publications has been increasing as more and more organizations seek ways to remain competitive during tough times.

Is there really a need for more books? Are there really new techniques that have not been explored? How much more can you write about a topic that at its essence is simple and timeless? Will more discussion about Lean lead to complicating the topic? Can you be innovative without inventing complications to the system?

Perhaps the answer we want to hear is that yes, you should buy another book about Lean (even if you got this one as a gift, please read it).

The purpose of this book was never to cover the well-covered topics regarding the "how-to" of Lean implementation, or the concept of the "complete toolkit" as Lean is often regarded, much less to teach you anything new about Lean methodologies. Also, it is not the goal of the authors to make you an expert on the topic they wrote about.

Rather, the purpose of each author was to share their own experience when they first learned the Toyota Production System (TPS) while working at their Toyota divisions. How they learned a specific methodology, technique, or concept that they chose to share with you. Because each author had a unique learning experience, you get the advantage of seeing the different approaches used to teach, as well as the unique way these authors translate that learning to the reader. The authors are not professional writers but consider themselves professional learners and students of Lean. Knowing this, they did their best to transfer what they learned to you, the reader. While each author has a unique approach, you will also see common threads emerge as they broke down their barriers of convention to accept a totally different way of thinking: The Toyota Way.

The most common thread that weaves together their stories is that they all had to learn the hard way. We wish we could tell you that by reading this book you will be able to learn the easy way. But alas, this is not possible. We do hope that you see yourself in our experience and struggles, that you are strengthened by the knowledge that you have many companions on this Lean journey, and that we all have stumbled. Those of us who have been on the path for some time also know that there is no magical, painless way to learn Lean.

Another common thread throughout this book is the utmost respect each author has for Toyota and our mentors, many times referred to as our Senseis.

In future books we will certainly cover additional topics, but we will also see some of the same topics being described by others who learned through different contexts and situations. The abundance of different and unique experiences can, by itself, be an effective Sensei.

Altogether, this book combines a total of 105 years of inside Toyota experience in divisions as diverse as sales, training, logistics, manufacturing, and human resources. It brings experience from people who worked closely with Taiichi Ohno, the greatest TPS Sensei, and those who worked with his direct students such as Fujio Cho. It brings experience developed over years of immersion at Toyota locations such as the United States, Brazil, Venezuela, Europe, and Japan. Finally, it brings the personal testimonials of those who learned by living the system.

For our students, we know that many days you are frustrated by the difficulty in learning Lean. We know that some days you wish we had not been so tough on you. It is our hope that by reading these chapters, you will see that the light bulb had to go off in our heads, too. We had our discovery moments too. We made our share of mistakes until we learned that humility and courage go hand in hand with the Kaizen spirit. And although situations may change, these principles will never change.

Enjoy!

Sammy Obara and Darril Wilburn

About the Authors

Stephen J. Ansuini

I started working at Toyota Motor Manufacturing, Kentucky (TMMK), in 1987 in the skilled trades development area with responsibility for the development of intermediate and advanced maintenance training. In 1988, I developed the initial TPS for the office (Office Lean) and TPS for Maintenance (also known as TPM). From there I started the TMMK Suggestion System in 1989, and supported Quality Circle deployment in 1990. During this time, I also supported the Toyota Motor Manufacturing, Indiana plant start-up by providing instructor development and training for the maintenance team members. I later provided pre-hire assessment and system development support for Toyota Motor Manufacturing Baja California, Mexico, in 2004. I supported the Toyota Motor Manufacturing Texas plant start-up in 2005. I then moved to the North American Production Support Center (NAPSC) located in Georgetown, Kentucky. I retired from Toyota in May 2007 with more than twenty years of experience. Prior to Toyota, I worked at Mack Trucks for ten years and served in the U.S. Marine Corps before that.

With Honsha I have worked with the State of Washington as well as one of the largest mortgage banks in the United States. I am also owner of the Center for Employee Development. I have had several Fortune 100 companies as clients in Lean capability building, realizing significant reductions of safety incidents, improved inventory turns, and reduced costs of operations. I am also working with Jackson Community College to establish a Lean Environment Simulator (LES) that will be available for classes in early 2012; it will immerse the participants into a manufacturing environment where they can experience Lean principles and tools in an eight-hour class.

s.ansuini@honsha.org
www.honsha.org

Gerson Valentim Damiani

Starting my professional career at Toyota Brazil (TBD) in September 1990, I had the opportunity to work at Toyota's Tahara plant, one of the premier plants in Japan. In Brazil I was able to work with Sakamaki-san, one of the people who helped Taiichi Ohno with the implementation of the Toyota Production System. I left Toyota in 2007 as a supervisor of the areas of press, forging, heat treatment, machining, and rear axle assembly.

Within a few months of leaving Toyota, I was granted the privilege to join Honsha as an associate. The first company that I began to support as a Honsha Sensei after leaving Toyota was The Tech Group, where I did not speak any Spanish, yet managed to learn it in eight weeks in Mexico—specifically in the beautiful city of Guadalajara—where I met the Virgin of Guadalupe, whom I keep close to my heart to this day.

One of the projects I think I can say made history was the work done at Carl Zeiss Vision Tijuana, where we changed a twenty-five-year-old process of how to make lenses for eyeglasses. For me it was a great honor to have worked with Sammy and Fukamizu in this project, but I cannot forget Rodolfo Moreno, the engineering manager who believed in the project from the beginning.

Another project that I cannot stop talking about is Mars Spain, where the plant manager Demetrio Otero, originally from Recife City, Brazil, had a very difficult mission. Demetrio invited Honsha to help change the company and culture of the people in the plant. After one year, the Spain plant became the Lean benchmark across Europe among the company's sites.

Now as a senior associate at Honsha, I can say that all the projects I have done in these four years have been a great honor, always visiting companies with a passion to teach what I learned throughout my sixteen-year career at Toyota. I would like to take this opportunity to thank the clients with whom I have worked in these past years for their trust.

I cannot forget to thank my Senseis who taught me so much at Toyota; they are Sakamaki-san, Ichii-san, Niyama-san, Torata-san, Nakata-san, Ando-san, Carlos (Coloral)-san, and Fukamizu-san. I believe these men are who taught me everything I know about Lean; I can say with certainty that I learned from the best Senseis in the world.

I want to deeply thank my wife, Solange Romera Damiani, who has been both mother and father to our children over the past four years while I spent many days away from home and abroad in order to teach what I have learned at Toyota. To you, my wife, I say, I love you as much as always. Thank you for being in my life.

To my children, Rennan Romera Damiani and Giovanna Romera Damiani, thank you for collaborating with your mother all these years that I have been far away, by studying hard, getting good grades in school, and mainly remaining humble, honest, and responsible. Dad loves you dearly. Remember this.

Special thanks to my good friend Francisco Estrada (Paco), for having helped me a lot in the translation of this chapter. Thanks, my friend.

g.damiani@honsha.org
www.honsha.org

Carlos Yukio Fukamizu

I worked for Toyota do Brasil from 1988 to 2004, and between 1990 and 1993 at the Toyota Japan, Kamigo plant.

As production manager, I conferred with management and production staff to plan, direct, and oversee production control of the consumer products manufacturing facility using TPS methodologies. The methods were essential to analyze technology and resources needs required for coordinating and directing projects, and making detailed plans to improve safety, quality, productivity, and cost reduction.

I was also responsible for QC circle activities focusing on the improvements of work conditions, and creating a good working environment for the employees resulting in improved safety, quality, and productivity.

To pursue a new challenge, I left Toyota in 2004 and moved to the United States to work as a Lean manufacturing engineer in an American company. Since 2008 I have worked as a consultant in Mexico, Spain, Lithuania, the United States, as well as South America. I have had great experiences and results implementing TPS concepts in various industries such as pet care, glass lenses, metallurgy, banks, restaurants, and electronics parts. In my experience, the implementation of Lean is the same for any kind of process, regardless of the type of industry. Of course all Lean journeys must start with a deep understanding of processes, customers, and culture.

c.fukamizu@honsha.org
www.honsha.org

Renato Eiji Kitazuka

Just after I graduated as a mechanical engineer at Faculdade de Engenharia Industrial in Brazil, I joined Toyota do Brasil for an amazing journey. Toyota had been in Brazil for fifty years, manufacturing the same product for that entire time. Then Toyota decided to expand its product portfolio by localizing the Corolla. I was hired to work with the localization of components as well as support and develop suppliers to meet the requirements of the famous Toyota Production System (TPS).

Prior to Toyota I worked in a very traditional mass production company. After joining Toyota, TPS became a passion for me. After learning TPS at the source, I decided to move to new challenges and learn more about implementing it outside the Toyota environment, so I joined Delphi Automotive Systems to lead the Lean implementation at a facility in Jaguariuna.

The work in Jaguariuna opened the world's doors for me and I worked at implementing Lean in companies in South America and Europe. After almost ten years in the manufacturing business, I decided to move on to a new challenge and implement Lean concepts in an education service business at my current employer CTB-McGraw Hill, in Indianapolis, Indiana.

As my passion for TPS guides my career, my passion for my family guides my life: my parents are the models who shaped who I am; my wife Alessandra is my other half, she is who gives me confidence to overcome all barriers and challenges; and my sons Bruno and Diego are my happiness, my major accomplishment still in progress.

r.kitazuka@honsha.org
www.honsha.org

Greg Lane

My twenty-two years of worldwide Lean implementation began while working with Toyota when I was one of a handful of people selected to be developed as a Toyota Production System Key Person through specialized training in Japan by Toyota's masters including Mr. Ohba, then returning to train others at NUMMI (Toyota and General Motors joint venture). I joined Toyota to learn their successful production system after working as an engineer (having a BS in mechanical engineering) for more traditional manufacturers, and then completing a Masters in business administration.

My Lean implementation work has taken me to thirty-two countries and allowed me to support diverse types of organizations. Continuing my Lean education has been significantly enhanced by personally buying and profitably transforming my own manufacturing company; this really connected the principles to my own profit and loss. The principal type of support I focused on during the past eight years has been "made-to-order" (job-shops) within small- and medium-sized businesses, including divisions of large corporations such as Continental and Whirlpool in areas where a traditional Lean approach has proven difficult.

I also share my experiences as a faculty member of the Lean Institutes in the United States and Spain, as well as lecturer of post-graduate Lean studies at the University of Barcelona and the University Polytechnic Catalunia. I have published two mainstream books and various magazine articles:

- *Made to Order Lean—Excelling in a High-Mix, Low-Volume Environment* (Productivity Press, New York: 2007)
- *Mr. Lean Buys and Transforms a Manufacturing Company—The True Story of Profitably Growing an Organization with Lean Principals* (CRC Press, New York: 2010)

glane@LowVolumeLean.com
www.LowVolumeLean.com

Robert Martichenko

I am the chief executive officer of LeanCor, LLC. LeanCor's purpose is to support its customers in preparing their people, perfecting their processes, and successfully implementing and operating the Lean supply chain.

To accomplish this purpose, LeanCor delivers Lean third-party logistics services, warehousing, and facility management; Lean training; and Lean supply-chain consulting services.

I have years of supply chain, logistics, and Lean implementation experience. This experience includes multiple Lean supply chain implementations supporting successful organizations, including Polaris Industries, Mitsubishi Caterpillar, and Toyota Motor Manufacturing.

I authored the books *Success in 60 Seconds* and *Everything I Know about Lean I Learned in First Grade*, both published by the Orloe Group. I also co-authored the logistics management book *Lean Six Sigma Logistics*, published by J. Ross Publishing, and co-authored the workbook *Building the Lean Fulfillment Stream*, published by the Lean Enterprise Institute.

In addition to leading LeanCor, I am a senior instructor for the Lean Enterprise Institute and the Georgia Tech Supply Chain and Logistics Institute.

In addition to my professional experience I hold a Bachelor's Degree in mathematics, an MBA in finance, and am a trained Six Sigma Black Belt.

Robert@leancor.com
www.leancor.com

Patrick Muller

As supplier development manager at Toyota Motor Marketing & Engineering Europe, I was introduced to TPS at TMC in Japan. During my eight years at Toyota, I lived and breathed the "Toyota Way" on a daily basis. My team was responsible for creating and maintaining a Lean European supplier base, focusing on quality, cost, and delivery by means of Lean technical support. It was key for my team to ensure advanced quality and capacity planning to enable on-time launches. I worked closely with Toyota Purchasing and Development as technical support using VE/VA methodology in the design of products and as a key player in supplier price negotiations.

I have worked as a Sensei in various business sectors' headquarters and sites around the world: automotive industry (Toyota, Ford), plastic manufacturing (Saint Gobain), food industry (Mars, Agrana Fruit), health care (CHCL), optical manufacturing (Carl Zeiss Vision), packaging industry (Portola Packaging), and U.S. defense electronics (Natel Engineering) and financial institutions.

I am currently employed at Rockwell Collins in Melbourne, Florida, as a principal Lean consultant.

p.muller@honsha.org
www.honsha.org

Alistair Norval

I graduated from the University of Toronto in 1979 with a degree in chemical engineering and began my professional career at Kodak Canada Inc. in Toronto, Ontario, Canada. I spent the early part of my career doing process engineering and moved on to quality assurance. I was very fortunate to be part of a division that was chosen to be a pilot on Lean implementation for the Eastman Kodak Company. After a successful pilot, Lean was rolled out throughout the entire company, starting in manufacturing and eventually moving to sales & marketing, research & development, and the support functions for the organization. During this time, I received in-depth training from leading international Senseis, including many Toyota veterans such as Pascal Dennis, author of several Shingo Prize-winning books including *Getting the Right Things Done* and *Lean Production Simplified*.

I was presented with a wonderful opportunity to join Lean Pathways, Inc., and have spent the past five years with them continuing my Toyota production system education. There I work with leading organizations worldwide on continuous improvement and assist them in using Lean to drive improved business results. These organizations are from a variety of industries, including discrete manufacturing, continuous chemical processes, new product development, health care, and service organizations. Kimberly Clark, Lockheed Martin, Magna International, Group Health Cooperative, and MultiCare Health System are a few examples of organizations I have had the pleasure of working with.

My passion is to apply Lean thinking across the enterprise to achieve consistently superior business results. I enjoy working with leadership teams and developing their Lean thinking and their Lean management processes to align, focus, and motivate organizations to become the best they can be.

al.norval@leansystems.org
www.leansystems.org

Sammy Obara

I was first hired by Toyota in Brazil as an intern for the prototype division of product development. The remainder of my thirteen years as a Toyota employee was split among different sites such as Honsha and Motomachi in Japan, Toyota de Venezuela (TDV), New United Motor Manufacturing Inc. (NUMMI) a Toyota–GM joint venture in the United States, and several other shorter assignments that included Toyota sites in Europe, Kentucky, and very recently in the Philippines. Although my education is in digital technology, information systems, and technology management, I use very little technology in my work as a Lean practitioner and in my day-to-day activities.

In mid-2011, I had counted a little over 300 companies that I had been to, on either a Gemba walk or doing hands-on Lean stuff. Some of my most memorable experiences include a great company that makes pet food and M&Ms. I have been to twelve of their sites from Brazil to Siberia, and they struck me as the model for Lean culture. Another company that I had the honor to work with makes diamond for the mining industry. In addition to its seriousness about Lean initiatives, it uses a good part of its resources (money and people) to help poor communities. Many of the senior executives spend weeks in Kenya every year in efforts to drive out poverty. Unfortunately, I was not given enough pages to list all the companies and their interesting characteristics, but I am glad to have been exposed to such a fascinating universe of Lean practitioners.

Today I help coordinate Honsha.ORG in North America. Honsha is an alumni association of former Toyota professionals. I also teach at San Diego State University, where I live and help other institutions in California. I would like to dedicate my chapter to my twin boys Andy and Ryan, and especially to my wife Miki, who gave me all the support (and brought ice cream) during my long battle trying to finish my chapter.

s.obara@honsha.org
www.honsha.org

Bob Plummer

I began my career with fifteen years of experience leading manufacturing operations, including Toyota experience at NUMMI, followed by fifteen years of experience as division president and CEO of both manufacturing and service companies. I have a Bachelor of Industrial Engineering degree from Kettering University and an MBA from Harvard Business School.

While in the roles of division president and CEO, I implemented TPS in several businesses. Two of my larger implementations included Portola Packaging, a $200 million global plastic packaging manufacturer, and Siegel-Robert Automotive, a $450 million automotive components manufacturer. When implementing TPS and Kaizen, I emphasize the important role of leadership.

As partner at The Stunsl Group, I consult with CEOs to develop and implement strategies to build and strengthen their businesses.

b.plummer@honsha.org
www.honsha.org

Art Smalley

I am a specialist in the area of world-class methods for operational improvement and have served numerous companies around the world. I was one of the first Americans to work for Toyota Motor Corporation in Japan, first studying at different universities in Japan and then learning TPS manufacturing principles in the Kamigo engine plant where Taiichi Ohno was the founding plant manager. During my stay at Toyota, I played an instrumental role in the development and transfer of both precision equipment and TPS methods to Toyota's overseas plants.

After a decade in Japan, I returned to the United States and served as Director of Lean Manufacturing for Donnelly Corporation. I subsequently joined the international management consulting firm of McKinsey & Company and was one of the firm's leading experts in the area of Lean manufacturing for a period of four years. During this time I counseled numerous Fortune 500 clients on operational matters involving Lean implementation and led specific cost, quality, and delivery improvement projects.

In 2003, I launched my own company, Art of Lean, Inc., and now divide my time serving a diverse base of manufacturing clients such as Parker Hannifin, Delphi, Schlumberger, Gillette, Sandia National Laboratories, and many other companies in areas of operational performance improvement.

In addition, I serve as senior faculty member and periodic advisor to the Lean Enterprise Institute and its global affiliates, delivering lectures to leading manufacturing executives around the world. Through the institute, I have published the definitive workbook guide on implementing basic pull production methods titled *Creating Level Pull*, which was awarded a Shingo Prize for distinguished contribution to manufacturing knowledge in 2005. In 2006, Art was inducted as a lifetime academy member of the Shingo Prize for Excellence in recognition of my contributions to manufacturing. In 2008, I also co-authored the Shingo Prize award-winning book titled *A3 Thinking* with my friend and colleague Professor Durward K. Sobek. In 2010, I published *Toyota's Kaizen Method: Six Steps to Improvement* with Isao Kato.

artsmalley@artoflean.com
www.artoflean.com

Darril Wilburn

During my seven-year stay at Toyota I was a leader in the development and implementation of some of Toyota Motor Manufacturing's highest profile leadership development programs including the Toyota Way 2001 (Toyota core values and principles) implementation at Toyota's largest manufacturing plant in North America. I worked with The Toyota Institute in Japan, assisting in the development of the Toyota Business Practice, and co-leading the global pilot of this program as well as the North American Senior Executive sessions. While at Toyota, I studied the Toyota Production System as a student of OMDD, Toyota's internal Sensei group. I was also part of the team that launched Toyota Motor Manufacturing Texas, where I led the assimilation and training of those new to Toyota management.

As a senior associate at Honsha, I have had the opportunity to work with the public and private sectors on projects that reflect the current global economic condition. Working with one of the largest mortgage banks in the United States, our team has implemented a redesign of the workflow to increase productivity and reduce cost and lead-times. I am also working with the State of Washington to develop a Lean culture that will help transform the way state government does business.

Other clients include M&M Mars, Valero Energy, Kimberly-Clark, Monomoy Capital Partners, and Toyota Motor Manufacturing. I am also an active speaker delivering presentations and keynote addresses on Lean Principles around the globe, including

- Harvard Business Review-Latin America, lecture series in Chile, Ecuador, and Mexico
- Lean Conference in Brazil
- M&M Mars Latin American Leadership Team Retreat
- Abu Dhabi Talent Conference
- Washington State Government Lean Seminar
- Lithuanian Prime Ministers Conference
- Minister of Defense, Lithuania
- ISM University of Management and Economics, Vilnius, Lithuania
- Monomoy Capital Partners Annual CEO meeting

Without the love and support from my family, Marcy, Sydney, and Ryan, I could not do what I love to do, so I thank you and dedicate this book to you.

d.wilburn@honsha.org

www.honsha.org

1

Courage, Humility, Kaizen

Darril Wilburn

I consider myself one of the luckiest people to have worked at Toyota. Everyone who works at Toyota receives invaluable training and on-the-job development, and I was no exception. What made me so lucky was the chance to work at three locations as well as being involved in high-profile projects. I had the opportunity to work at Toyota Motor Manufacturing Kentucky, the largest plant in North America; the North American corporate headquarters; and finally to be part of a new plant start-up team at Toyota Motor Manufacturing Texas. In addition, I worked on significant projects such as The Toyota Business Practice and The Toyota Way 2001. Most significant was the opportunity to be trained by Toyota's internal TPS group, Operations Management Development Division (OMDD). I am forever grateful for the opportunities afforded me while at Toyota and thank all the wonderful teachers and leaders who did their best to teach me The Toyota Way.

With a background in education, process improvement, and leadership coaching, I was hired in the late 1990s as a Development Coach at the Kentucky plant. My job was to teach and coach members of the leadership team on how to improve their "people" skills. I was assigned several managers to meet with and develop strategies that would allow them to work with their people more productively. My typical manager was one who was quite good at the technical aspects of the job but had a more difficult time developing the type of relationship that fostered mutual trust, a key component in the Toyota Production System (TPS).

The position of Development Coach at the Kentucky plant was a new position and one that was established by my first Sensei. She believed strongly that Mutual Trust was a key in the development of a TPS culture. She also believed that we could develop people in leadership positions who did not naturally possess the skills needed to build mutual trust. When assigned a new leader to coach, I chose to spend much of my time on the floor with these leaders in order to understand their work conditions and the situations that they were in every day. My Sensei insisted on the Gemba (Japanese word meaning "where the work is done") approach, and I came to understand why. The Gemba approach allowed me to gain true insight into their situations, where they struggled and where they excelled. They were proud to show me their production lines and introduce me to the people they worked for. Yes, I said the people they worked for; it was common for Toyota leaders to consider the people on the teams they managed to be people they worked for and not people who worked for them. This was a new mind-set for me but I came to see it as an essential element in establishing a TPS culture.

These Gemba sessions with the assigned leaders became something that looked forward to to every day. I hope I was able to add some value to those I was assigned to help, possibly through new insight and improved working relationships. But I am also sure that I learned much more from them than they learned from me. These Gemba sessions were the beginning of my journey to learn TPS from the people perspective as well as the technical manufacturing perspective. It was fascinating to see how TPS functioned. Not to be too dramatic, but it was like hearing a symphony with many components, parts, and people coming together at the right time to produce a quality product. When I work with clients today, I strive to help them develop this rhythm of work and unity of purpose.

I became more and more fascinated with TPS and had a strong desire to learn more about not just the production part of TPS, but how it evolved and how people functioned within the system. I shared this with my Sensei and she said, "Darril, you have the people part of the TPS equation. If you can combine that with the technical aspect, then you will have a powerful combination. Learn the principles behind the tools and how respect for people (customers, team members, society) drives the system." And so that became my objective: to understand this connection between people and process, the elements that make TPS one of the most studied but least understood work systems.

THE TOYOTA WAY 2001

In 2001, Toyota developed the internal document called *The Toyota Way 2001*. Toyota had grown very quickly around the world and struggled to convey the essence of what makes the company great to its newer associates. When Toyota was a small company and centrally located in Japan, it was possible for senior leaders to teach team members in groups or one-on-one. The rapid growth made it impossible to disseminate the Toyota Way in the same fashion. Under the direction of then Toyota Motor Corporation President Fujio Cho, Toyota's Global Human Resources Division researched and developed *The Toyota Way 2001* as a way to communicate to global Toyota team members the "DNA" of Toyota. In the introduction, Mr. Cho states, "In this booklet we have identified and defined the company's fundamental DNA, which summarizes the unique and outstanding elements of our company culture and success. These are the managerial values and business methods that are known collectively as The Toyota Way."

In true Toyota form, the "Way" was condensed into a thirteen-page booklet. Someone once told me that they heard that the booklet took ten years to write. I told them I was not sure but it sounded right and added that it probably took one year to write one-thousand pages and nine years to condense it to thirteen pages!

Once published, Mr. Cho challenged each global region to disseminate the Toyota Way to the people at their locations. I was fortunate enough to have the responsibility to develop the program we would use in Kentucky to teach members of the management team. During the development process, I was able to meet and learn from the great leaders at Toyota Motor Manufacturing Kentucky.

Here I share the Honsha version of The Toyota Way that is based on the foundational Lean principles of Continuous Improvement and Respect. Within these two principles lies the heart: Courage, Humility, and Kaizen. Toyota uses slightly different words; here I have attempted to take the original concepts and find the deeper root.

An example is Genchi Genbutsu. This is a key element of The Toyota Way and is often quickly translated into "Go and See." As with many Japanese words, the quick translation fails to capture the essence of the word. At the Kentucky plant, many people used the phrase "Go and See" in place of Genchi Genbutsu but often the action was "Go and Watch" or "Go and Do," neither of which captured the essence of Genchi Genbutsu. When I asked one senior executive, Hiro Yoshiki, what Genchi Genbutsu meant to him, he explained the purpose [my paraphrase] as follows: "The most important reason to 'Go and See' is to learn, learn deeply about the situation and what is needed from you. The second reason is to teach by asking the questions that lead team members to correct answers. The third

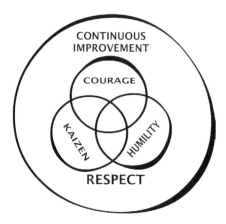

reason is to be seen." This third reason did not sound very humble to me but I came to realize the meaning. By being seen, you are able to convey to everyone that the situation is important to you and that the people working on the problem are important. You and others also build a mutual understanding of the situation and thus can arrive at solutions quickly. This was a key learning point for me. The fourth reason to go and see, said Hiro, is so you do not have to go and see anymore. This sounded very strange to me until he explained further. "We want to go and see but not the same problems again and again; we want to see new problems. Plus, if the time is taken to teach, then problems are avoided in the future because team members have a higher skill level."

If we are to learn, teach, show respect, and develop others, we must go to the part of our business where value is created for the customer. In manufacturing, we call it the "Floor"; others call it the "front line." Whether it is manufacturing or service or a nonprofit agency, the message is still the same: Show your learning spirit, your humility by practicing Genchi Genbutsu!

COURAGE, HUMILITY, KAIZEN AT THE HEART

When we develop Courage and Humility we will then be able to practice Kaizen. These three elements work together and allow us to show respect for people and to develop a culture of Continuous Improvement. It was during my study of TPS with OMDD that Courage, Humility, and Kaizen came to life.

OMDD uses emersion as the preferred way to teach TPS. My first lesson was early one Monday morning at a parts supplier's plant location. With little more than an introduction, we started and I was taken to a work cell that made hinge parts for car seats. My Sensei told me, "Darril-san, this is your work area; please find 100 problems, I will return in 2 hours to see your list." This was all very new to me. I had spent many hours observing the well-oiled, highly efficient production line at Toyota. But this was obviously not Toyota. The production area was a mess; there was no standard work and no hint or any kind of order. In this case, it seems that identifying waste would be even easier. But it was not. I do not know if it was a lack of experience or a lack of confidence but I found it difficult to see any problems, let alone a hundred problems in two hours. How would I do that? Just getting organized as to how I would observe was difficult so I observed the team members and the machines from outside the cell, pacing around it like a timid puppy for two solid hours, looking for the elusive problems. At the end of the two hours, my Sensei returned to find that I had exactly two problems on my list. I was ninety-eight problems short of the goal!

He looked at me and then wiped his hands over his head and down to his face. He must have been thinking, "Oh my, what kind of idiot do I have here?" After he composed himself, he said, "Tell me what you see." So I described to him what the team members were doing but that I did not see any problems. I still struggled to identify the problems. My skill level was so low that one obvious item not on my list was a neatly hung mallet that was used to slam each part into one of the machines. This problem should have been obvious to anyone! At least they had it on a string so the team member did not have to reach very far for it; that should make it good, right? I was so naive.

At this point he was even more frustrated. "Darril-san, come with me," he said. In a private meeting room with a flipchart, he started to explain to me how to observe in order to deeply understand the work. He explained that at first that it is not my job to correct the work but to understand it, then to make improvements. I had long been an admirer of Dr. Stephen Covey's *The Seven Habits of Highly Effective People* and what he was explaining to me was Habit 5, "Seek First to Understand, Then to be Understood." From this perspective it really made sense to me. This was also a fundamental lesson in The Toyota Way element of Humility. Humility insists that we understand so that we may develop better solutions. Taiichi Ohno said, "Observe the production floor without preconceptions and with a blank mind." This is what my Sensei was trying to teach me with actions, not just words.

He continued to teach me his approach, and he wrote the word "Muri" on the flipchart. He explained that Muri is part of the three Ms of waste: Muri, which translates as *overburden*; Mura, which translates as *unevenness*; and Muda, the most famous element, which translates as *waste* and has seven components. He explained that we must approach our deep understanding of the process first from the perspective of the people doing the work. We must look for Muri and eliminate it from the process. We must also send the correct message that our purpose is first to improve the work for the people doing the work. This will help us gain buy-in with the team when we go deeper into the improvement process. At this point we only looked at Muri. He asked me to list what I observed in the process that could be considered Muri. I recognized that using the mallet to hit each part, several hundred times per day, would be considered overburden, so that finally made it to my list. I could see walking inside the cell as overburden. My list had grown somewhat, but from my Sensei's perspective it was still incomplete. "Darril-san," he asked, "what is the best way to increase your understanding of the process and your ability to see the Muri?"

"I will observe more closely and with an eye for Muri," I replied.

"This would of course be helpful, but what can you do that would deepen your understanding more quickly?"

"Are you saying I should actually learn the job?"

"I am not saying, I am asking."

"Then I will need to learn the job in order to more deeply understand the process and to see the Muri more closely."

Now the lesson of Humility was even more profound. Not only was I learning new skills from a Lean/TPS perspective, but I also needed to learn how to do the manufacturing job I was observing. I was not only a student of the Sensei, but now also a student of the team members I had been observing. I approached the team and asked if they would teach me their work process. They all smiled as if to say, this is going to be fun! "Of course," they said.

After donning the appropriate personal protective equipment, I started on the first machine in the process that connected the first two flat steel plates and began to turn them into seat hinges. This had looked so easy from the outside looking in. The team member teaching me the job had several laughs as I fumbled to keep up with the speed of the process. I would turn the raw material the wrong way, drop the parts, and was very slow and awkward. After a day on the job, I was able to pick up the process and do it with help from the team member assigned to me. I was not able to do it as quickly or with the quality of the team member, but with her help I understood the process much more deeply. Looking through the lens of Muri, I was able to add many problems to my list.

The next machine was the infamous "mallet hanging from a string machine" that I mentioned previously (Figure 1.4). The first action was to pick up a flat steel part, apply gooey lubricant with a brush to the section that would be moving against the previous piece; then put this into the machine by placing a hole in the part onto a small peg in the machine, and then smack the part with the mallet so it fit tightly even if it was already tight. Well at least it was standardized. This seemed very wrong but I wanted to learn from the worker perspective so I did as instructed. As I did this process, I realized that smacking the part with the mallet was indeed overburden and caused a bit of pain at the end of the rotation—not to mention the possible damage to the part itself. I also realized that the reason the parts did not always fit snuggly on the small peg was that the peg had become worn over time and when the part was even slightly off center, the peg might not allow the part to fit correctly. The mallet was obviously a countermeasure to this problem but it was not the result of deep, 5-Why problem solving. In this case, as in many others, the result of shallow problem solving is more burden on the worker. This was powerful learning for me.

One process called for the worker to add pins and grommets to a machine for processing. The hand motions used required reaching, handing off the parts from one hand to the other, and crossing arms to place the parts in the machine. This is also a burden on the worker...my list was growing.

Over the next couple of days I learned each process in this same way. When my Sensei came back and asked me what problems I had on my list, I showed him that the list had grown, and he seemed a bit more pleased. He asked me if I had not seen these same things before. Of course, I had seen the steps in the operation while I observed the process, but not through the eyes of Muri. I also discovered that I was hesitant to judge the steps in the process. When I observed the process and saw something question-able, like the mallet, I told myself, "There must be a perfectly good reason for doing that." When I told my Sensei about this rationalization of what I was seeing, he said, "When you observe the process, look for fact; don't be concerned with whether there is a good reason for the action or not. If the action causes burden, then write it on your list as a problem. If the action is wasteful, then write it on your list as a problem. Maybe it will turn out to be a problem we work on now or one we don't work on for a while, but put it on the list anyway." This skill took the combination of both Humility and Courage—the humility to understand the process and the courage to identify the problems. It is not common practice to gladly raise problems to the surface in most work environments. I have observed that we are more likely to place a mallet on a string and smack a part than we are to actually recognize the problem and solve it at its root cause. I realized that I was very timid in my observation and that I must be more courageous in challenging myself to see more deeply.

Muri was an important lesson. Not only had I gained so much insight into the work itself, but also the process we were using to eventually make improvements. I was able to build strong relationships with the team members, thus setting us up for rapid Kaizen in the near future. This step of building the relationships with the team is not to be skipped if you are an "outsider" coming into the team. Learning from the perspective of Muri is a great way to foster relationships.

Several years later when I was beginning my consulting career, I had a client who made cast aluminum parts. It was a hot and dirty job, and I remember being a bit intimidated by not only the work, but also the seasoned veteran workforce. The plant was nearly sixty years old and many employees had been there for more than forty years.

On my first day at the plant, I immediately thought back to the lessons I had learned from my Sensei. Observe from the perspective of Muri: learn the process deeply. One of my first actions was to find the most grizzled veteran on the process I was assigned to and ask him if he would be willing to teach me the components of the position as if I were a new hire. He growled but agreed. I mustered as much humility and courage that I had and began to learn the job. Because of the inherent danger of the job, I was never allowed to do it alone but, with the veteran by my side, I eventually was able to accomplish most of the tasks. After that first week, the general manager of the plant sent a letter to the managing consultant stating that "We really liked working with Darril. He immediately developed an excellent rapport with the caster operators; in fact, he ran the casters for a bit (under the operator's supervision) to learn the job." I was obviously pleased that one of my first consulting jobs was going so well but I was shocked that the act of learning the job before attempting to help improve the process was seen as so unusual. What other way would be effective? It was growing up at Toyota that taught me the power of small things such as learning the process, working at the Gemba, and building relationships. These small things are really the big things.

Having exposed me to the concept of Muri, my Sensei now moved on to Mura and Muda. There was a great example in this plant of how Mura or "unevenness" can lead to Muri. There was no set work pace or takt time established in the cell. The goal was seven pallets of parts on the dock by the end of the day on Friday. The practice was to work as fast as you could until you achieved the seven pallets and then take it easy for the rest of the week. This usually happened at some point on Friday morning, depending on how the machines ran. Quality was also an issue. I asked the area supervisor about the quality measures for this operation and he expressed that there were many issues with rejects and scrap. I asked the team about the safety record for the area, and they expressed that they had a new person in the cell because one person was out on medical leave and that they had many missed days on the team due to injuries. It does not take a rocket scientist to see the possible correlation between increased work speed and the quality and safety issues of the cell. We would not be able to attack all the issues during our stay but we could set up the process to minimize both Muri and Mura.

This fit well with my next learning: Muda, or the seven types of waste. In order to see waste, my Sensei helped me and the team begin standard work. We established the takt time and developed a pace setter, which for us was someone standing at the end of the cell with a stopwatch and not allowing the worker to put a part in the box until the appropriate time. Eventually, this method led to the team working at a steadier pace that was not prone to cause injury. It also helped us see the waste as it happened. We also helped establish standardized work for each of the processes in order to more closely match the cycle time with the takt time. Once we were working with a standard, my Sensei and I returned to the training to discuss Muda. I knew the seven types of waste but had not really been trained to use them in any meaningful way. He explained one of the wastes and asked me for examples from the process. Because I had spent so much time learning the process, it was much easier to develop examples. After I exhausted examples from memory, we walked out to the floor and he asked me to find more examples. I think he was testing me to see how deeply I understood the process by asking me to first work from memory. The first waste we focused on was waiting. I was able to see people waiting on the machine to finish cycling before they could work, or waiting to put the part into the box at the end of the cell. Before we established standard work in the cell, there was lots of activity; it looked very busy all the time, except for Friday afternoon. Was all the work actually adding value? It was hard to tell before the standardized work. Taiichi Ohno once said, "Wasteful action is not work." This was a great example of just that. In a sense, the team was saving up all the wait time in the process until Friday. By developing the takt time and standardized work, I was able to see the waste as it occurred and not have to wait myself until Friday to see it.

Before we moved on to the other types of waste, my Sensei made a point about the person standing in front of the machine. He explained that this waiting is one of the worst types of waiting. He said, "When we allow a human being to wait for a machine and just stand there, what we are saying is that the machine and the human are of equal value or maybe even the machine is more valuable since the human is waiting for it. Never allow this to happen. It does not show respect for people!" Today, when I am with a client and touring a production area, I still see this and am quick to challenge the leadership to develop ways to engage the person in other work while the machine is working. It is better for the machine to wait on the person than for the person to wait on the machine.

We rotated between the meeting room and the floor with each of the other six forms of waste and each time the list of problems grew until eventually there were more than 100! Before this experience I could only see with the eyes I had developed over my lifetime—eyes that were trained, by my upbringing and the places I had worked, to overlook problems. Now I was developing a lens with the knowledge of Muri, Mura, and Muda. It reminds me of the movie "The Sixth Sense," about a boy who had a special ability to see and communicate with people who were no longer living. This was his sixth sense. In the movie, the boy mumbled to his doctor, "I see dead people, they're everywhere." After learning to see the workplace through the lens of Muri, Mura, and Muda, I find myself mumbling, "I see waste, it's everywhere."

As illuminating as it was to begin the development of an "eye for waste," just seeing the problems and not solving them would itself be a waste.

It was this phase of my training that was even more challenging than the first. Now I actually had to work with the team to develop and implement improvements. Many of the people going through this program at the same time I was had much more experience on the floor and were also

very good at fabricating in the maintenance workshop. They could conceive of something that would help improve the process, like a gravity-fed chute for parts delivery for example, and then quickly produce the device after cutting and welding the metal.

The team and I had developed several ideas that we wanted to implement but we needed help to fabricate the items. Usually you can work with the plant's maintenance department for help but in this plant the resources were scarce. I spoke with my Sensei about this problem, and he brought me a pair of scissors and some heavy yellow tape. He then pointed me to the stack of used cardboard in the corner. "Darril-san, be creative!" he said. Again, this was my opportunity to practice both Courage and Humility. The Courage to find another way and the Humility to be the guy using cardboard and tape while the others were welding and fabricating!

Soon the work cell resembled a police crime scene with all the yellow tape. We made a small box out of tape and cardboard to hold lubricant to improve the process of brushing lubricant on each part. We made parts chutes for one machine so we could load parts from outside the cell to the operator. This was the machine that required the operators to cross their hands and reach often to complete the process. We dropped the cardboard and tape chutes into the machine and placed them near the point that the parts would be loaded in order to complete the process. This, combined with new standardized work for this process, allowed us to reduce operator time from over thirty seconds to less than fifteen seconds with a higher degree of ergonomic safety.

Some interesting developments resulted from our use of cardboard and tape in our Kaizen efforts. After a few days of cutting and taping and changing the designs several times and re-cutting and re-taping, my Sensei took me to one of the other cells where the students were fabricating metal and welding. He asked me if I saw anything different there as compared to my cell. Obviously there were lots of nicely constructed parts chutes and tables made from metal. It did not resemble a crime scene because there was no bright yellow tape. It did not have piles of failed attempts as seen in my cell with the ripped-up cardboard and peeled-away yellow tape. It was the failed attempts that my Sensei asked about further.

"Why do you think there are no failed attempts here?" he asked.

"I guess they got it right the first time," I responded.

"Maybe so, maybe so. I want you to think about this question and get back to me later."

I kept working that day but the question was on my mind. Had I failed that much more than the other students? Were they really that good? Or, had they invested so much time and effort in the construction of these beautiful works of metal and welding that they were reluctant to try something else if the results were not what they expected? I shared this with him later in the day and he responded, "I think you are correct. They did not adopt the true spirit of Kaizen. Humility says that we don't really know so we must understand and then try many things to see if we have the right solution. If we don't, we try again. That is the beauty of cardboard and tape; you are demonstrating that you are not quite sure and you want to be sure before you make it permanent. If I have invested so much in my idea and I have not trialed my idea quickly and inexpensively first, then I am reluctant to change my plan and will try to make it fit. I think they approached Kaizen with only Courage and not a good combination of Courage and Humility. You may think you failed more than they did but actually you were able to learn faster and make improvements faster. This is Kaizen."

The lessons were clear. If we want to build a culture of long-term, sustainable continuous improvement, then we must first develop the Courage to challenge our thinking, to expose problems, and to solve them. It is also vital that we combine our Courage with the Humility to deeply understand the current situation, including the needs of the customers. If we can combine these two principles, it is then that we can Kaizen and develop the culture of continuous improvement.

When we attempt to Kaizen with just Courage, we may find ourselves in a similar trap as my fellow students. Kaizen in that case may look like

a bully trying to prove that he is right. Kaizen with only Humility is too slow to act and is always looking for more and more understanding before action. It is the combination that makes Kaizen work.

TEACHING OTHERS

Several years later, I remember those lessons along with many others as I teach those outside of Toyota. Inside Toyota, we take many things for granted, not the least of which is the culture of continuous improvement that has been developed over the years. In Toyota, problems are readily exposed so they can be solved. Visual management is a key component in exposing problems as they occur. Tracking visuals such as Andon boards and production count boards are commonplace.

I have had the opportunity to work as a consultant in many non-manufacturing but still production-related businesses. One example, and you might be surprised, is a mortgage banking company that works to modify mortgages. It is no secret that the U.S. mortgage industry has been in financial upheaval for several years. The volume of requests for mortgage modifications far outpaced the capacity of banks to process them. In a sense, these were production facilities with information coming in one side, and the product, an approval or denial, coming out the other. Activity takes place between the beginning and the end of the process, and in that way it is much like constructing an automobile. If this is true, then the same principles of Courage, Humility, and Kaizen should also apply.

Honsha was asked to assist this company in increasing its capacity as well as maintaining high quality. We began with one group so we could understand the current capacity as well as the work itself. With this in mind, one of the first questions I asked the management team of this area was a seemingly simple question: "Are you ahead or behind?" I was surprised to see the surprised looks on their faces.

"What do you mean?" they asked.

"Are you producing your product ahead of your demand, with your demand, or are you behind your demand?" I replied. Still they were confused.

"I guess we are behind because there is no end to the work," one said.

"Will you be able to catch up?" I asked.

"I don't know," one replied.

With this exchange I knew we had a lot of work to do. As we toured the workplace, there was a glaring lack of visual understanding of the current condition. Employees were simply doing what they do with little knowledge of how the company was performing. I talked with other members of management as well, and it seemed that no one had a clear understanding of their condition other than it was "bad!"

We worked closely with one particular manager and his group to develop clear measures of productivity. We dug deeply into the process, becoming humble students and learning the process almost as well as the people doing the work. Working closely with the manager and the team, we established pilot process improvement experiments that allowed us to understand and increase capacity, while maintaining high quality. We asked that the team visualize its production progress with simple whiteboards showing plan versus actual and the difference. This was a culture change for them, exposing problems, understanding capacity and if we are ahead or behind, and allowing anyone who walks by to see this information. The act of visualizing their status took a combination of Courage and Humility—the Courage to show current condition and the Humility to admit there was a problem. It was not unusual to walk around the

workplace and see production tracking but it was always just one number: what was produced, not what should have been produced and comparing the two. One without the other is meaningless.

This was made evident during one meeting with a group of managers at this same location. There was a crisis, and they had to develop a plan to process a large number of modifications in the next two weeks. A member of senior management gave a pep talk explaining the importance of getting this work done and how she knew they could do it, just like they had done it in the past. She encouraged them to try really hard and maintain a great attitude. It was much like a pregame speech that a high-school coach might give. It was very inspiring, and everyone left feeling great. I could only assume that there was additional strategy beyond "You can do it." I was not a regular attendee at this meeting so I did not know what to expect.

The next Monday we had a status meeting to see how we were progressing on the "crisis." The meeting consisted of the managers and the same member of senior management. The process went like this. The member of senior management asked each manager what the production was for that day. She then recorded the number on her sheet (their ability to get real-time data from the computer system was limited). After each number, the team would clap for the reporting team. I did not clap; I was not sure what to clap for. Were these good numbers? Were we ahead or behind plan? For someone with a Toyota background, it was very confusing. We also discovered that the original goal was not static, that new requests were coming in each day, so not only did we have to eliminate the "crisis" number but we also had to outpace what was coming in with increased productivity.

After this meeting I asked to meet with the member of senior management. I asked her if the meeting had gone as planned and if she was confident that we would be able to make the goal. She assured me that all was well. I then asked what the plan was, how could we be sure that we could make the goal. As it turns out, there was no plan beyond the pep talk and hoping that we made it. This was very frustrating but I remember the patience my Sensei had shown me in the past. So I asked her what she might expect from each person in production. Her expectation was ten per day per person. So if we multiply this by the number in each group, can we consider that our plan? If there are seven in the group, then the expectation is seventy per day? She agreed, although this was not really a plan and not really a reflection of the reality of production. She had not spent much time on the floor and did not have a clear idea of actual productivity. She only had reports. Taiichi Ohno once said, "Data is, of course, important … but I place greatest emphasis on fact." Reading reports at your desk will give you the data. Only going to the floor will give you fact!

Regardless of this disconnect, I decided to use the numbers she supplied for the next step. I asked her if I could facilitate the production meeting the next day and actually compare planned production to actual production. She agreed.

The next day I started the meeting with a flipchart with a grid of each group number, and a space for Plan, Actual, and Delta (the difference between the plan and actual) next to the name. I asked the first manager, "What was the production of the group today?"

"Seventeen"

I posted the number under "Actual" and I asked him, "How many people do you have in the group today?"

"Eight at work today," he said.

I multiplied eight by ten and placed eighty under "Plan" and sixty-three under "Delta." I smiled and thanked him. There was no clapping. This went on for the next seven managers and each time it was like the air was being sucked out of the room. In the previous meeting we were just looking at production and had no way to know if we were making progress against the goal. Now we were dealing with reality, with fact, not just data. At the end it was clear that we would never reach our goal without a different strategy. This was a very humbling exercise and the point was well taken. We must be humble and accept the facts, and we must be courageous and solve the problems, through Kaizen, that arise from our new understanding.

It took several months but this team eventually developed and began to understand their work in a new way. The success was evident when one manager we had worked with in the pilot group was asked in a meeting with his senior manager about the possibility of adding a component to the current process. Once the request was made, he outlined the process for the senior manager on a flipchart and how much time each step took. He estimated how much time the new element would take and added it to the process time. He calculated the impact on productivity and then said, "We can do this new element but it will cost us, in the short run, X amount of production per day per team. Is this a price you are willing to pay?" The senior manager was a bit astonished at this display of facts and said, "No, not at this point but can you work on the Kaizen of the process so that we can add this element in the future and not risk production or quality?" His answer was, "Of course!"

I had witnessed him a couple of months before in a similar situation. He was asked about his team's production during a meeting, and he was immediately defensive. After complaining and making excuses, he gave in to the request and then complained about senior management to his people. We coached him on these points. He must have deep understanding of his team's capacity as well as the work process. Only then would he have the

information he needed to respond with facts, not with emotion and excuses. He obviously learned a great deal and was able to put it into practice.

Lean is simple as a concept, but practicing Lean is difficult. When we focus on the foundation of Courage, Humility, and Kaizen, we can begin to learn it deeply and make our practice more meaningful.

2

Stability and Standardized Work

Gerson Valentim Damiani

Standardized work is one of the techniques that the Toyota Production System (TPS) uses for joining optimum operators, machines, and material, to provide products with quality and low prices to their customers. The standardization of operations seeks to maximize productivity by identifying and standardizing the work elements that add value, eliminate waste, level between processes, and define the minimum level of in-process stock. A standard routine for operations flows in a steady and leveled stream of production, requiring a small amount of parts and different machine layouts.

When I (Gerson Damiani) worked at Toyota, I learned the importance of having the work standardized; it helps leaders and managers recognize where the wastes are and how to quickly act to eliminate them. I learned standardized work very oddly; I was just beginning as a Group Leader in Production when something very interesting happened in my life, which I wish to share with you now.

After obtaining my Engineering degree at Santa Cecilia dos Bandeirantes University in Santos, Brazil, I spoke to my manager to request an opportunity to work in Toyota's Engineering area. That was when Niyama-san asked me, "Why do you want to be an Engineer of the Press line?" I replied, "Because I think there are many wastes that we can eliminate more quickly using PDCA (Plan-Do-Check-Act) and Kaizen along with the Production operators."

After many conversations, Niyama-san said, "Gerson, I have a position for the area of Engineering, but I also have a position as Group Leader of the Press line, for which I believe you fit the profile I've been looking for." Then I said, "No, wait; I had only made the request to be an Engineer, not a Group Leader. Besides, the escalation process always starts as a Leader, then Group Leader, then flow Supervisor; am I right?" Then my manager said, "Gerson, you don't need to be a Leader; I have a plan for you. First,

I'll transfer you to the Press area, for you to help the Press Attendants, and then we will see about your promotion, all right?" So, we moved forward.

After a week, I was transferred to a Press area to then discover that the Manager was retiring, and that the other Group Leader would be leaving Toyota. So, I would be responsible for the area along with another Supervisor named Nakata-san, one of the best leaders I've ever worked with, along with Niyama-san, because we always worked together throughout the transition of the SBC Toyota Plant from a car plant to a plant for making car safety parts. The transformation was very complex because we had to greatly improve employees' awareness about how to make products with excellent quality.

Then after making changes to the plant, one day Niyama-san asked me, "Gerson, how was it today in the Press area?" I said, "Fine, we complied with the plan from production scheduling, no accidents occurred, no incidents (Hiyari Hato: the possibility of an accident), and we had a 0.05% rejection of parts today." Then Niyama-san said, "Gerson, I did not ask you this. This is the minimum a person in charge must know at any time of the day. I'm inquiring about the problems that occurred in the area." Then I said, "I do not know what problems you're talking about, boss." So, Niyama-san said, "Very well. Tomorrow, I want you to define an area where you can observe all the employees working. You'll stay there for thirty minutes and then tell me what type of problems occurred within the thirty minutes." I said, "Very well. I will do this tomorrow."

The next day, after defining the tasks for each employee, I went to an area where I could watch the employees for thirty minutes. I looked and looked and found nothing; Niyama-san appeared and asked, "Well, how many problems did you find?" I said, "None. Everything is perfect." Niyama-san said, "Of course not; twenty problems occurred right in front of you, and you did not see one problem? I said, "Where were you standing to detect twenty problems? Because I was here and did not find any." Niyama said, "Gerson, tomorrow, you'll stay in the same place and observe more closely. Try to find them, because they are happening right in front of you."

The next day, I was at my post to observe for another thirty minutes. I tried with all my might to identify the problems, but could not find anything, and once more, there appeared Niyama-san, asking how many problems I'd found, and my response was none. Again, he informed me that there were twenty. This took place throughout the whole week. On Friday, I detected one problem, whereas he observed seventeen. Niyama-san then said, "Gerson, why are you not paying attention to the Operation? Look, you must pay attention to how each operator is working. You should know the operation standard. If you do not know the standard, you'll hardly be able to see problems. So, here; take the standard work instructions (450 in total) and study them one by one." Then I said, "All right, boss, I'll study all of the work instructions."

After a week of studying all the operational standards at home, I think my son Rennan was ready to work for Toyota, because he was always at my side asking how things were, since I had to read the work instructions. For me, it was very good because I was able to teach my son and also study.

After a week, I returned to the same point of observation, ready to detect the problems on the line. I stayed for thirty minutes and could not see anything; then my boss came to ask how many problems I'd detected. I said none, and I had studied all the steps, and yet I still could not see. His answer was, "Because you still have junk in your mind. Gerson, you have to concentrate on the movement of the operators' hands, the sequence of the operation. This is important to ensure the stability of the line and guarantee good products."

During the week, I stayed at my post to see where the problems were, talk to the operators, and follow the production standards. On Friday, I had found seventeen problems and my boss had found eighteen. He then said, "Now, every time you come to see me for a signature, you have to bring me five problems that you saw on the line, and not only problems, but also the actions you will take to solve the problems."

When I started to look at the process, I discovered that for a work instruction to be well-followed, it depends on the head of the area overseeing each of the steps written in the standard, because people always want to change something to improve the way of performing the operation, and with a lot of discipline, this is possible. It's not a problem to change things, but first we must test to know if the change will be beneficial.

When working on a line where the takt time is very low (i.e., fifteen to twenty seconds), any change you make can reduce the cycle time by one to three seconds, which can unbalance the line, which in turn will result in the accumulation of work-in-process (WIP) inventory between workstations.

Takt Time: Takt is a German term for speed, pace, or rhythm. Production time (takt time) is the reference used for the production line (finished product) market demand; hence, it associates and determines the pace of production to the pace of sales, represented by the following equation:

$$\text{Takt Time} = \frac{\text{Available Production Time per Day}}{\text{Customer Demand per Day}}$$

Example:

$$\text{Takt Time} = \frac{27{,}600 \text{ seconds}}{460 \text{ pieces}} = 60 \text{ seconds/part}$$

To use takt time, it is necessary to know the "actual work time," that is, the time from the beginning to the end of the shift, subtracting the operator's line stops for coffee, meetings, cleaning, etc.

I'll share with you something that happened to me when I was assessing a medical components company. While on the shop floor, I noticed that there was a great deal of WIP inventory between each operation; but why would this happen? At Toyota, being trained to look for waste, it becomes somewhat logical to identify where problems may be.

When I was training people in standardized work according to Toyota standards, I could see that people were already accustomed to problems, and then I remembered my lessons from Niyama-san. Although the waste was apparent, people did not believe that more waste could be found; for this, I had to prove to them that there was much waste on the line, as evidenced by the following:

- *Waiting:* There was no workload balancing between the operators. One operator produced less than the others; therefore, this operator was the bottleneck in the process.
- *Inventory:* There was a lot of inventory between operations.
- *Overproduction:* Producing faster than the takt time to generate WIP inventory.
- *Scrap/Rework:* The people who were the bottleneck in the process had to work at a faster pace, frequently causing the product to require rework or to be scrapped.
- *Motion:* The person who replenishes the assembly components must perform his or her cycle more times than the standard dictates due to the rejected products on the line.
- *Overprocessing:* Due to the amount of rework, there was a quality inspector performing 100% inspection of the parts.
- *Transport/Conveyance:* Production was often stopped to check the quality of the finished product, which had to be taken by forklift to a separate area and await its release by the Quality department.

Notice that for this one example, we can see all seven wastes occurring on the same line.

After pointing out the waste to the people being trained, I had to prove that it was possible to better balance the line, thus avoiding the waste. Then after watching the videos, we filled out the Standard Work Combination Sheet and did a Yamazumi chart before going to the shop floor to do Genchi Genbutsu (which refers to evidencing for oneself where and how problems are occurring).

On the floor, we began to balance activities by operator according to takt time, where the variation between operator times could not be greater than two seconds. We practically stayed all day at the line, testing and proving that it was possible to improve the operation without the operators having to work excessively on the line.

By the end of the day, we were able to balance the line, yet we still needed to validate the positions and standardize the activities of each operator on the line. On my visit the following month, I found that people were not inspecting the consistency of the operation and that the Standard Work Instructions were not in the work area. I asked why they were not working according to the procedures. The reply was that they did not have time to standardize the operation as per the performed test.

For me, the following was the greatest lesson I received from Niyama-san: Regardless of what you do now, do it in accordance with the standard.

People lose sight of the importance of standardized work for operations. With a standard, it is much easier to find waste.

Stability in the process will be based on how the work instructions are written, how the operators are performing the operation based on the standards, and, of course, it will depend heavily on the leaders, managers, and supervisors making daily checks (hour by hour) of how the operators are doing the work. Do not worry about this taking a long time; when we already know the standard, a noncompliance error can be detected within a minimum of cycles of the operator.

After learning this lesson from Niyama-san, the company sent me to Toyota Japan to learn more about standardization and TPS.

When I was at Toyota in Japan in 2001 to receive training on how to prepare the plant to produce the redesigned Corolla, the following occurred to me: I was in Engineering, which was on the mezzanine above the production lines, with glass windows that enabled everyone to see the production. I looked for my boss and asked where the coffee machine was. My boss, Ando-san, said, "Gerson, before answering your question, may

I ask you a question? Who is the king in a factory?" I said, "That's easy—the president, for he can command and dictate here at Toyota." Ando-san shook his head and said, "Gerson, think a little more before answering. I'll ask again: Who is the king in a factory?" I thought harder, but could not find an answer, yet I didn't tell Andon-san that I did not know; I said it was the director. After the president, the director is the one who has the most power. Ando-san, again, shook his head. He said, "Gerson, let's go to the factory for a tour, so you may understand some basic things about the culture of Toyota."

We went to Production, where we went through some lines, and during this time, Ando-san did not say one word. Then we reached the coffee break area in Production, located between the production lines (assembly, welding, bodywork, painting, etc.). Ando-san then said the following: "Gerson-san, I will ask again, and if you do not respond correctly, you have to pay for the coffee; if you answer correctly, I'll pay for the coffee. Now respond: Who is the King in a company?" I thought about it with all my might to avoid paying for the coffee, but I did not know the answer. While I continued thinking, Ando-san said, "I want a cappuccino" and laughed at the situation. I was trying to find an answer that was right in front of me, but could not see it because I was thinking with reasoning instead of with my heart. In the end, I could not continue and told Ando-san, "Though I've tried to find the answer with all my strength, I do not know the answer." Then he said, "The first great virtue of man is to recognize when he does not know, in order to learn; but many men always say they know and then they disappoint later, because no one can fool everyone forever; remember this always, Gerson-san."

After this happened, I asked Ando-san what the answer was. He replied, "You have to discover it for yourself; it's around you all the time. Look, Gerson-san, if you think with your heart, you will find the answer." Then I looked ahead, and there was a machine operator with a stopped machine, and it took less than a minute for several people to approach to help him with the line that was down. Then I thought, it can only be the operator. Ando-san then asked, "Well, what's the answer?" I said, "The operator." "Why?" he asked. I replied, "I think it's because it is the operator who produces the product, and looking at these people helping with the line, I got that impression." Then Ando-san said, "Excellent observation; but there's something more that I will explain now. If the operator wants to build a high-quality product, he will; if he wants to make a product that will have to be reworked, he will; if he wants to make a product that will be rejected at the end of the line, he will. But how do we have the operator make only top-quality products? The answer is to help the king. If we help the king, he will only make products of excellent quality. For example, now the line has stopped; he saw what had happened and could not identify where the problem was, so he sought help, and see how many people wanted to help the king. Gerson-san, this is the essence; do not forget. Now, pay for the coffee; I have to work." After this, my perception of my employees changed dramatically. Not that I did not care about my employees, but I would have to pay much more attention than I had thus far.

This is why it is very important to involve employees in the development of procedures for the operation of the plant—so they will feel like they are owners of their process and strictly follow the procedures to ensure stable operations.

IMPORTANCE OF STANDARD WORK

Standardized work is a technique whereby you are in the base of the Toyota Production System. Standard work is a reference in Toyota and is considered one of the most important techniques of TPS because we know that when we have a standard procedure, we can adequately maintain quality products from the beginning to the end of the project; that is, the first car is as good as the 500th or 500,000th car.

For this purpose, Toyota's assembly lines train people in a line parallel to the actual production line, performing the same activity as would be done on the assembly line. They also teach the operators skills. For example, putting their hand inside a box with screws and having to remove five screws; this should be repeated twenty times, and the operator should not remove more or less than five screws. Operators must repeat this process again and again until they remove the five screws consistently in twenty repetitions.

On the assembly line, before the worker enters the line, he or she must pass several skill tests; operators cannot proceed to the next training event until they have passed these tests.

But why is this important? At Toyota, every second of production is extremely important, because each activity described in the work procedure has a time to be executed. If an operator fails to remove the five screws from the box, this may delay the flow of production.

WHY WORK USING STANDARDS?

The first question we have to ask ourselves is why should we do standard work? If the answer is "to do our jobs better," this is partially correct; if the answer is "to maintain a standard in our daily activities," it is also partly true; but if the answer is "we want the work of our operators to be easily implemented and easily trained," then it is correct

Whenever we think of standard work, we want to have repeatability in the operation, where it depends on the person carrying it out. That is, the operator must perform the operation repeatedly without making any mistakes in the sequence of the operation.

Many companies spend a lot of time trying to create long trainings, where the employee ends up abandoning a Just-In-Time (JIT) work experience due to the high demand and many documents and regulations that he or she must fill in the manufacturing process. More questions that we must ask include: Does it add value to our product? What is the purpose of taking several hours or weeks to train an operator? Without these questions, we would not find that the hours of training are too long, and at the end, after weeks of training, the operator joins the line and cannot perform the activity that was defined. But why does this happen? The answer is very simple: Our training has no objective. We train because we have to meet the company equipment, yet ultimately, we do not manage to reach the goal.

We have several ways to do standard work, but we must never forget when doing standard work that we have to think simple. This means creating a procedure where anyone can be incorporated at any point of the assembly line and perform the activity with only a simple explanation so that we succeed in maintaining the operators' repeatability in each activity.

If we make a standard operating procedure in which the operator has doubts regarding how to perform the operation, then our standardized work is half done. This is why it is important for the leader or line manager to create the standard. The knowledge acquired during years of experience can help make a simple and objective standard.

In companies where it is the operator who may have more experience than the leader or supervisor, you need to make use of the operator's experience to develop operational procedures.

In many companies, the standard is defined by production engineers who know how to do an activity but do not know the details of how to make a quick and repetitive activity ensure the quality of the products or services to be performed.

When it comes to standardized work, we must ask ourselves the following: What is the work that I do on this machine? At my workstation? If we do not create a standard manufacturing process, this will never change. What changes is when you increase or decrease the takt time, place more people in the process, or remove people, but the activity itself never changes; hence, the importance of standardizing the manufacturing process is to ensure repeatability and quality processes.

OPERATIONAL PROCEDURES, WORK INSTRUCTIONS, AND WORK AND LABOR PROCEDURES

Operational procedures, work instructions, as well as work and labor procedures all refer to the same thing; their objective is to standardize the operation.

People often think that to do standardized work is only to standardize the operator's tasks, but in this case we want to standardize the manufacturing operation because the goal is for anyone to arrive at the location where they need to make a part, read the work procedure, and perform the operation only with a simple explanation from the leader of the production line.

What is the procedure for training? After describing the work procedures, with the description, key point, quality, and safety, the leader goes to the operator who has to perform the activity and carries out step-by-step instructions of the transaction by reading the procedure and explaining it to the operator. Then the operator must perform the operation by reading the work procedure. After performing the operation, the operator repeats the operation, but this time he or she must explain to the leader what to do; that is, the trainee becomes the trainer. This method eliminates several hours of training that a person usually requires in other companies.

I have a brother-in-law named Marcelino Edjalma, who worked at a vehicle assembly plant. He assembled the car's seat belt. When he would need to go to the bathroom and had no other person to cover for him, he would start working ahead in the seat belt assembly line to allow time to go to the bathroom. When he returned, he would be behind by three to four vehicles, so he would take the belts that he had not fitted and enter the assembly operation of other workers in order to mount the belts until he reached the point where he had left off. But the question is: How could he manage to do this?

I think the time of his operation was faster than the takt time of the process because if he had only the precise time, he could not perform his activity more quickly, even if he wanted to. This is because when we do operator balancing, we must take into account all the movements of the operator. In case there are any operations that could fatigue the operator, Kaizens are made during the tryout and Goshi.

A tryout is different from Goshi. Tryouts are used, for example, to test some production jigs. The quality process never uses tryouts to verify production capacity at Toyota. Goshi, on the other hand, is a simulation of the maximum production capacity, to observe how operators are working by checking the product flow and operators. This event takes place in an hour. While the operators are working on the production line, the leader, chief, supervisor, manager, engineering, maintenance, and quality control are outside the line watching all the items that need improvement as soon as possible to achieve the line speed according to the takt time defined by the customer.

In Goshi, we also check how the movement of material near the line will work, as logistics personnel will replenish the line and remove the product from the line to where the product will be taken, to the one responsible for its release and dispatching. So you see, the entire process is verified from the material input to the delivery of the product to the customer.

At Toyota, we would generally perform two or three Goshi before filling the line. Usually, it takes an average of two to three days to reach the ideal production. Depending on the process, this is achieved after three hours of production; hence, the customer takt time can be reached very quickly.

Usually, people agree that companies have a learning curve; thus, it takes one or two weeks to reach the takt time. This occurs when the operating rules are unclear to the operator, and when the training system is not optimal, such as providing the procedure to the operator and saying, "Follow the process and give it your best!" How can a person do his or her best if he or she has never made this product before?

I was at a company once where the supervisor seemed like a foreman with a whip in his hand; if the operator did not make the part on time, the supervisor would shout and insult the operator, calling him a "jackass." I asked the supervisor why he reacted this way with the operator. His answer was, "If there's no whip, things don't work." It was then that I started training them in standardized work and explained the importance of following the standard operating procedure, which was designed to perform the activity within the takt time. Then the operators began to offer suggestions for making activities faster and with less physical effort, to help all operators achieve the defined takt time.

Sometimes, bosses forget that they have to assist operators, because if we help the operators, we will achieve greater productivity.

A problem in many companies is that they do not know the purpose of applying Seiri, Seiton, Seiso, Seiketsu, Shitsuke (5S). They think that it is just to make areas more beautiful and orderly. Of course, after the implementation of 5S, everything will look neat and better overall, but what is the purpose? For those of us who work at Toyota, it is simple: It serves to make sure that waste can be seen in less than ten seconds. With this, one can work to quickly eliminate waste and avoid a costly operation.

HOW THE WORK WAS DONE AT TOYOTA: STANDARD WORK BEFORE TECHNOLOGY

Before, without any technology to help standard work activities, the staff of Toyota developed a technique to time the activities performed by the operator; but how was this done? Let's look at the detailed steps.

First, one would write what the operator does for each activity and then time the activities ten times consecutively, and consider the time that was repeated the most during the ten repetitions. This is how I learned it at Toyota Japan, as it was explained by my Sensei. The idea was that I learn from Toyota's history and experience, and ensure that more attention be placed on the standardization in order to eliminate waste.

I learned to check the process without using a stopwatch. It is very simple; you count 1,001, 1,002, 1,003.... When you pronounce the numbers, it takes the same amount of time as using the counter. It is important for leaders to check the operation time without using a stopwatch. Nakata-san would stop in front of the line with his arms crossed and start to count the cycle time for each operator. If he discovered any unbalance in the line, he would call me to ask where the problem was. I needed to identify the same issue, but without using a stopwatch to check the operators' cycle time in the process. After discovering the problem, I would call my group leader and ask him the same question: Where is the problem? The group leader needed to find the problem without using a stopwatch either. When the group leader found the problem, he was required to call the production team leader to ask the same question; the team leader, using the same process, once he found the problem, was required to talk to the operator regarding the unbalance in the line and explain the importance of following the procedure.

This was the most challenging part of standard work, as there were many activities performed by the operator; but with a lot of persistence and perseverance, it was the beginning of the first standard work activities in the machining area and, later, in other departments.

Once the standard time was established, there had to be a written work procedure, so the operator could do the same repetitive activity in the same way. But how could this be done without technology?

The staff began by describing the operation step by step, and after timing each step that was taken, the problem was that oftentimes the operator did not perform in the same sequence as in the previous repetition. This initially made it a bit difficult to standardize the activities.

As the years have gone by at Toyota, some things have changed, but we have never forgotten the initial basis set by our Senseis Taiichi Ohno and Sakichi Toyoda.

HOW STANDARD WORK WAS DONE AT TOYOTA AFTER THE INTRODUCTION OF TECHNOLOGY

After technology (video cameras, computers, etc.) arrived, standardization activities became easier to perform. We could use video to record an activity and then describe the operation being performed.

Toyota has developed a system whereby after making a video, it can be played back in a program that displays tens of seconds. You may wonder, why tens of seconds? The answer is simple: because every second you can win at Toyota is like finding gold. Let's do an exercise now to clarify what I am saying.

Imagine that we conduct a Kaizen that reduces one second in a final assembly line. If we do the math, we'll find gold. Here we go:

1 second × 400,000 vehicles produced in a year will give me 400,000 seconds gained in a year, right!

We divide the gain by the takt time of the production line to see how many cars we can produce in the time we have gained. Here we go:

400,000 seconds / 60 seconds (takt time = processing time of the assembly line for a car) = 6,666 cars a year

Now multiply this number of cars by the sales value, and we have the following:

6,666 cars × $ 18,000 (value used for reference only) = $119,998,000

After this calculation, I think everyone will be thinking: How can I save one second in my process? Well, it takes us awhile to understand our needs.

But let's return to our current era at Toyota Brazil. We are using the concept to evaluate a video recording of five repetitions (cycles) of the same operation, then discarding the longest and shortest times and averaging the three remaining times. This is very different from what Toyota was doing previously. We learned this new methodology with Sakamaki-san in Brazil as demonstrated in the following figure. This must be done for manual, movement, and automatic activities.

After describing each activity, we will have to standardize the activities, and for this, we must consider some important factors before starting the standardization.

To begin the preparation of standard operating procedures, the first thing we must verify is the lead-time (total execution time of the operation), that is, adding the complete cycle time of each operation plus the times that do not add value. The latter are called non-value-added times because we must do them due to their importance for the continuity of the process, but add nothing to the product. For example, exchanging a barrel of welding wire and doing inspections during an exchange of carbide inserts for machining are the activities for which we have to stop the process to carry out the task, in order to maintain the quality of the manufactured products.

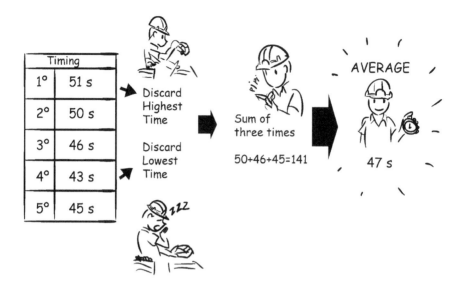

Timing	
1°	51 s
2°	50 s
3°	46 s
4°	43 s
5°	45 s

Discard Highest Time

Discard Lowest Time

Sum of three times

50+46+45=141

AVERAGE

47 s

Once the lead-time is defined, we need to set the number of operators needed in our process. How do we do this? We take the lead-time and divide it by the takt time as follows:

$$\text{Operator Quantity} = \frac{\text{Lead Time}}{\text{Takt Time}}$$

After defining the number of operators on the line, we must balance each activity that the operator must perform, using the Yamazumi diagram, which means balancing the workforce as in the example in Figure 2.1.

With the graph, we can divide the operations among the operators so that their workload is exactly the same, because if this does not happen, there may be dissatisfaction among some operators that may cause delays in production and a revolt, causing a problem for the area chief, which would then be difficult to reverse.

Once a balance is established between the operators, they must define the flow, which should follow the balance achieved before, as in Figure 2.2.

Note that the layout of the production cell shows how the operator must walk during the operation, but we can also see a cross figure, which means that we must be aware of operator safety. There is also a diamond figure, which means that these points in the process require that inspections be carried out during the manufacturing of products. We also have an X figure inside a circle, called Temochi, representing the standard inventory

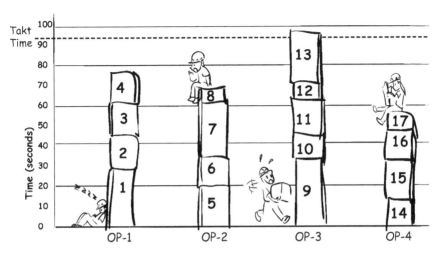

FIGURE 2.1
Yamazumi diagram.

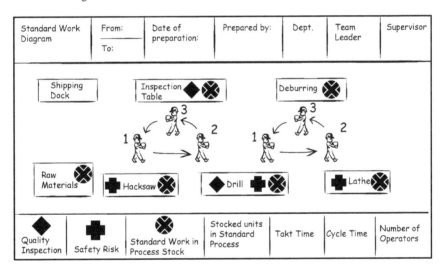

FIGURE 2.2
Standard work diagram.

within the process, which we use to provide faster part changing on the machine or to guarantee the number of parts that the machine requires, as some machines are made to produce more than one piece in the process.

Factory Layout

The layout of the factory determines the way in which the resources of materials, information, and customers flow through operations. What I learned at Toyota was that a good layout can bring many benefits to operators and productivity by reducing waste.

The key point to creating a good layout is to think simple and not complicate the task. To think simple, we must always consider the movement of the operator's hands as well as the operator and product movements.

I have made many changes in layouts since leaving Toyota. I have taught people that you always have to find an easier way of doing things in a production line.

I undertook a project at a company in Guadalajara, Mexico, where we needed to increase productivity to meet customer demand and decrease scrap at the line. Looking at the layout, there were two separate areas performing sequential processes of a product (a press and an assembly operation), with five days of WIP inventory kept between them. The actual problem, I found, had more to do with a myth: people were told that the two processes could not be physically connected due to the presence of a vertical injection machine in one of the areas, although there was sufficient space to place the assembly line adjacent to the vertical injection press.

The problem was that no one considered calculating the takt time to verify whether the line had capacity before attempting to locate the two areas together.

After two days of observing the areas separately, taking time for each activity, and documenting the movements of the operators, we began to draw the new layout with the vertical press. After defining the new layout, we discovered that the old layout required ten operators. By balancing the line activities according to the takt time, we estimated that the new layout would need only five people.

The key point was to take the time of the injection molding and the curing time of the rubber element applied to the product, which, after application, required a twenty-minute wait in order to dry the product, before the testing process could start the testing process. In order to wait twenty minutes for the product to cure, we created a standard inventory called *Temochi* in Japanese.

Before moving the layout, we performed trials in some points of the layout to verify if the line balance was right and define the standardized work procedure for each workstation.

Immediately after moving the layout, the operators felt uneasy with the new way of producing; but after showing them the importance of following standardized work procedures in the operation, they started feeling more confident in their ability to achieve productivity without rejections, which is what occurred through the implementation of standardized work in their area.

The experience was very good for me because it was one of the first companies that I worked with after leaving Toyota, doing what I had always learned: *Find the easiest layout for the operation, using standard work as the basis.*

Layout changes such as the location of a machine in a factory or a product in a supermarket may affect the flow of materials and people throughout the operation, impacting the cost and overall efficiency of production.

An improvement in the layout of the production line yields the following benefits:

1. Elimination of transport man-hours
2. Faster feedback regarding quality to help reduce defects
3. Reduced man-hours by reducing or eliminating waiting for a batch or process
4. Reduced production cycle

When we arrange the layout of a production line, not only must we think of the flow of the operator, but we must also consider how the product flow in the line should be. We must think of how to make the operator exert minimum effort and, if possible, have something to move a piece from one machine to another.

Objectives of the Layout

The objectives of developing a proper layout are as follows:

1. Minimize the size of the plant, therefore reducing the costs of operator motion, transport, space, and capital for facilities.
2. Remove the excess centralized inventory of materials, components, and units purchased or manufactured.
3. Minimize disruptions to the factory due to change and to enable future growth.
4. Avoid locating offices or support services in the perimeters of the factory.
5. Reduce the space occupied by the formal corridors of the factory in relation to those occupied by the production processes.

One day, a friend invited me to verify the layout of a press factory that made products for automobile assembly and computers. When I entered the facility, it seemed to me like a messy factory producing inventory, with no production flow. There was too much waste of transport and operator motion.

He asked, "What did you see in my process?" I replied that I did not see anything because it was very difficult to observe something with all of the disorder and lack of organization. Then he said, "Seriously? I thought the layout of the factory was much better now." To this, I replied, "Better for whom?" For the operators, it was much better because they did not have to work much; they were always moving to find something, not to mention the waiting time for a press change, etc.

My friend looked me in the eyes and said, "Then how would you change the flow from what it is now?" I said, "Very simple. All you have to do is think simple; don't complicate things. Make the flow visible, simple for the operation, where the operator can work and not have to walk all day."

He then said, "Gerson, I have a new plant that I want you to see to verify how the flow is. Can you take a look?" I said, "Sure!" When he showed me the layout, I could not believe it; the same mistakes that the old plant had, the new one had, even before starting the process. Why was this happening? Often, it is very complex for people to think simple; they always want to make more complex things that do not work and only bring more waste into processing.

I told my friend that he should change the layout to have more flow and arrange the machines to make it easier for handling forklifts. After six months, I visited my friend again to see if he had taken my advice. To my surprise, he had not changed anything; it was a new factory with the same mess as the old one.

I asked him why he had not changed anything as per what we had discussed. His response was that there was no time to think of another mode despite his attempts to change.

Sometimes, what is easy for one person is too complex for others. At Toyota, we received training to look at the problem and solve it as fast as possible, always avoiding waste in the process, so that the flow is the simplest and easy to visualize.

Human Factor

In TPS, productivity is a key factor, and its increase is a constant target. Meanwhile, the human factor in TPS is closely correlated with productivity.

PROBLEMS IN THE IMPLEMENTATION OF STANDARD WORK

Problems that occur in the implementation of standard work are typically simple to solve. The problem is that people do not want to make the necessary improvements because they take time, and in the end, you lose the implementation.

In many companies that implement Lean, there is standardized work. The problem is that it is implemented badly. Quite often, the standardization is not done by the Leader or Supervisor of the area, but by the Engineer of the area, who does not possess the same type of experience as the Leader and Supervisor of the area.

The Engineer does not know the details of the operation; the Engineer often has excellent technical knowledge but does not have all the details on how to make the operation faster and more appropriate. But why am I writing this? When you have to write the key points of the operation, the Operator and Team Leader possess much more knowledge with which to define the standard operation, as mentioned previously.

Another question is: Why do people not want to stay within the standard? The answer is simple: Because we forgot to explain why the operator must follow the standard.

In a company in Mexico, after the implementation of a standard, the Operations Leader would audit every line operator to verify whether or not they were all following the work procedure according to standard work. At first, the Leader had to review every thirty minutes, then one hour, and then every two hours, four hours, until she reviewed only once each shift.

She reviewed the work standard and hours of operation (the takt time was 10.5 seconds). The operators initially had trouble with the operation sequence because they were already accustomed to operating the wrong way, but the Leader, upon detecting a deviation, would talk to the operators about where they were making the mistake, and then stayed close to the operator until more than ten parts were produced, to see if the operator had understood the explanation.

An extremely important point refers to the photos that are placed in a standard work procedure. Many companies use pictures taken from too far away or that are very difficult to make out. This is why, often, the operator does not follow the standard.

The pictures must show how to perform the operation. They must offer details to achieve a good operation so that there is no doubt in the operator's mind at the time of the operation.

Toyota rigorously follows its standards; at all times, the Leader is reviewing the work of each operator.

WHERE TO PLACE STANDARD WORK INSTRUCTIONS

Where to place operational standards is the big question that everyone asks. The answer depends on the process you have, because there are operations in which the standard cannot be physically placed in front of the operation. So, the answer is, "It depends." But if you ask where the best place is to put the work instructions, the answer is, "where the operator has to perform the task." This is so that if an operator has a question during the process, he or she can look at the standard and perform the activity safely.

The problem occurs when there is a Kaizen done to the line; one has to change the standard work instruction so that other employees can perform the task in the same way. But why is this a problem? You need time to make a change to the standard work instructions, and quite often, we have no time to change them, which then makes the daily checks useless, and the Kaizen is lost over time.

At Toyota, when we want to do Kaizen on the line, first we test to prove that the Kaizen is really going to bring a benefit to the area. Then we check to see that it will not cause an imbalance in the line. When there is an imbalance, we need to redistribute the activities between operators, which may generate another change in the standard work instructions. This is why standardized work is not easy to do, and why so many companies have their procedures in a binder—to avoid seeing that they need to make revisions.

Toyota's operational standards are in front of the operator. In the case of forging and foundry, they are next to the operation, because the heat can burn the instruction sheets. But before doing the activity, the operator must see how to do the operation, and then the leader or manager must observe whether or not the operator is following the work according to the standard.

I hope this chapter on standardized work has helped answer any questions you had regarding this topic.

The most important point is to make things as simple as possible first, and then think of how to improve the process.

I have no doubt that if you do not have good standardized work, you will certainly have many quality problems in your process. If you do have standardized work, be certain that it is being followed correctly; use the experience of the "king" to help create good standardized work procedures.

Just to finish, I want to make it clear to you that for the implementation to have passion, you must perform the implementation of each technique with joy, not simply implement because you must. Remember that Lean is for the organization; once it is well-implemented, it does not fall back. The implementation of Lean may be lost only when the system depends on a person. We must acknowledge that the system cannot rely on a single person; the system depends on all employees every day, hour by hour, minute by minute. When I left Toyota, nothing was lost with my absence; do you know why? The system was all standardized. It does not depend on a person; it depends on the operators wanting to perform their tasks according to the standards.

3

Jidoka

Renato Eiji Kitazuka, with Carlos Moretti

More than a technique or a tool, Jidoka is the principle that pursues quality production and decouples the process from direct supervision. Over time, Jidoka became one of the two pillars of the Toyota Production System (TPS) (Figure 3.1).

ORIGINS

By the end of the nineteenth century, years before Toyota Motors Corporation was founded, the principles that guided its famous production system were already being practiced by Sakichi Toyoda, a visionary man considered by many as the Father of Japan's Industrial Revolution and the inventor of Japanese inventors.

In his childhood, Sakichi observed his mother working very hard making cloth for the family on a manual loom. It troubled Sakichi to see his mother working so hard to produce such a small quantity of cloth. This led him to invent a loom that eliminated some of the wasteful motion in traditional loom work. He continued to build on this initial invention, and he eventually developed a loom company. As the company grew, he was perplexed by one of the biggest issues in looming: If one thread broke without being noticed, hours of precious work and much raw material would be scrapped. To prevent this, a person was dedicated full time to monitor the machine and stop it when a thread breaks. Sakichi realized that just adding extra workers to the job would not solve the problem. He figured out that one possible solution could be to decouple the looming work supervision from its operator, and by doing so, free him/her more time to perform value-added work. Step by step, he implemented small changes and identified new opportunities to improve the process' design. This technique, of achieving higher levels of efficiency and quality through small

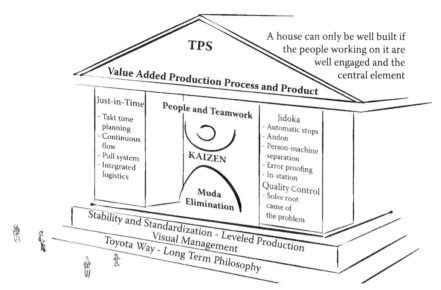

FIGURE 3.1
House of TPS.

improvements, became his legacy, the Kaizen Culture. Finally, after many attempts, Sakichi developed a mechanism that would automatically stop the loom if a thread broke. Far beyond a simple quality device Mr. Sakichi introduced a guideline, a principle adopted by Toyota as the essence of TPS called Jidoka, a Japanese word for automation that has a deeper meaning at Toyota: *automation with a human touch* or *autonomous automation*.

JIDOKA AS A PILLAR OF THE TOYOTA PRODUCTION SYSTEM

At Toyota, people know that "the right process will produce the right results." Therefore, one of the main goals of Toyota's management teams is to improve processes by eliminating waste. On the other hand, predicting all the potential failures of a given process is nearly impossible. So, the best way to achieve the "perfect process" is to stop the process and fix every small error immediately after it occurs and before it reaches a critical level.

I used to work in a fastener company, and I can recall an example where an oil leak was identified within one of our main client's assembly lines. After our client's final inspection team detected a certain number of defective components, the whole batch of parts was segregated. As our client pointed to one of our items as a probable source of problems, we started a problem-solving process.

There were many different parts that could have caused the oil leak—for example, gaskets, joints, bolts. I was assigned to support the problem-solving process focused on the bolted joint.

It took us a few weeks to finally find the "root cause": a variation in the torque control system, which was not assuring the proper pressure over the joint, thus leading to the oil leakages.

As a solution, the torque control system was adjusted accordingly and new parameters of inspection were added to the process.

Although, at the time, it sounded great, deep in my mind I was not sure that the root cause had really been eliminated. "What if the inspection fails?" I wondered.

A few years later, when I was working at Toyota, one fact called my attention at the engine assembly line: to my surprise, other than sophisticated torque control systems, I had seen in many engine assembly lines that Toyota was using very simple and cheap mechanical torque wrenches to ensure proper torque application.

I asked the assembly line leader why Toyota didn't use electronic or pneumatic devices. He told me that some time ago, Toyota had also run a similar problem-solving project due to an oil leak issue.

I didn't know it then, but I was about to learn a more effective way to run a *real* problem-solving project!

Toyota had never considered any component as being part of the problem! Using the Jidoka concept, after the torque inspection failed, they immediately realized that there was an issue with the torque application system and the assembly line stopped. The team in charge of solving the problem identified that the pneumatic system adopted to apply the torque over the fasteners was highly susceptible to variations within the air pressure lines and that jeopardized the stability of the whole process.

As a countermeasure, for small production volumes, they adopted a very reliable and well-known technology: a simple mechanical device that did not depend on air pressure.

Experts in the matter might say that I am oversimplifying the technical part of this case, and indeed I am. It is not my goal to discuss the problem and solution, but emphasize that it merely took Toyota a few hours from the moment they detected the problem to put the countermeasure in place. Thanks to the Jidoka principle, they were able to stop the process, narrow it down to the specific cause without being diverted by other potential factors. The result was that the problem's analysis was drastically simplified.

At Toyota, the elements of building a solid process are compared to building a solid house. This is visualized in the House of the TPS, built over a strong foundation of process stability, with two strong pillars—Just in Time and Jidoka—that sustain its protective roof (competitive cost). (See Figure 3.1.)

As with any house, the roof will only be as steady as the pillars are strong. But what we experience when working with companies outside of Toyota is that they love to implement Just in Time, because of the inventory reduction they experience. On the other hand, these same companies are reluctant to stop the processes when something goes wrong. "The show must go on," they say.

We call this the "toolbox approach," that is, choosing the tools and techniques that help solve an urgent need, but do not look at building a sustainable culture of Lean. There is no doubt that this approach will lead to the construction of a weak house!

Lean techniques should be used in the same way as when you start a course of antibiotics: You take them all as prescribed and not just when you want to or because you like or dislike them. Fujio Cho, former president of Toyota Motor Company, said the following:

> Many good companies have respect for individuals, practice Kaizen and other TPS techniques. But what is important is having all the elements together as a System. It must be practiced every day in a very consistent manner—not in spurts—in a **concrete** way on the shop floor.

I've been deploying the Lean Culture over the past ten years, working with different business and cultures. I must confess that I am still learning the TPS through the House analogy. Ironically, I was a little bit disappointed when I was introduced to it.

My first weeks at Toyota were incredible! Every day, I learned new business administration techniques. My boss, a patient teacher—or *Sensei*, in Japanese—spent a great deal of time with me. During one of our learning sessions, I asked him for something to read about the TPS. He gave me a copy of Toyota's internal handbook. After reading it, I thought, "How is that possible? One of the most powerful production systems in the word is based on a house analogy? What about the 'do-it-yourself instructions'?"

After that, I started searching for explanations everywhere, except among external sources, but I found no descriptions of techniques.

A few years later I left Toyota to be a Lean Agent in an auto parts company. It was a brand-new facility, built over Lean concepts and considered by many as a model Lean plant. In truth, I was seduced by their outstanding Lean structure and their amazing, fully detailed Lean manual, *The Lean Production System Manual*. This handbook had complete, detailed instructions on how to implement a Lean system. All the requirements for a Lean company were listed there. The company also had lots of experts running training sections and developing Lean projects. I had definitely not seen that structure at Toyota. In fact, at that time, I could say that their Lean system was better than Toyota's.

On the other hand, something was intriguing me; despite the fact that the above-mentioned structure had been implemented, the basic concepts were not in place! There was a huge distance between what they had written and what they *really* did. The procedures that were performed at Toyota in a natural way were just neglected.

I started asking myself, if the structure here is so great, then why has Toyota had more success deploying Lean than my new company has ever dreamed of?

After experiencing failures and successes in deploying Lean techniques in different processes, I learned that the simplicity of Toyota's TPS material was actually its major advantage. The principles embraced by the House of TPS guide workers to drive their efforts to strengthen the system's foundation and pillars, without inducing them to apply a specific technique. I had just underestimated the power of that analogy!

We still observe companies that focus their efforts on deploying Lean techniques. Thus, Lean becomes another program for "specialists," and department performances are measured by the number of Lean techniques that are implemented.

The bad news about this approach is that when Lean becomes a task for specialists instead of everyone's duty, your Lean deployment process will need *direct supervision* to achieve the desired quality level. And as we see below, the Jidoka principle is just the opposite: We should decouple the process' quality from direct supervision.

When deploying Jidoka, the Lean expert does not play the auditor's role, but rather the teacher's role—a Sensei who imparts knowledge and shares his experiences. Instead of using books, the Sensei guides his pupils through "learning-by-doing sessions" and then makes *the technique's purpose* very clear to everyone.

This may be considered one of Toyota's major success factors—no matter which Toyota facility you work in, the House of TPS is present.

SO, WHAT IS THE PURPOSE OF USING JIDOKA?

1. *Built-in quality.* This is ensured by preventing the defective products/services from being delivered. This technique means that you are going to dedicate yourself to only obtaining products/services with the customer desired quality level. The process should be designed to identify problems immediately after they occur and induce workers to always follow the correct procedures. Although it sounds simple and obvious, in most cases, this feature is neglected.

2. *Decouple quality and process flow from direct supervision.* The poka yoke, developed by Shigeo Shingo, is a Japanese term meaning mistake-proofing, and is a key technique to decouple the quality of a process from direct supervision by stopping operation as an issue arises and to request assistance to correct the process. As Shingo used to say: "Most people know how to ride a bike. But it doesn't mean that they know how to fix it. So, why would it be different with a process?". The Jidoka principle provides for autonomy. When we manage to decouple the execution of a given task from direct supervision, we better utilize resources and free up time of skilled workers for more value-added tasks, and thus, improving the process.

Years ago, I worked for a fastener manufacturer. This company had a very skilled group of engineers working in the Production Planning department. They were supported by many technicians working on the shop floor, monitoring the production and inventory levels and providing vital information to develop the Material Requirement Plan. All their tasks were aided by powerful production planning software.

The production plan team was considered by many to be "the company's brain and heart." They were respected by all other areas. I also have to say that they were the most stressed team in the company, always working extended hours under high pressure. Unfortunately, despite all the resources and efforts consumed by this structure, it was not error-proof! They frequently experienced planning reviews, extra freight, and fines for late deliveries. At least a quarter of the whole facility area was dedicated to staging the finished goods. Considering the "in-process inventory," we could say that more than half of the floor space was dedicated to inventory.

Later, when I started working at Toyota in Brazil, I almost went into shock when I met the single engineer who was responsible for planning the parts production and the whole assembly line.

As a matter of fact, in Sao Bernardo, Brazil, we had small production volumes but the complexity of a car assembly line is much bigger than the complexity of a fastener production facility.

I thought, "How is it possible? My friends from my previous job were always complaining about how hard it was to keep things running and how busy they were. How could a car manufacturer run *the entire* planning department with a single engineer? I mean, just one person was assigned to dealing with forecasting, production orders, machines' schedules, follow-ups, inventory control, etc.!"

A tour with Toyota's production planner revealed to me many of Toyota's world-famous techniques. When I was introduced to Kanban, a technique developed to support the Just in Time pillar, I understood that it was also applying, in full, the principles of Jidoka. A Kanban system is designed to be run by workers from the shop floor, as it decouples the production's control from the production planner's direct supervision; there is no need for "experts" or follow-ups. The complex "puzzle" of adjusting the production planning is replaced by a very simple task that is executed by the workers in real-time (see Chapter 4 for more details about Kanban).

Here, we must emphasize the importance of understanding the purpose of Jidoka. If Toyota had applied Jidoka according to its direct translation—automation—as most companies actually do, they would have developed very complex software to plan its production. By adequately understanding the technique's *purpose,* Toyota aimed its efforts at decoupling the Production control from direct supervision.

Using Jidoka

When I worked at Toyota, I had one of the most valuable experiences during the launch of a new engine's assembly line. I was working as a Product Engineer. My office was located in an administrative building far from the manufacturing site, and I was required to deliver training at the assembly line. It was my first long visit to the manufacturing site, having spent only a few days there since I had been hired. It would also be my first real contact with Jidoka. When I visited the assembly line, the first thing that caught my attention was that the line was mostly manual. Just a few very complex tasks were automated with very simple devices. I really was expecting robots and very high-tech machines in the assembly line. "The Japanese are the experts in automation," I thought.

So, I asked a friend how they could have Jidoka in place if there were no electronic devices running on that line. My friend told me that there were just a few robots on the whole site, and they were mostly dedicated to hazardous tasks or high-precision-level activities. The other activities were manual, but that, indeed, Jidoka was in place on that assembly line.

I have to confess that I became a little bit frustrated when he told me that Jidoka was a cord hanging over each workstation, used to turn on a lightboard, the Andon board. These boards were used to show when a workstation needed support.

Actually, I didn't understand my friend. How could those simple cords ensure the quality of the whole process? As an engineer, working in a fastener manufacturing company, I visited many assembly lines, where I saw very sophisticated and automated equipment used to control the processes. Could it be possible that a cord attached to a red ball was the great secret of the famous TPS?

When you look at an iceberg floating in the sea, you can't see what lies underwater. Likewise, at a glance, I could not see all the details hidden in that process. After spending some time observing the assembly line activities, I understood why Toyota was so confident in its production system: Those cords were just symbols—symbols of everyone's commitment to quality.

Looking "underwater," I understood that the behavior and the culture were much more important than fancy high-tech equipment. At Toyota's assembly line, everything was inducing the correct activities. On the floor, there were indications and borderlines used to show the workflow to the operators. Each workstation had the correct material and tools for its application. There were few opportunities for mistakes. In fact, making mistakes was more difficult than doing the right things.

After all, if those features failed, a new opportunity for improvement was identified—an opportunity for all team members to work and design a better process! That's why the Andon cords were so important, and interrupting the process was an expectation when problems occurred. I was fascinated by the concept of the Andon cords being quality gates, where operators verified their work and decided whether the product would move on or if assistance would be needed.

So, you may ask, "When should I start implementing Jidoka?" Well, without knowing your process, this would be a very difficult question to answer. There is no strict formula, but there are a few guidelines.

Implementation Stages of Jidoka

Most companies fail to implement Jidoka because they do not fully understand the principle, and as a result, they misunderstand the basic needs of implementation. A quick assessment will be very useful in identifying the stage of implementation that a company has reached.

To start the implementation of Jidoka, let's go back to the "House of TPS" analogy. You will only be able to build the pillars—JIT and Jidoka—when the House's foundation is solid. Thus, we could say that, first of all, you and your team should have *systematic problem-solving skills*. This is a very important landmark because, in fact, all of Toyota's techniques are countermeasures established after problem-solving processes (see Chapter 5 for more details about PDCA problem solving). Trying to implement Jidoka before having *basic stability* will compromise the whole structure of the House.

Once you have team members who are able to solve problems by eliminating their root causes, you should start developing processes and methods that detect problems as soon as they occur.

Although problems occur daily, it is not so easy to see them happening or learn from them. This probably happens due to the heritage of our childhood, when errors and problems were subject to punishment. As a result, we perceive problems as our personal faults and we tend to hide them. As managers, it is our duty to show our team members the benefits of bringing problems to the surface. Taiichi Ohno, the father of the modern TPS, stated that "No problem is the biggest problem."

Bringing "problems to the surface" is the greatest challenge in building the Jidoka Culture. It will take time, discipline, and effort to gain people's trust and confidence that the revelation of problems will not result in punishment. One of the best ways of empowering Jidoka's implementation is to deploy a Kaizen Teian program (see Chapter 7).

But how can we ensure that all the problems of a given process will be discovered? Utilizing inspections is a possible answer. Although inspection is one of the seven wastes—overprocessing—it is almost impossible to recognize problems if we don't use inspection procedures. The third stage of Jidoka is implementing effective quality gates or inspections points to identify process errors.

We can classify inspections into three types:

1. *Judgment inspections:* Where a finished product is compared to a standard. If anything goes wrong, the product is scrapped or reworked.
2. *Informative inspections:* Where feedback is provided on the process and corrective action is taken. The informative method may also prevent errors by using statistical tools and analyses to predict process tendencies.
3. *In-source inspections:* The most used methodology at Toyota, where simple devices make the 100% inspection feasible and reliable, without the interference of human fatigue and attention.

In-source inspections are the most powerful techniques used by Jidoka implementation. The basic principle is to "discover" the errors before they even occur. We can achieve this using Poka Yokes. As stated above, these devices induce the correct execution of the process or stop errors from occurring. Poka Yoke is the key technique used by Toyota to make problems visible. It is also used as fuel for the Kaizen Teian, promoting the best utilization of team intellect.

We must remember that we are susceptible to mistakes. As a matter of fact, whenever the circumstances and environment induce *mistakes,* sooner or later, they will occur. To reach the fourth stage of Jidoka and create an environment and circumstances that *induce* quality, we should ally Poka Yoke devices, 5S, standardization techniques, and the Built in Quality process.

At a pick-and pack-company that I visited years ago, one common issue was that incorrect material was shipped to the wrong destination due to material being placed in the wrong package. In fact, the process was not badly designed. They did have software to control the operation and a good control method was in place: After scanning a package identification label, a worker would assign a shipping order to it; the system listed the order's contents, and as the worker scanned the package with the required material, it was marked as completed by the system. All these procedures would assure a good process, except by the line organization, that is, a poor 5S. Multiple packages were opened, and the workers were easily confused.

Wondering which package was under work, it was easier to place materials in the wrong packages than to place them in the correct ones. Was this an issue of bad people or bad processes?

After we have gone through all of those steps (a built-in quality environment, which means an environment with a strong 5S, a high level of standardization, *in-source* inspection methodologies, and Poka Yoke devices in place), we can reach the final level of Jidoka: decoupling the process' quality from direct supervision. At this level, you and your team will reap the biggest benefits of Jidoka and will be able to put Andon boards, escalation charts, and the ultimate interruption cords in place, minimizing the chance of errors and reducing skilled labor waste.

It Was Too Early

In the past several years, Lean practices have spread around the world to many different fields. As a result, it is not difficult to find a company that uses Lean techniques to promote the continuous improvement of its processes. I have had the chance to visit many of them, and I'm happy that I learned a little bit about their different processes. I love to understand, or at least, try to understand, how the raw material is transformed into a part. I love "seeing" the flow of people and information inside a bank or an insurance company.

During one of these visits, something very interesting caught my attention. We were walking through the maintenance department of a company that produced hinges, and I saw an Andon board, covered with dust, in the corner of a small room, buried under three or four boxes.

The production manager, one of the three people with me, noticed that I was looking at the board and said, "Ah! That board…. It did not work at all!" Actually, what really caught my attention was the lack of 5S within the room, but of course, I asked him why it did not work.

He replied, "Because, after the Andon board was in place, we had to stop the assembly line at least five to six times per shift. This tool really does not fit our company."

"So, tell me about your team's problem-solving skills," I said.

"Two of them are going to complete the training sessions next month. The others are going to begin their sessions after them."

Well, blaming the Andon board for "stopping" the assembly line is the same as blaming the knife that you used as a screwdriver for cutting your finger. As James Womack says, "We are stuck in the Tool age."

Unfortunately, that manager, like many people, misunderstood the Andon board's purpose: to stop the process in order *to solve problems.* By misunderstanding it, he did not notice that his team was not trained properly in problem-solving techniques. They were barely dealing with the problems' symptoms, let alone eliminating their root causes. Another point that should be highlighted is that they decided to put Andon boards in place too early, before the process was stabilized. Worst of all, in that manager's mind, stopping the process was not good at all. In order for Jidoka to work, the company must see problems as good to have and work diligently to uncover them in order to solve them from the root cause.

CONCLUSION

Many companies deploy Lean techniques in a random sequence. Specifically talking about Jidoka, this "toolbox approach" leads them to use fancy Andon boards, escalation charts, and to stop the processes whenever a problem is detected, even though those companies don't have basic skills in problem-solving techniques. As a result, management teams will deal with a problem's effects instead of seeking its root causes. This superficial approach jeopardizes Jidoka's reliability, as the process becomes ineffective and unpredictable. Ironically, having a predictable process is all that we want when deploying Lean techniques.

In order to enjoy all of Jidoka's greatest benefits, a given process should naturally induce its correct execution—*built-in quality*—without direct supervision. This high maturity level will only be achieved when you and your team deeply understand the process, know all of its fragilities, and realize that stopping it and effectively fixing its problems is a health habit.

Indeed, this is a long journey. Nevertheless, "short-cuts" *must* be avoided. The more deeply you understand your process' weaknesses, the easier it will be to have a strong Jidoka pillar for your House of TPS!

4

Just-In-Time and Kanban

Carlos Yukio Fukamizu

My first contact with the methodologies of Lean Manufacturing happened in an American company, not at Toyota. After obtaining my degree in Production Engineering, I was in doubt as to where I should start my professional activities.

Shortly thereafter, I received a job offer to work in Recife, a town in the northwestern part of Brazil; this place was known for its famous beaches and 365 sunny days a year. Of course I accepted the offer, initially thinking of the time at the beach I could have every day.

I started my job as a process engineer. I was responsible for defining the stages of heat treatment between the steps of aluminum sheets lamination, and I realized this company had a method of work that made me curious; work teams were tasked to improve devices, processes, tools, etc. The teams were composed of people from different areas and responsibilities with a common goal of continuous improvement; each one had a leader responsible for the team, including organizing meetings, materials, schedules, classrooms, etc. The activities of each of the members were discussed according to the tasks and goals set in previous meetings, there was visual control of the activities of each group member, and they were very strict with the dates of beginning and end of each task.

The methodology used in this company at that time left a very good impression. After researching more, I realized it was deeper than I imagined. It was aimed not only at continuous improvement but a whole philosophy of implementation of a production system; it was the culture based on the improvement of man with the obsession to always be improving the processes to pursue waste elimination.

The vision of this company for continuous improvement in the elimination of waste radically changed the way I used to think and act as a process engineer.

Years later, while working at Toyota, I learned more about the culture and principles this company was implementing; it was clear they already used many of these principles of Toyota Production System (TPS), in particular, Kaizen, or continuous improvement.

JUST-IN-TIME

Introduction

The concept of Just-In-Time (JIT) at Toyota was established after years of continuous improvement within the production processes, aiming to manufacture the vehicles demanded by customers in a fast and efficient manner, making the delivery time to be as short as possible.

JIT was not simply an inventory reduction, or the solution to bad management. It focuses attention on how the skills and knowledge of employees can best be used to improve productivity, safety, and quality. It is also about how to engage and commit all levels of the organization to aim toward the same objective.

JIT is one of the pillars of the TPS and Kanban is a means of application to reach the concept of production in Just-In-Time.

In this chapter we also examine case studies and projects I developed in non-automotive companies using the Kanban system.

INTRODUCTION OF JIDOKA AND JUST-IN-TIME AS THE PILLARS OF TPS

Both concepts are deeply connected; it is not possible to have JIT production if Jidoka's concept is not efficiently deployed in the productive processes.

Jidoka

This concept was applied to the first mechanical loom developed in 1896 by Sakichi Toyoda, founder of Toyota Motors Corporation group.

The traditional looms from that time used to waste materials due to the poor quality of products; such things used to happen when the cotton threads got broken, creating noticeable defects in the manufactured woof, which was very frequent at that time.

To eliminate the defect, Sakichi Toyoda installed various mechanical devices made of metal plates on the cotton threads and in case any threads got broken during the manufacturing, the metal device slid and automatically stopped the equipment without the operator's command, thus avoiding the production of a defective woof.

Therefore, Sakichi Toyoda's concepts and ideas resulted in machines capable of automatically stopping in case any defects occurred. The separation of man and machine becomes possible; the quality process is made within the productive processes by operators, avoiding that the production of defective products is sent to the next process, a crucial rule for JIT production.

Just-In-Time Manufacturing

Before the beginning of World War II, Kiichiro Toyoda, Sakichi Toyoda's son, traveled to the United States to study the American automotive industry, especially the Ford Motor Company, and returned to Japan carrying a deep knowledge about Ford's Production System and was determined to adapt a system of production that aligned the Japanese market and its low demand.

With his experience acquired in the United States during his studies, Kiichiro Toyoda started the automotive operations utilizing JIT in 1937.

Kiichiro's system was to provide the sub-steps of the productive sub-processes for the production sequence (e.g., machining, painting, welding, etc.). The JIT concept was to eliminate the waste, producing only the necessary, when necessary, and just in the necessary amount. Nevertheless, it was still hard work because American production was eight times bigger than that of the Japanese; increasing the productivity was a matter of survival for Toyota.

Another major milestone in the development of TPS was the work of Taiichi Ohno. Kiichiro Toyoda invited Ohno, machines manager at that time, to develop a more efficient production system in order to increase productivity.

In 1956, with the concepts taught by Sakichi Toyoda (Jidoka) and Kiichiro Toyoda (JIT), Ohno traveled to the United States to visit auto factories, intending to improve the Japanese low productivity when compared to the American one.

At this opportunity Ohno observed countless opportunities to improve productivity, such as production cells full of inventory (WIP), vast storage areas, excessive movement of parts, long setups, high rejection levels, etc.

However, his most important discovery in the United States was not made during his visit to the factories, but rather when he got to know a supermarket. Self-service stores virtually did not exist at that time in Japan, and Ohno was very impressed. He was amazed by the way customers chose exactly what they wanted and in the amount they wanted it. He admired the way supermarkets restock goods in a simple, efficient, and effective way.

At this point began the concept of pull production systems and that Kanban will be a crucial technique for the success of the JIT concept, which is discussed on page 64.

JUST-IN-TIME (JIT)

Concept

As discussed, the JIT concept was created due to the necessity of eliminating waste, producing only the necessary, when necessary, and just in the necessary amount.

In August 1988, I took a position as process engineer at Toyota do Brasil; at that time, I met Haraguchi, general production manager. Haraguchi-san had solid knowledge about the TPS (Toyota Production System) concepts he was taught by Taiichi Ohno, founder of the TPS.

Haraguchi-san used to teach new engineers everything concerning the TPS, and I owe much of my professional life's development in this area to his teachings. At that time, I was assigned responsibility for the processes of heat treatment, casting, and forging, and tasked with elaborating and improving these production process areas.

Toyota do Brasil was inaugurated in January 1958 and was the first factory built outside of Japan, starting the manufacturing of the Land Cruiser, which later would be named Bandeirante, a name sold only in Brazil, and finishing its assembly in 2001 with the building of the new factory Corolla in Indaiatuba, São Paulo.

Although producing the Bandeirante, an old-fashioned vehicle, for more than forty years, Toyota do Brasil was loyal to the concepts taught by Sakichi Toyoda and Kiichiro Toyoda. The most interesting process in understanding the JIT concept was that the whole daily production plan was sent only to the vehicle assembly line; we knew exactly how many vehicles, types, colors, accessories, etc., should be assembled that day. The assembly line used to work on a moving conveyor belt, where operators assembled the parts as a function of each step of the subassembly according to a standard time: the takt time.

Takt time was a number defined as a function of the available time of daily work divided by the daily demand. With it, it was possible to determine the production time necessary for each vehicle. This number was essential to the production subprocesses, such as machining, welding, painting, chassis, etc., processes that supplied the parts for the assembly operation, determined their production capacity in terms of human resources, production, productivity, machine capacity, etc. Every process was initiated in the final phase of manufacturing, that is, the assembly operation used the necessary parts as a function of the daily production plan and the subprocesses only supplied the amounts used by the assembly operation. There was the rule of the subsequent process to ensure that only the necessary amount used by assembly was supplied; in this case, the assembly operation was responsible for getting the used part, thus deploying the pull system. In this manufacturing process, Kiichiro Toyoda's concept of producing only the necessary, when necessary, and in the necessary amount (JIT) becomes very noticeable.

Obviously, today this concept is widespread in Toyota's whole operational chain, from suppliers, dealers, on through to the final customer.

It is also evident that now the production chain is very clean; any problems in the production chain, such as missing parts, broken machines, inefficient processes, etc., could generate a complete stoppage of production. Therefore, Sakichi Toyoda's concept (Jidoka) of never sending defective parts to the subsequent process becomes crucial to JIT production.

Total Customer Satisfaction

My prior idea of *customer*, working at an American company, was more directed toward the final customer, that is, the one at the last phase of the operational chain, not worrying about how the intermediary processes were being made. Many times, these processes were inefficient; each one was interested only in meeting production targets assigned to him or her and with a huge amount of inventories between the processes that hid the problem and the urgency reaction about solving the problems was not a common practice among employees. I could only understand better the idea of *customer total satisfaction* working at Toyota.

The JIT production concept requires the production chain operational processes to be efficient and effective. Toyota has a different idea of "customer." The idea was that every prior process had a subsequent process as its customer. Forging, for example, had machining as its main customer and this last one, in turn, had assembly as its main customer and so on, thus operating systematically in the pull system process, that is, producing exactly the amount spent by the subsequent process.

This system of JIT, combined with the pull system, required that the processes be highly efficient; that process quality be inserted in the production process, such as operational rules, error-proofing devices (Poka Yoke), operators training according to operational rules, TPM, etc.; and that such processes ensured that defective parts were not sent to the subsequent process.

More Evident Waste in the Manufacturing

Producing with a JIT system has as a goal the complete elimination of waste. In my opinion, the definition of waste is any unnecessary input or any undesired output in a system, specifically in the manufacturing process. Thus, waste is any resource spent in the production of a product or service beyond what is strictly necessary.

Eliminating waste means analyzing every activity performed at the factory and eliminating those activities that do not add value to production and product.

Working as a process engineer at Toyota, Haraguchi always encouraged us to use the practice of Kaizen (continuous improvement); our group of engineers had as its purpose reporting to him at least five daily Kaizens deployed in production.

At that time, the Kaizen concept at Toyota do Brasil was to build a culture of continuous improvement; the idea was that everything could be improved. With almost 500 employees, the participation rate in Kaizen exceeded 90% of employees with an average of five Kaizens deployed by employee per year.

The work method in the JIT concept requires deep teaching and learning about waste, being able to recognize that it is an essential step and that Kaizen practice is very important in order to recognize and reduce waste to a minimum.

Following is a description of the most common types of waste found in a manufacturing process. The manufacturing in JIT processes makes the waste noticeable in every process and creating a culture among employees that says waste can be eliminated or reduced to the maximum is fundamental in the JIT production concept.

1. *Waste of waiting:* This type of waste refers to the operator who is waiting for the execution of a task, due to, for example: machines breakage, not balanced processes, missing raw material, or simply because he is looking at the machine while it processes the product.
2. *Waste of transportation:* This type of waste refers to the activity of transportation and movement of materials that does not add value to the manufactured product and is necessary due to process and facility restrictions, which impose great distances to be traveled by the material during processing and also accumulation of inventories in the sub-processes, generating significant movement of materials.
3. *Waste of processing:* This type of waste is more common than we imagine. I believe everyone has already seen cases in which an additional process is aggregated in order to solve a quality problem. I had an experience like this in Forging, where we were manufacturing the forged front axle of the vehicle. The process did not provide deburring after forging, but we used to do it due to a clearance of the tool that generated the burr in the forging process. The solution was simple: promoting a system of preventive maintenance of the tool. So any element that adds cost and does not aggregate value to the product is subject to investigation and elimination.
4. *Waste of movement:* This type of waste is always present in operational tasks performed by operators in production processes. The ideal way of analyzing the waste of movement is with the deployment of Standardized Work, thus it is possible to analyze and reduce to the maximum the movements that do not add value to product and process.
5. *Waste of inventory:* This type of waste refers to any material or product in an amount superior to the one immediately necessary to the subsequent process (customer). In an ideal state, if the flow between processes is balanced, the inventory would not have to wait until the material or product was processed.
6. *Waste of reprocess and defects:* This type of waste refers to products out of specification, and also includes reworking and products returned by customers.

7. *Waste of overproduction:* This type of waste refers to producing more than necessary, faster and before the necessary term required by the customer. Toyota believes this is the most critical waste and considers it the main cause of all types of waste.

Continuous Flow Process (One-Piece Flow) and Pull System

As discussed, in the JIT concept, the purpose of production is to manufacture products demanded by customers in a fast and efficient way with the shortest delivery time possible, and the process with a continuous flow (one-piece flow), in its optimum state, means that products are processed and transferred directly from one process to the next, one part at a time. Additionally, it is the most effective way of processing and transporting products and materials, having as a result a minimum use of resources as manpower, machines, raw material, auxiliary material, space, and short manufacturing lead-time, thereby obtaining in this way a better knowledge of customers' demands.

Obviously, the flow process of a part is an ideal state, but Toyota's goal is to reduce the batch size between productive processes.

One-piece continuous flow deployment depends on processes. Machining, for example, was one of the processes that could apply this concept. Machining production process layouts were designed in the shape of U cells, with inflow to raw material and outflow with the finished product. There were cells in which an operator handled more than twenty machines and devices; however, these productive cells were not dedicated only to one type of product and with this my job as a process engineer was to promote the continuous improvement, particularly in the setup of machines and devices of the productive cell—it was common to have more than ten setups per cell.

Other processes, such as casting, forging, stamping, and so on, did not have this possibility of one-piece flow; it is impossible, for example, to stamp a part of the vehicle and do the setup for the manufacture of another part. The idea here is to use the concept of one-piece flow with a dramatic reduction in the size of the batch, and it can only be achieved by reducing setup times.

With the size of the part batch scaled for these processes, the pull system automatically made the production orders to be scheduled as FIFO (First-In-First-Out), and here Kiichiro's JIT concept is also evident once only required items are manufactured, in the time and quantity demanded.

Lean Methodologies for Waste Elimination

According to Taiichi Ohno, 99% of the activities of a production chain, for example, are activities that do not add value to the product, and only 1% are activities that do add value to the product manufactured. How many of us have assessed a manufacturing process from its order to the finished product? Do we produce inventories that will only be used long after? Is rework a constant? And is the level of rejection beyond acceptable? Do we have over-process due to process and quality deficiency? Is the breakdown of machines a constant? Are there operations with unequal activity time cycles, causing the operator to wait? Large and uncontrolled setup times? So, how can we improve continuously? Learning to see the waste and to recognize waste is opportunity for improvement.

The "hunch" of Taiichi Ohno was to analyze such wastes more deeply, aiming at their total elimination and thus reducing more and more the lead time of the process.

We know many Lean techniques today, such as: 5S, SMED, PDCA, Standardized Work, TPM, Jidoka, Kanban, Poka Yoke, Kaizen, etc.

What would be the purpose of the creators of these methodologies? The answer lies precisely in the analysis of Taiichi Ohno, in his relentless pursuit of the total elimination of waste.

Examples

SMED: This methodology was created based on the extensive tooling changeover times in the stamping processes that used to take hours, sometimes days, thus leading to high inventories of raw materials, WIP, finished products, and a logistics structure too large for handling, and theses are all non-added-values that only increase the costs and lead-times of the process.

Standardized work: Standardizing the operations process, analyzing in detail the operator's movement, standardizing work sequence activities, standardizing quality processes within the process, performing an ergonomic and safety analysis on every operation activity, etc.

Kaizen (Continuous Improvement)

Since joining Toyota, this method of ongoing improvement is taught to all employees. Toyota understands that those who do the work are the experts and can detect waste and abnormality quickly. Using this potential of human resources as a basis for ongoing improvement and problem solving was essential for the strengthening the TPS.

Toyota, in my opinion, does not seek cost reduction with Kaizen activities; rather, it aims at introducing the culture of total elimination of waste, that everything can be improved from the implementation of good ideas that will become Kaizens.

KANBAN AS A TECHNIQUE OF JIT

The Kanban system was inspired when Taiichi Ohno went into a supermarket in his visit to the United States; and today we see that many of the characteristics of supermarket systems are embedded as rules in the Kanban system. Some examples include

- *Consumers choose what they want, in the amount they want, and buy.* The analogy here, in the manufacturing process, is a pull system, the subsequent process search for the required amount in the previous process and it manufactures only the amount withdrawn when necessary, and the production order of the products follows the typical sequence in which the products were withdrawn by the subsequent process.
- *Customers minimize the activities of the employees at the supermarkets by carrying their own goods to the cashier.* The analogy here, in a manufacturing process, is that human and transport resources are used with greater efficiency; only the products and materials needed for that production moment are handled and transported.
- *Instead of using large inventories of products for item replacement, the supermarkets replace only the products that were sold, reducing the stock and the physical space of such products.* Analogy with the pull system.

As seen previously, the most efficient method of JIT production is continuous flow, that is, to connect the processes with standardized inventories calculated so that the operating cycle is completed.

However, it is not always possible to connect the manufacturing processes, due to the distance between the processes, unequal cycle times, factory layout, work shifts, etc. Kanban artificially aims at the connection of those processes that, for some reason described, could not be connected.

Taiichi Ohno clearly describes that TPS is a production method, while the Kanban system is only a means of applying the method. Therefore, the Kanban system is a means of application for the JIT production method. Many times we mistakenly hear that Kanban is an inventory control system.

Kanban is a programming system drawn to meet customers' needs and facilitate the visual management of the production throughout its processes; in other words, we can visually manage activities related to transport, manufacturing, operation, and prompt response to demand fluctuations; decentralize factory control by assigning the production/ inventory control to supervisors/operators; provide the production with a greater reactive capacity due to changes in demand; supply materials synchronously in time and quantity as needed at a given process; etc.

At Toyota do Brasil, I had my first experience with the Kanban system; the project was to connect the forging, heat treatment, casting, and subsequent processes with the Kanban system.

At this time I met Mr. Sakamaki, who was also himself a disciple of Taiichi Ohno, receiving his knowledge of TPS directly from the master. Sakamaki-san had been sent from Japan to Brazil so that he could have a deeper understanding of what TPS was. He was a very strict person when it came to teaching and applying the method, as almost all Senseis and disciples of Ohno were.

We started by implementing the Kanban system in the forging process, which was provided with two presses of 1,600 tons and 2,500 tons only; at the time, the forged parts were exclusively for the single model we manufactured in Brazil, the Bandeirante. And within his first visit to the process, Sakamaki-san identified that the inventory level was too high, there was a load unbalance between the two presses, and the tool setups required too much time, thus generating a very high batch production per part. Therefore, our major focus before implementing Kanban was making the process stable, leveling the loads of the two presses, and making improvements for the dramatic reduction of setup times on both presses.

The Bandeirante was composed of about 120 forged parts, with a demand of 25 vehicles at the time. The balancing was performed by taking into account the work hours of the morning and night shifts based on the daily demand required by production planning. With that we dedicated two families of forged parts: one to the 1,600-ton press and the other to the 2,500-ton press.

The next step was to improve the times for tool setups on both presses. The application of the SMED concept and definitions of *internal* and *external setup*, coupled with Kaizen, were important for the significant reduction of tooling changeover times.

- *External setup:* Activities that can be performed while the equipment is working, for example, preparing the next raw material in the process area.
- *Internal setup:* Activities that must necessarily be performed with the equipment stopped due to safety and process constraints and process; for example, we cannot manually adjust the tooling with the machine in motion.

When we started, the average setup was around forty-five minutes per tool, and there was a standard heating process to normalize the temperature of the tool before starting the forgery, which was very important, because if it was not done well, there could be a breakdown in tooling; this step utilized almost 50% of the total setup time; the process was considered an internal setup because it was held soon after the assembly of the tooling in the press and used gas burners for doing so.

First, we started listing all the setup activities and split them into *internal* and *external* activities with their respective times; after that, we analyzed which internal activities could become external activities with the Kaizens.

Having this definition in mind, we promoted countless Kaizens in the setup process; the main one was building a second base with a rotating device where we could assemble the tooling of the top and bottom table off the machine and, once the entire tooling had been assembled, we could also preheat the tooling outside the machine; all these previously considered internal activities were now external ones. Thus, we achieved an extraordinary reduction in setup time of over 90% with these Kaizens implemented.

We could now think of how to implement Kanban within the forging process and, for the kind of forging production that was produced in batches, the Signaling Kanban (Triangle) was ideal, because it created the connection between the forging process and the subsequent process with a continuous flow of production in small batches. With the dramatic reduction in setup time, now it was also possible to reduce the size of the batch and create the desired flow.

The next step was to calculate the batch size for each part based on production's average daily demand, which at that time was twenty-five vehicles a day; batch sizes ranged depending on the quantity of parts used per vehicle (e.g., two parts per vehicle for a same forged item). The calculation of the batch size was as follows:

1. Demand (25 vehicles/day) × Quantity of parts/vehicle (120) = 3,000 forged parts/day
2. Calculating the number of setups per day:
   Mean time for production of 3,000 parts = 910 min
   Available time for setups = 960 min (2 shifts) – 910 min = 50 min
   Setup mean time = 5 min
   Number of setups/day = 50 min/5 min = 10 setups/day
3. Calculating the batch size:
   Daily demand/Number of setups = 3,000/10 = 300 parts
   Note: For parts needing, for example, two parts per vehicle, of course, the batch size was 600 parts, and so on.
   The batch size computation, as we saw previously, refers to an optimum condition in which the process does not have line shutdown problems, so it is important to know the production efficiency to add a safety inventory for each batch size.
   In the optimum state, for example, for a batch of 300 parts and a daily consumption equal to the demand (twenty-five vehicles), we have in this case (300/25 = 12), twelve days of inventory turnover—this means that for an optimum state, we would have to produce the same part every twelve days.
4. Calculation of Order Point (OP):
   We can imagine the OP as a Kanban trigger; that is, it is the computed and defined inventory so that the production operation of the part begins.
   The calculation of the OP took the preparation time of the raw material; for the forged parts, it was required to cut the rolled steel bars into the corresponding sizes and weights, the setup time of the tool on the press, and the predetermined safety inventory.
   For example, let's assume that the batch size is 300 forged parts, the OP computed is 50 parts, and the Kanban attached to the container is for 50 parts. When the first part was removed from the container, the trigger was activated as production order a forged part.

The next step now is to build up the inventory fluctuation based on the spin of the forged parts.

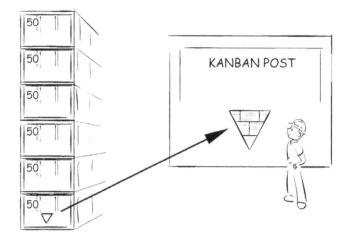

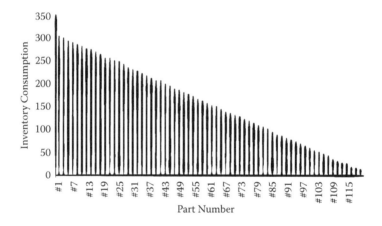

Above shows the part numbers for the inventory consumption and as the stock of the parts reach the respective OP, the Kanbans are raised to a production Kanban position and usually the part's production sequence is in accordance with the Kanban's raising sequence.

As said before, Kanban decentralizes the factory's production control by assigning this responsibility to the supervision and the operators; but for this to happen without any failures, it is critical that the rules of the Kaban system are followed:

- Defective parts are not to be passed on to the following process.
- The following process goes to the preceding process to withdraw parts.

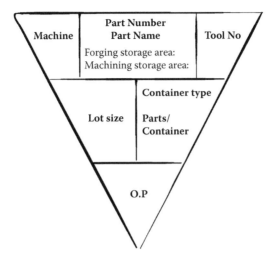

- The quantity of parts produced must equal the quantity of parts withdrawn by the following process.
- Parts must not be produced or conveyed when there is no Kanban.
- Kanban must be attached to the actual parts.
- The number of actual parts must be the same as specified on the Kanban.

The following are the required pieces of information that a Kanban should have:

1. Part number
2. Part name
3. Location in the inventory area (subsequent and lower process)
4. Machine where the part will be manufactured
5. Number of the tool corresponding to part
6. Batch size
7. Type of container and quantity of parts per container
8. OP (Order Point)

CONCLUSION

Kanban is an alternate solution when continuous flow is not possible; in cases where continuous flow is present, there is no need for Kanban signaling.

Kanban is not a technique for reducing stock, it only manages the inventory. In some cases, by implementing the Kanban system, we can even increase the inventory; the quantity as seen above depends on the calculation of batch size.

The implementation of the 5S methodology is important to keep the system working.

Standardized operation works regarding Kanban's working; rules and flow are important for the system to work out.

5

Problem-Solving PDCA

Sammy Obara

Albert Einstein has been attributed to having said, "We can't solve **problems** by using the same kind of thinking we used when we created them."

DEFINITION

Simply defined, a problem is a deviation from a standard. Failing to see the elements that are intrinsic to a problem can cause us to lose focus on how to solve the problem. For example, a common step to most people is to jump into a solution before analyzing what is really causing the problem. Another mistake is not identifying the standard or not understanding its deviation. Typical assumptions like these can cause the best-intentioned team to lose focus and get lost along the problem-solving effort.

WHY PROBLEM SOLVING IS SO IMPORTANT ALONG A LEAN TRANSFORMATION

When introducing and implementing Lean techniques, a set of challenges inevitably comes attached. For example, we cannot connect processes without hitting several problems; we cannot lower inventory levels without unveiling new problems each time we try.

With so many new problems being created so fast, solving them in an effective way becomes vital to solidify the success of each step in the Lean journey. Adopting early a methodology that has been proven effective can avoid the frustration of the constant hitting or missing. In today's competitive environment, the winner is whoever misses the least, and thus the need for a proven scientific method to solve problems.

I received one of those chain e-mails recently with the following methodology to find the root cause of a problem. The person who sent me that e-mail said: Here is a "scientific method" to problem solving. The e-mail read as follows:

> "FACT: England and the US have the highest rates of heart attacks
> The Japanese eat very little fat
> The French eat a lot of fat
> They suffer fewer heart attacks than the British or the Americans
> The Japanese drink very little red wine
> The Italians drink excessive amounts of red wine
> They suffer fewer heart attacks than the British or the Americans
> CONCLUSION: The Root Cause of Heart Attacks
> Eat and drink what you like. It's **speaking English** that kills you."

Jokes aside, that e-mail made me pose two questions: First, how well are we using the problem-solving methods that are widely available and have been proven effective? Sometimes the impression is that we overlook the connections between the facts and always end up with the solution we had preconceived way before we started.

The second question: Why are we so afraid of problems? In many organizations I work with, they simply abolished the word "problem." This forbidden word has now officially been replaced by "opportunities." And shame on you if you still use the old-fashioned word "problem." This attitude tells me that people really have a great fear of problems.

My colleague Darril Wilburn always tells his class that "Problems are NOT opportunities. Problems are problems!" He explained to me that his Japanese Sensei (EVP Nate Furuta at Toyota Motor Manufacturing North America) used to say that to make sure people understood that there is a totally different sense of urgency and importance depending on which word you use.

I had to meditate more on that as I too became used to calling problems opportunities. It took me a while to get back to the original terminology.

Human nature has a tendency to disguise words so that they become appealing. It happened with words such as "used cars," which became "pre-owned" (same thing, more appealing); and if you put the word "certified" in front of it, it is almost better than new. In the corporate world, the "inspection" department became "quality control," then "quality assurance" department, and it is still changing.

Today, when I hear the word "opportunity," I always think of those people selling time-share resorts. Not only do they use the word "opportunity" every few minutes, but they also make it sound like there is a sense of urgency: If you do not buy it now, you will be forever frustrated; you will be the only loser around.

I think the point is exactly that with opportunities. It may even sound like there is a sense of urgency, but there is not. An opportunity—you can choose to take it or leave it. Thus, some people choose not to buy the time-share, regardless of how good the sales pitch was.

A problem, on the other hand, does not leave room for choice. You must solve it because if you don't, it will only grow bigger and more difficult to face. A problem does not leave you a choice of running away, no matter how bad the sales pitch was.

Do you really want to disguise your next problem? Are you that afraid of it?

Before switching gears, we still have to figure out why we are so afraid of problems.

Let's ponder: For one, the concept of problem itself tells us it is not a good thing. We always relate problems to very visible and negative consequences whenever there is one occurring: low morale, high pressure, time consumption, and so much more.

Another reason for the fear of problems is the frustration of having them come back constantly. Former Secretary of State John Dulles once said, "The measure of success is not whether you have a tough problem to deal with, but whether it is the same problem you had last year." In other words, what makes your mechanic good is not how many times he has fixed the same problem in your car. Perhaps by solving problems, we mean that the same problems will not come back the same way again.

So, if people are afraid of problems because they keep coming back, what would it be like if they could solve problems once and for all? Would people lose their fear and become problem seekers?

There are certainly other reasons why we are afraid of problems (some will stem from punishment from the boss, retaliation from customers, etc.); however, at least we can eliminate one of the reasons if we use an effective problem-solving method—one in which problems can be solved once and for all. One that ensures a thorough application of a key element called root cause analysis.

Of course, a good and proven scientific method to solve problems will prevent the same problem from happening again. But finding such a method among so many others available may sound like a daunting task.

WHAT IS PDCA?

PDCA is one of those methodologies that has been proven effective by world-class organizations. The letters stand for Plan-Do-Check-Act. Used correctly, it can ensure that you never have the same problem again. Used wrongly, however, and it may lead you to trying to banish the English language from the planet in the name of preventing heart attacks. For even a scientific method can be applied in the wrong way.

DO YOU REALLY NEED A METHOD?

We have been solving problems since we were babies. During this period, we solved problems such as hunger, pain, and tiredness just by adjusting our crying volume and frequency. We grew a little older and started playing with toys that stimulated trial and error; we had to pass geometric

shapes through holes that resembled a star, a hexagon, and a circle. A little later in life, we came across real problems at school, work, and in other situations. We may not realize it, but what we have been using to solve today's problems are the same techniques we learned in our early lives, namely, trial and error, forcing a result, and in a more adult version, crying at times. This is what inspires many of us to look for the best methodologies or techniques to solve a problem.

HOW AND WHERE TO FIND PROBLEMS

We tend to solve problems that are imposed on us via a crisis: the equipment broke, the material is defective, the delivery is late. Out of curiosity, what is really the proportion of problems that we need to solve right away against those that we can solve in a proactive mode?

At Toyota, many of its problems come from internally created crises. From corporate tops to local departmental supervisors, each level creates higher standards that they want to meet each year. To close the gap in all levels, smaller teams are formed to attack the problem. This methodology of continuously improving standards has been largely studied under the label of "Policy Deployment."

This approach allows, to a certain extent, proactivity within teams and establishes a culture of working ahead of the problems to prevent them from becoming problems. So, it is natural to say that if you are bad at finding problems to solve, policy deployment will help you find several.

But never mind if you still do not have a Policy Deployment approach in practice at your organization. There are other ways to find problems, and an easy one is when you stop running away from them. When you stop neglecting them, you start seeing them as problems rather than as a timeshare opportunity that you can pass if you do not want it.

THE MOSQUITOES CASE

When I was an intern at Toyota, based out of Honsha headquarters in Japan, I was assigned to work for a few years at the Overseas Planning Engineering Division. Our division had Toyota transferees from more than twenty countries, and many of us became quite good friends.

A vivid example from those days that my colleague Bunchai-san, from Toyota Thailand, shared was how they used PDCA to reduce the number of mosquitoes in the plant. Although this happened in late 1993, the structured method made such an impact on me that I still think of that example when tackling highly technical problems.

I use this example to point out how I solidified my PDCA understanding. I hope it has the same effect on you.

HOW WELL DO YOU UNDERSTAND THE PROBLEM?

Toyota Thailand, also known by the initials STM (Siam Toyota Manufacturing), is located in a country with a tropical climate, and mosquitoes are a common nuisance.

Through employee surveys, STM found out that 65% of the employees were complaining about the high incidence of mosquitoes in the factory. Compare that to the second-highest problem—noise in the factory—with a mere 24% of the complaints, or the third one—too much dust—at 8% of the complaints.

The first thing they did after realizing the magnitude of the dissatisfaction was to form a PDCA team comprised of people who could add to the

scope of control over the problem—the people related to employee relations, to environmental affairs, and to facilities. Although they did not enlist a mosquito expert to be part of the team, they invited such an expert for a small lecture and Q&A session.

They chose a fun name for the team: Doctor Smile.

They also investigated the point of cause.

GENCHI GENBUTSU: THE POINT OF CAUSE

In Japanese, Genchi Genbutsu roughly translates to "real place, real stuff." Only by going to where the problem is really happening can we thoroughly understand it.

Point of cause helps to understand the what, where, when, who, why, and how of the problem:

- Where mosquitoes would be more common (a few areas were more prone to mosquitoes than others).
- What types of mosquitoes were there, and which ones would bite (it turns out that only female mosquitoes bite).
- When the mosquitoes were more active (from July to November, the rainy months for that region).

- How they bred (that type of mosquito had a fast life cycle, where, in just a few days, an egg would become a mosquito and lived for just a few weeks).
- How they lived, entered the plant, bit employees, etc., etc. (the findings were too numerous and could fill this chapter).

The team even set up a sticky screen that would enable them to count how many mosquitoes were caught in each area and when. This screen proved essential to do a later checkpoint and compare the results of each of the countermeasures they were testing.

All these answers together directed everyone's attention to the right places. I learned that planning to solve a problem was a critical step. If they were not capable of counting mosquitoes, how would they know if their solution was helping the problem or making it worse? And if it was helping, by how much was it helping? Imagine them adopting some solution that was, in reality, not affecting the real problem. For how long would they keep that fictitious solution given the not-so-fictitious cost to keep them?

Sometimes, we get caught in the fast lane and do not plan how we will solve the problem. We end up shooting in all directions very fast, hoping that one of the bullets will hit the mark.

The point of cause, or Genchi Genbutsu, will determine how well your problem will be solved. Therefore, Genchi Genbutsu should never be replaced with other artificial methods such as collecting information from your computer screen, reports, phone calls, hunches and guesses. You must go to the floor; there is no substitute for it.

HOW WELL CAN YOU STATE THE PROBLEM?

The planning phase continued. Because they took serious care as to how the problem would be stated, the problem statement kept everyone's efforts focused on the single problem.

A good image to remember is of a mountain that we must climb. But there is so much clutter, fog, and many obstacles that we are discouraged from taking on the journey. Now imagine that on top of it all, we cannot even distinguish what is the real mountain that we will climb.

A problem statement can be compared to a flag on top of the mountain, very clear and visible so that all of the members of the team will be clear as to where to go, joining forces instead of dividing and getting lost.

A problem must be stated clearly, accurately, concisely, and in such a way that it can be measured. Having met these criteria, the entire team will be able to attack the same problem, or in this analogy, climb the same mountain.

Another benefit to having a clear statement is that it removes clutter from the long path of solving a problem; on the other hand, a mountain path that is full of obstacles will discourage and distract people on the team.

An example of clutter that can harm this first step is when there is what I use to call "junk words" (I substantiate this concept in an experiment that I share in the following pages). Some well-intentioned problem solvers may get intimidated just by the amount of clutter (or complexity) that appears to be on that mountain. They also get discouraged and, therefore, disengaged in the problem.

I have seen problem statements that simply read "too many customers complaints. We need to pay more attention when we take the orders and deliver the products."

Let's review the issues with such a statement:

It is too broad a mountain to allow anyone to focus on what the issue really is. Remember that if the team cannot clearly see the mountain they have to climb, then they may be all climbing different mountains. And dividing people on the team in these early steps means dissolving the brainpower needed to pursue the one problem you want to solve.

Another typical aspect of this problem statement is that it thinks it is bringing the solution already. Interestingly enough, even good managers still think that problems can be solved by this magic command: "Pay more attention." They have been trying that command for centuries; it has not worked well, but they just keep insisting on it.

One of the toughest aspects of following scientific methodologies to solve problems is that most of them require you to collect data and information to a great extent before you get into the solution phase. They forget that we are wired to always be a step ahead and ready to implement something fast. This is because we need a sense of accomplishment, and collecting data for hours on end does not give us that sense. Remember how successful that motto of Nike was? "Just do it." I think it would not be too successful if it said, "Just plan first."

Another aspect of that statement is the clutter that I mentioned earlier: The term "too many" is formed by junk words. Here is my take on junk words:

I did an experiment in my classes where students had to answer how much is an expensive car. The only thing I said was, "Luxury cars are just too expensive."

Answers varied from $35K to $150K (a factor of five times). This was a huge variation especially considering it was a class of well-educated Lean practitioners from the same country and exposed to the same markets.

When hearing that sentence, nothing struck us as weird or odd. As a matter of fact, it is such a common communication pattern that I took that one straight from the headline of a leading newspaper that distributes almost two million copies.

Junk words can be identified by their effects on the statement. They add to the length but do not add to the value of the sentence. In the case of the car, we can eliminate the word "just" or "too," and chances are we still have the same variation in the answers. How about if we switch the word "expensive" to "cheap?" Will the variation still be there? (The answer in my experiment is yes.) And note that we switched the word not with a synonym, but with something exactly the opposite. How about if we eliminated the word "luxury?" Would the answers change much?

The experiment indicated that for some people what can be a real bargain, such as a $35K luxury car, to others can be "just too expensive."

What would have happened if we had just eliminated everything that is not adding value to the sentence? Would we still have variation? (Again, yes and high.)

Does that not mean that we can eliminate three quarters of the sentence and still get the same flawed perception? Perhaps this is the reason our problem-solving meetings are taking sixty minutes while we could do them in only fifteen minutes. Perhaps this is the reason why problems are difficult to solve; the thinking inside the head of each team member can vary by factors of several times.

We all have our own perceptions and that is not going away anytime soon as our perceptions come from personal experiences, expectations, education, values, gender, age, and the list goes on. Still, by being aware of that can help us improve the way we approach a problem. Eliminating such "junk" is crucial to bring everyone to the same mountain; it is like eliminating the obstacles on the way so they can all join the hike.

Being measurable in a problem statement can eliminate this variation in perception. On top of that, it will allow you, in the progress of solving a problem, to check against the initial condition to see whether or not you are closing the gap between the current and ideal situation. Finally, combining a measurable statement with all the data (exhaustively collected during our point-of-cause phase) will let you establish what a reasonable goal can be.

GOAL: A plan with a deadline. A common practice in solving problems is that goals are set by the "bosses" according to factors totally disconnected to the problem, such as quarterly numbers and other metrics for their managerial performance report. Rarely do we see goals being set by people who did diligent investigation of the problem. The farther away you are from the point of cause, the more unrealistic the goals tend to be. This may be the reason why Toyota lets teams that are actually hands-on solving the problem, establish their own goals. Naturally, those teams will know what is realistic after they have been through the Genchi Genbutsu exercise.

The goal statement always carries a strict deadline and consequently it keeps the team focused on the climbing of the mountain.

To me it still sounds weird to put the word "strict" together with the word "deadline" as I just did, but I use that redundancy on purpose. You will see why on the quick note about deadlines in a few pages.

HOW WELL DO YOU UNDERSTAND THE CAUSES?

The planning phase still remains crucial when you start pursuing the possible causes of the problem. A fairly simple method to dig deeper into the causes and get to the root cause is the Five Why's. By simply and continuously asking "Why?" to a cause, we can explore the causes down to their roots—the cause behind the cause.

Back to our example from Bunchai-san, his team first asked why people were complaining so much about mosquitoes. The obvious answer came from their trap device: there were too many mosquitoes inside the plant. But, why? The answer was because they bred too fast during the rainy season. But the team, knowing that this was a superficial cause, asked why they bred so fast. Among other logical answers, one was that there were too many breeding spots near the factory. A few more "whys" later, they identified the main breeding points as being some of the gutters as well as a small pond behind the building.

My colleague at STM mentioned the long ordeal, preparing to prove (or disprove) the root causes; after all, going after the wrong lead could end up being costly and useless.

Their PDCA mentality drove them to do small checking events after testing localized solutions. By temporarily deactivating some gutters, they evaluated the effectiveness of that countermeasure.

By checking the amount of mosquitoes close to the pond, they evaluated how much evidence there was that would prove this to be a real breeding site.

Another critical element in describing the problem and its causes lies in how we display the findings from the extensive data collection/Genchi Genbutsu. Contrary to traditional beliefs that a good report is a thick one, the PDCA method forces us to weigh in on the importance of each contributing factor to then decide what to leave out and what to make part of the vital few indispensable pieces of data.

Something I really learned to appreciate was how effectively Toyota can communicate via charts, diagrams, and graphs; provided of course that you have good data, charts are a much faster and accurate means to convey information. They also help eliminate misinterpretation, which is so common when working in a diverse team. And their objectivity helps condense lengthy explanations of the data.

My colleagues from STM used Pareto charts to show the quantity of mosquitoes per area. The Pareto chart makes it easy to distinguish the areas that had more mosquitoes, thus helping them decide where to tackle first. They believed that by attacking 20% of the areas with more mosquitoes, they would be reducing by 80% the number of complaints. Their belief was derived from the Pareto law, which states that 20% of the causes are responsible for 80% of the problem. They also used trend charts showing when along the year mosquitoes would be more active. This gave them a clear indication as to the best time to test their countermeasures. It also helped them determine breeding cycles and elements that could affect the incidence of mosquitoes in the factory, such as weather and factory conditions.

Another chart they had was called the cause-effect diagram, commonly known in Toyota as the Ishikawa diagram (probably because the person who popularized this diagram was Mr. Kaoru Ishikawa—not Mr. Fishbone as some might think). They used the Ishikawa diagram to plot the results from their extensive brainstorming session where they asked the five whys. Once neatly distributed across the diagram, it was easy to understand the probable root causes for the mosquito infestation. I learned that brainstorming for causes can only be effective if the people participating in it have been through their Genchi Genbutsu (yes, to the point of cause). How else can they contribute to the "whys" if they do not understand the what, when, where, how, and who? Brainstorming for innovation and revolutionary ideas may benefit from the wild guesses of diverse contributors. But the same thing is not true when you want to collect probable causes of a problem. As a rule of thumb, if you want to participate in a 5 whys session, you must first perform a proper Genchi Genbutsu.

Only after the extensive checking stage did they take the next step: Implementation, the "Do" part of PDCA.

Doing Well What Does Not Need to Be Done

The "D" part of PDCA. Trystorming, the hands-on version of brainstorming.

Our human nature brings satisfaction when we see things getting done. It is that pursuit of a sense of accomplishment that many times supersedes the inquiries to check and evaluate if what we did had a positive and sustainable effect. As most brainstorming sessions, theirs generated several potential root causes and I guess this can be seen as the good news. The bad news was that there were several potential root causes. Yes, too many root causes can cause overwhelming workloads involving the selection, prioritization, proving and disproving them, etc.

In our story, they used a mini-PDCA method, testing out their root causes until they could prove or disprove each of them. Their proven root causes led to testing some countermeasures that included these three: (1) installing fly traps in the entrances to each of the buildings, (2) weekly application of an insecticide in certain spots, and the one I liked the most, (3) contemplated bringing fish and raising them in the pond behind the plant so they could eat the mosquito larvae before they hatched.

Each of their countermeasures was proven on a small scale prior to execution and next I use the three countermeasures I described above to show what I mean by small scale. I call it trystorming, which is trying quickly several countermeasures, almost as if you are in the middle of a storm.

Trystorming is the antidote when team members are already exhausted from meticulous and thorough brainstorming and they are borderline becoming too comfortable in their chairs. I think there is some truth to the adage "analysis paralysis," in that after some time sitting, thinking, and talking, we become paralyzed by the inertia and our bodies are numbed up like zombies at the end of a long movie.

That is why, back in our example, their trystorming occurred quickly with several trials at the same time. Needless to say, they took good care not to cross-contaminate their results with the results from parallel experiments. The way they used the trystorming concept on those countermeasures I cited included them installing one fly trap first, and checking results before they bought several more for all buildings. The next one, they checked the effectiveness of different brands of insecticide and applied them in different corners of the plant to see how they worked before they made it a weekly practice. The final one, they checked if the fish would really eat that type of larva and survive that type of water before they bought and released 200 fish into the pond.

It becomes clear that the implementation phase must be done in a way such that it constantly checks for the effects of what is being implemented. Imagine what it would be like bringing hundreds of fish to the pond all at once, only to later find out they could not survive that new condition. Chances are that dead fish would attract even more mosquitoes and other insects.

This careful process of planning, testing, and checking for results before standardizing a solution is exactly like having mini-PDCAs within a PDCA.

PROJECT MANAGEMENT

Once the team had a consensus on what had to be done, they distributed those countermeasures among themselves and each responsible team member established his or her own timeline, always observing the deadline in the goal statement.

Although each team member is responsible for implementing and checking the effectiveness of his or her own countermeasures, once they are all implemented, they collectively check the results against the goal.

In this case, the goal was not to reduce the number of mosquitoes—or mosquito bites for that matter. It was just to reduce the number of complaints from workers by August 1994. And that, they did!

A QUICK NOTE ON DEADLINES

When a team commits their goal to a deadline, it should mean that they would do whatever it takes to keep to what they committed to. I hear frequently a variation of that term as the "drop dead date."

It is funny to me to see so often people misusing the term "deadline." Sometimes they even use the term "strict deadline," as if there was another type. They commit to one but when it is the due date, they justify their missing the date and propose a new "deadline." But is a deadline not something definite? Finite? Does it not imply an end to it? As many other things that are about to die, you can do whatever it takes to prevent it from dying but once they are dead, they are dead. You mourn the loss, you learn from it, but normally you do not resuscitate a dead pet, person, or line. I mean, a line for some reason is often resuscitated in many organizations

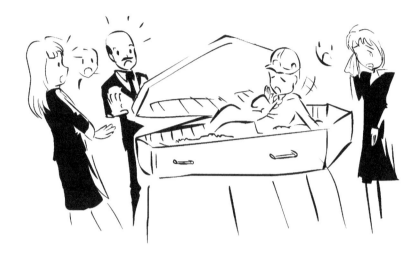

out there. I wonder if people do not respect deadlines just because they know they can keep postponing them. Should that date then not be called "faintline?" If you cannot make it, you can still keep coming up with new dates; after all, that date is not really dead, it just passed out for a while. What would it be like if we all started calling those dates what they really are, faintlines? When they are to be seriously respected, then we can call them deadlines. No need to distinguish deadlines as "strict" and "flexible."

Continuing with our case, their after-PDCA survey showed a drop from sixty-five to twenty-one complaints in the same time period. Quite an impressive number, judging by the fact that this had been a problem plaguing that site for so many years.

STANDARDIZATION

One thing that still fascinates me in every Toyota site I visit is their level of standardization. I see that as one of the keys to Toyota's success.

STM used standardization in several ways to ensure maximum return on their PDCA as well as to pave the way for the continuous improvement cycle.

For example, to make sure that the insecticide countermeasure would be consistently applied, they created a chart showing where to apply and with what frequency, depending on the time of year. To make sure the fly traps never lost their effectiveness, they had a calendar reminder showing when and who should be emptying and cleaning the trap. In addition to that, there was a standardized instruction sheet showing how to clean and hang the trap.

Also, to maximize their gains, they presented their PDCA to the neighboring plants: an electronics manufacturer, an engine plant, a consumer goods plant, etc.

I am not sure how much further they could have driven down the number of mosquitoes, but it is reasonable to expect more positive effects for STM and for the entire region once the other companies implemented Toyota's solutions.

The standardization is the "A" part of PDCA, and we can only standardize what has been validated along the implementation-check phase (or "DC" part of PDCA). Standardizing without checking for effectiveness is a mistake that, if ignored, can perpetuate bad practices for a long time.

RECOGNITION

Rewards and recognition is a two-word term that I rarely heard being used together in Toyota. Perhaps this is because they perceive these words as not being related to each other, or perhaps because they think rewards reach the intellect and recognition the soul. (I heard that one from my first Toyota Senseis, Mr. Sakuta, in 1986; he is no longer with us but his teachings impacted several lives in our production engineering division.) What I noticed about rewards is that there is a huge difference between monetary rewards at Toyota and that of other big companies. While most companies reward employees with enticing monetary prizes, sometimes proportional to the amount of money they saved, in Toyota the rewards could many times be less than a fraction of the huge savings. Often, the rewards would even be the same for a $1000 savings as for something two or three times as much.

It seems that what they would consider more was the effort, the teamwork, the correct use of concepts such as standardization and Yokoten (which is explained next).

The result of this was a reward amount that seemed just symbolic compared with other companies. With that, they created a culture where money (or reward) is no longer the major goal in improvement efforts.

Now on to the recognition aspect. In a highly standardized environment, it is easy to identify changes; no matter how small they are, they stand out. Add to that the culture of Genchi Genbutsu where leadership is on the floor frequently, and they can observe those improvements within the day, if not in real-time.

This combination of improvement visibility with the constant presence of leadership on the floor allows for prompt and frequent recognition from the manager to the person executing the improvement.

Immediate recognition methods vary from public praise all the way down to positive coaching where the operator is asked why she did it the way she did it, what kind of waste she thought she was eliminating, how she would ensure that the improvement stays in place, etc.

At least from my own experience with my Sensei, the Socratic coaching was more common than the praises. Very early in my career, I had to learn to be prepared for the series of questions my Sensei would challenge me with, and the best way to be prepared was to anticipate the questions and have the answers built into the improvement I was implementing. So instead of letting him ask me how I would ensure consistency in that new process, I would have already created a standardized document for him to see. Instead of waiting for him to challenge me with the "whys," I had already prepared the "becauses." Sometimes I wonder if they perpetuated this practice to create a culture of thinkers, because it really does increase the sense of preparedness in the workforce.

It is interesting to me that well-schooled managers sometimes fail to understand that if they do not recognize the efforts of their people, their people will fail to understand what is important to the manager and consequently to the company. Culture is only reached when values are shared, and how in the world will the masses share the same values of the company if their leadership does not recognize what is valuable? By the same token, praise is often mistaken as the only means of recognition, and managers do that often to motivate their people. The key mistake is that they miss great opportunities to develop their people through good coaching.

A HIGHER LEVEL OF RECOGNITION

In addition to instant and constant recognition, Toyota also excels in the higher levels of recognition, the other end of the spectrum.

One of the ultimate ways to recognize a good PDCA project, such as the mosquito one, is to bring it to Toyota Headquarters in Toyota City. Every year, Toyota sponsors the annual Kaizen and PDCA convention, where only the best PDCAs from each plant around the world are presented before the highest executives in the company.

Those ten minutes of fame are so coveted that teams go beyond their regular functions to win a ticket to present their projects. I frequently have seen teams meeting on weekends at someone's house, or taking evening classes to better understand the details of their projects. I am not sure the team at STM took classes, but I know they found an insect expert and got a few learning sessions from him.

This annual event in Toyota City has been happening at a global level since 1986, and I think it was easy to understand why it became such a desired event to attend.

Right when you enter the Toyota Hall where the event takes place, you can see the amount of planning and importance they put into this single day. You can see the signs and distribution materials exclusively prepared for the convention, the staff impeccably rehearsed to make this a flawless event, the agenda detailed down to the minute of each presentation. By the way, STM's presentation was scheduled to start precisely at 10:23 a.m. and finish at 10:39 a.m., including a time for comments from Toyota execs and hand-off. The commemorative photo was planned from 4:08 p.m. to 4:13 p.m.

Everyone knew that that day would not bring in more business to Toyota, nor would it increase its sales or benefit the bottom line. In reality, it is a day devoted solely to recognition. Toyota could easily save a lot of money by not bringing so many people from all over the world and tying up so many executives for the entire day just to listen to what had been done, for something they had already capitalized on.

The constant coaching leading to that one day of recognition was a clear demonstration of how much Toyota cared about the development of its collaborators.

Now, make no mistake, STM did not get to that ultimate recognition point without a lengthy process of instant recognition sessions. For several months and iterations, the team probably had to hear constant questions such as: What did you do to prevent mosquitoes from coming back? How will you spread this learning to other companies and also to other Toyota plants? Needless to say, Senseis do not expect verbal answers but, rather, concrete displays that all challenges have been satisfied.

This solid demonstration of value and care can be summarized as genuine recognition and not just as a "feel-good" event.

YOKOTEN: SPREADING THE LEARNING LATERALLY

Very common to companies that are bigger, we see the same processes done differently depending on the person, department, site, etc. The bigger the company, the more different ways of doing the same thing. One of the smallest companies I worked with had only fifteen employees. It was a surfing school in San Diego where, in addition to the owners, everyone else was a surfing instructor. After a day of learning their procedures, I came to realize that all the instructors did exactly the same thing, just in different ways. They had fifteen different ways of conducting the warm-up exercises, of teaching the hand signs, of covering the land lesson, of coaching students in the water, of repairing a board, of... you name it; in all cases, there was no reason why they needed do it in different ways. They just did not know any better. But a reasonable assumption is that among those fifteen ways of conducting a class, there would be an optimum one, perhaps combining the warm-up from an instructor with the coaching from the other and at the end, you would have the standardized module with the best timing, customer satisfaction, cost, quality, etc.

Worthy of pointing out, even in a micro-sized, single-site business, there are difficulties in adopting a standard procedure. Now imagine scaling up that size a few thousand times.

A company as large as Toyota, with full plants located all over the world, has a much more intimidating challenge. To capitalize on the efforts of one improvement in the welding of a bracket for the Corolla in Turkey, they would need to report that to all plants that use the same process and produce the same vehicle.

The same thinking goes for the PDCA on mosquitoes. Once STM's PDCA had concluded (which means tested and validated), STM sent its report in A3 format (approximately our 11×17 paper size) to Toyota headquarters in an overseas department that could identify what other locations could benefit from such an initiative. Also, those neighboring plants that received STM's A3 were also part of the Yokoten activity. Sharing the learning was done on at least two levels, wherein STM independently helped local companies and also at the corporate level where Toyota would help them spread the word to other sister plants.

Yokoten is key in implying a faster speed in Lean transformation. The efforts invested in the sharing of best practices in a Yokoten fashion will pale in comparison to the benefits from the accelerated learning.

WHAT IS NEXT?

When referring to PDCA, we always do so as if it was a cycle, something that never ends. So it would be natural to think that we should do another PDCA on the mosquitoes so we lower the complaint to a better level.

Because the metric chosen was not number of mosquitoes, but the number of complaints, in this case the complaints about mosquitoes became second to complaints about noise level.

The PDCA cycle continues, and it is still attacking the same metrics: Complaints.

The major cause for complaints has now become the noise level, at twenty-four complaints. Time to start the cycle all over again.

Well, that is how I learned the essence of PDCA. Thanks for letting me share this with you, and I hope you learned something new too.

6

Toyota Kaizen Methods[*]

Art Smalley

The topic of Kaizen is not new or unique to Toyota Motor Corporation. The term "Kaizen" roughly translates to "change for better" and is normally equated with Continuous Improvement in English. The concept of Kaizen inside Toyota has various roots that should be mentioned for reasons of clarification. Also unlike the Western world where Kaizen is typically a big event over a fixed period of time (e.g., five days), Kaizen in Toyota is more a process consisting of six basic steps that anyone or any team can do over any period of time. In this chapter I briefly introduce the background of Kaizen methods inside Toyota, some of the origins, key concepts, and the six basic steps of the process.

The word "Kaizen" in Japanese is written with two kanji characters meaning to change and for the better. Unfortunately, the origins of the term are not exactly clear in terms of etymology. The word "Kaizen" is Chinese in origin and has roots as far back as the Qing Dynastic period in China from 1644 to 1911. The term has always meant improvement although it was not used exactly as in the specific sense we use it today in Lean manufacturing, business, or process improvement.

In the early part of the twentieth century, the term "Kaizen" gradually started to appear in published Japanese works. However, it was not a word widely used by the general population. "Kaizen" was mainly used as a technical term in books and did not cross over into the modern spoken vernacular. Starting around the early twentieth century, the industrial engineering movement in the United States and other countries made methods-based improvement a priority. Works by Fredrick Taylor Frank, Lillian Gilbreth, and others in the field became popular topics. Translations of these books into Japanese no doubt spurred the need for

---

[*] *Note:* This chapter is condensed from a previous work titled *Toyota Kaizen Methods: Six Steps to Improvement*, authored by Art Smalley and Isao Kato and published by Productivity Press, Inc. in 2010. For parties interested in a fuller treatment of this topic, please refer to that work.

a specific word to mean improvement in this sense and adaptation of the Chinese characters representing "Kaizen" likely occurred. Indirectly, all these works affected Toyota and other companies inside Japan.

In terms of specific direct influences, there were several particular items that influenced the development of Kaizen inside Toyota. Kaizen methods inside Toyota are chiefly a logical extension of Sakichi Toyoda's founding precepts, the Training Within Industry (TWI) Job Methods course, and several classroom lectures known as the P-Courses taught by Shigeo Shingo from 1955 to 1981 inside Toyota. The Kaizen course borrows elements from each of the preceding training courses and also adds unique Toyota elements.

Before diving into the basic steps of Kaizen at Toyota, there are some related topics that are worth highlighting in terms of general positioning that affect thinking patterns concerning this topic. Kaizen training at Toyota identified some specific beliefs about how improvement should be carried out. For example, a typical question posed for discussion was, "How do you increase productivity?" Participants normally responded with typical answers such as increasing the number or workers, adding machines, working overtime, or working harder. From a sheer numbers point of view, those answers might deliver more units of production but they do not qualify as true Kaizen. In an ideal case, Kaizen seeks to produce greater quantities of quality product that can be sold using existing manpower, machines, and time constraints. None of the first three typical answers accomplishes that goal and the fourth one—working harder—is neither sustainable nor desirable.

In Kaizen, Toyota wanted leaders to be able to separate work quantity input-based improvements (more machines, more time, more people, etc.) from work quality or method-related improvements, for example, change the nature of the work to be easier and better. In other words, leaders driving Kaizen needed to eliminate waste or unnecessary details in the existing process.

It is possible to make more items by increasing equipment or personnel, but those come at an obvious drawback—increased cost! There are two ways to improve production that do not add cost to the equation but only one of those ways is desirable from a Toyota point of view. By improving the *quality* of their work, teams can in fact produce greater quantities of quality product using existing resources. In modern-day terms, this is of course often referred to as "working smarter" and not "harder."

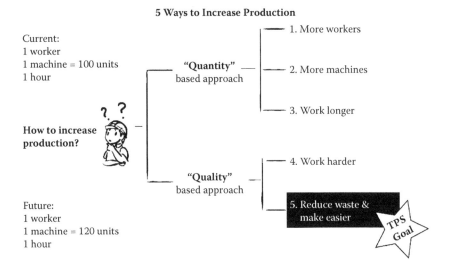

5 Ways to Increase Production

Current:
1 worker
1 machine = 100 units
1 hour

How to increase production?

"Quantity" based approach
1. More workers
2. More machines
3. Work longer

"Quality" based approach
4. Work harder
5. Reduce waste & make easier — TPS Goal

Future:
1 worker
1 machine = 120 units
1 hour

A second preliminary concept discussed in the Kaizen skills course was the notion that how you performed work eventually affected cost. The previous discussion point often drives this point home, but for confirmation the following content was also discussed.

At the time this course was developed, the intended audience was almost exclusively from the manufacturing ranks. As such, the typical graphic used was a manufacturing flow sequence that highlights contrasting styles. Whether or not you are in manufacturing today is not of any consequence. There are ways of doing work that involve inefficiency in your current style of operations. That inefficiency might be rework, downtime of machines, delays in response times, waiting by personnel, or other problems. It is a leader's task to identify more efficient ways of doing things that involve a better sequence and quality of result.

Sometimes, discussion of these previous concepts caused some concern on the part of employees. For example, "I work hard for the company," "I do my best all the time," and "I am very efficient in my day-to-day work routine" are commonly held beliefs. To help reconcile this subjective self-held viewpoint versus reality, Toyota developed the following concepts over the years of the Kaizen course and Toyota Production System (TPS).

Most people feel they are very busy at work and sometimes overwhelmed during peak work hours or rush periods. The reality is that most of what people consider "work" is not value added from the customer point of view.

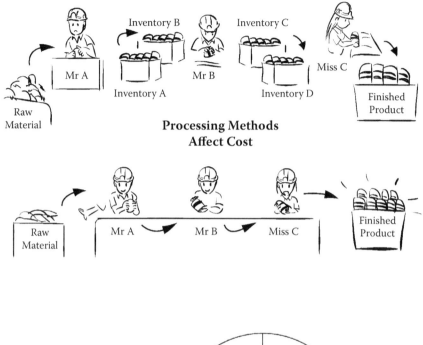

**Processing Methods
Affect Cost**

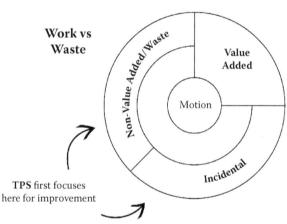

Toyota taught leaders to think of work as true value-added operations to the customer, incidental items required in the current state of operations, and pure waste in the operation.

In reality, true value-added work is quite a small part of our normal jobs. Customer requirements spell out the form, fit, content, function, etc., of what they desire. The intermediate steps we use to get that end result are usually not specified. A machine such as a lathe, for example, might remove metal to a certain final dimension and surface finish required by the customer. Which exact type of lathe, the tool, the holder, the storage location of materials, or the exact program used to make the part, is normally not specified. Only making the required final dimensions and specifications as indicated in print in this case are value added to the customer. The rest of the operation is not entirely value added and can be studied for improvement. In reality of course, the value-added portion can be analyzed for improvement as well but that is usually not the initial starting point for Kaizen.

Incidental waste pertains to work that is required in the current state of the operation that is not valued added but still must be done in the current process. For example, the movement of material is not value added to the customer but still some minimal amount must be done in order to get parts from the delivery truck to the process and back again to the shipping dock. Pure waste, on the other hand, is excessively moving materials from one storage location to another location multiple times.

To help leaders and employees see that not all work is value added, Taiichi Ohno coined the terms Muda, Mura, and Muri to explain the concept he was articulating. Muda is waste, Mura is un-levelness, and Muri is overburdening the person or process. All three of these different phenomena are disruptive to efficient production operations.

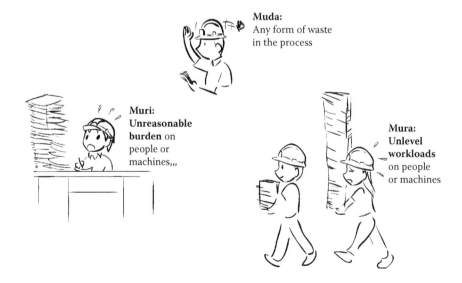

Muda: Any form of waste in the process

Muri: Unreasonable burden on people or machines,,,

Mura: Unlevel workloads on people or machines

Even more specifically, Taiichi Oho codified seven typical types of wastes in the mid-1960s:

1. Over-production
2. Excess inventory
3. Scrap and rework
4. Wait time
5. Conveyance
6. Excess motion
7. Over-processing

As the original list of seven wastes was created inside Toyota, many companies have altered the list and added their own forms of waste as well. Failures to utilize human potential, inefficient systems, wasted energy, etc., are frequent additions to the list. The original list is not perfect and was intended to serve as a way to highlight examples for employees to identify areas for improvement. For parties outside of manufacturing, the list requires translation into relevant examples. For example, waiting for material might instead relate to waiting for documents to arrive or be processed. Scrap and rework might pertain to mistakes in documents or transactions.

The final critical concept that relates to the introduction of Kaizen is the principle of *cost reduction*. Kaizen can be conducted for a variety of reasons, including quality, lead-time, productivity, safety, and other items. Ultimately, however, in Toyota we were also crystal clear about the need for cost reduction.

As mentioned earlier, the automotive industry is a highly competitive industry with many complementary products. Establishing a reputation for quality is critical for any industry. In the long run, companies must also make a profit. A former president of Toyota Motor Corporation, Taizo Ishida, used to remark frequently about the need "to defend your castle by yourself." By this comment he meant that it was proactive and helpful to take your destiny into your own hands and not leave your personal fate up to others. One of Toyota's methods of embracing this concept was the principle of cost reduction.

In the simplest sense, profits are determined for a company by three factors: sales price, cost, and volume. For general discussion purposes, these three elements can be represented by the following equation:

$$\text{Profits} = (\text{Sales Price} - \text{Cost}) \times \text{Volume}$$

Cost Reduction Principle

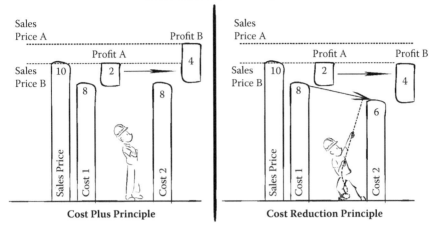

Cost Plus Principle | Cost Reduction Principle

Given this simple equation, how can a company earn greater profits? There are only three levers for the equation: increase the sales price, increase the number of units sold, or reduce the cost. In general in competitive industries, raising prices is difficult and customers may simply turn to alternative offerings from competitors. Simply making more products is no guarantee of making money either...the result may just be excess inventory or waste. The only sustainable way to increase profits is to focus on cost reduction.

Importantly, reducing cost does not mean simply cutting costs or jobs. Reducing costs means eliminating waste in any process that does not add value to the customer. Less inventory, fewer defects, less waiting time, etc., all lead to greater productivity of the factors involved in production. This is the true spirit of Kaizen—establish more efficient uses of existing resources by taking out the waste or unnecessary details that do not add value. Companies that can accomplish this goal will reduce costs and help improve profits. By emphasizing this formula, Toyota made sure that everyone realized they had a direct hand in the success of the company.

In general, there were six main steps to Kaizen inside Toyota and the steps are related to other methodologies, such as the scientific method and general problem solving. The big difference is that in Kaizen, as we will observe going forward, there are more degrees of freedom and greater emphasis on generating original ideas. In general, all improvement methodologies follow the pattern of Plan-Do-Check-Act (PDCA) in some basic fashion and in this sense Kaizen is fundamentally the same.

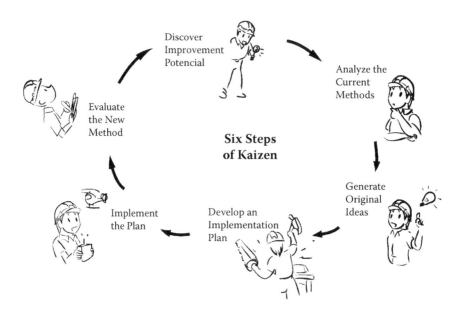

Six Steps of Kaizen

- Discover Improvement Potencial
- Analyze the Current Methods
- Generate Original Ideas
- Develop an Implementation Plan
- Implement the Plan
- Evaluate the New Method

STEP 1: DISCOVER IMPROVEMENT POTENTIAL

The first basic step of Kaizen at Toyota is to discover improvement potential. There is a slight technical difference between problem solving and Kaizen that is worth emphasizing. In problem solving you are typically trying to close a gap to a known standard. The root cause for this gap is pursued until the gap is closed. In Kaizen there does not technically have to be a problem or a gap from standard. Process performance might be fine or at standard, however you still need to improve for some reason. For example, you might be at 100% on-time delivery but with a lead-time of five days. A good example of Kaizen would be to maintain 100% on-time delivery with a lead-time of two days or less.

Discovering improvement potential is sometimes obvious but helps to embody certain attributes when pursuing improvement. Negative defeatist thinking will never lead you to any gains. Here are some basic things to keep in mind when searching for improvement opportunities.

Always keep the spirit of inquiry alive when you are conducting Kaizen. Do not settle for simply understanding "what" is going on in any process. Seek to understand "why" it is the way it is and exactly "how" it works.

Often this process of investigation takes some time in the beginning, but in the end it always pays rewards.

Practice the Toyota concept of "Genchi Genbutsu" at every opportunity. That is, go and see the actual objects in question at the actual workplace. Don't accept second-hand information or reports, as these often will mislead you or fail to ask all the right questions. Just as detectives visit their crime scenes for investigations, you need to visit your worksites for detailed observation as well.

I also suggest that you throw away all preconceived notions about the process or situation you are facing. There is nothing wrong with having opinions or hypotheses when you start out. However, be careful that these do not function as blinders that limit your ability to obtain better ideas or different points of view. Sometimes the best ideas are not always the first ones you come across.

When assessing improvement potential, always practice thorough observation of the work site. This is related to the concept of Genchi Genbutsu but do not fall into the trap of seeing things once at a high level and thinking that you understand all the details. It often takes multiple observations to understand the details of any process, so plan on spending some time "getting under the hood" of the process and learning what makes it tick.

The final point regarding attitude and posture toward discovering improvement potential is to strictly adhere to the concept of "AQD." By this acronym I mean that you should strive to be *analytical, quantitative,* and *detailed.* The term "analytical" means, roughly, to break things down into smaller pieces for study. This helps tremendously in Kaizen if you can break things down into understandable, interrelated components. Second, strive to be quantitative and measure things accurately. Do not accept verbal qualitative statements such as "good," or "long," or "hard," for example. Learn to measure things and be precise. Finally, I also suggest being as detailed as possible. Practice the technique of peeling back the layers of the onion until you are very clear and close to something that can be improved.

If you embody all these attributes, they will make it easier to conduct Kaizen in general and also easier to identify improvement opportunities. Of course these attributes do not generate ideas or answers for you but they help stimulate the mind in a positive direction that will be of benefit during the entire process. In addition, there are also some traditional techniques that Toyota often employed during Kaizen activities to help generate improvement areas. I will outline several of the more common ways to find improvement opportunities.

One of the simplest ways is to compare performance or any process or area to the existing standards and look for opportunities to improve. Technically, if you are short of the standard, you are in problem-solving mode but that is okay if you are looking to improve. If you are meeting all or many of your standards, then you have to question if the standards are now too low in terms of difficulty and need to be raised. This is an excellent way to create the need for Kaizen in many instances.

Additionally, a great way to find opportunities for improvement is to create something we called a "production analysis board" at Toyota. Write down the expected production rate for the shift in small increments, such as every fifteen minutes or at least every hour. Then for one day collect data about how well the process is able to meet the expected rate in terms of actual output. Also note the reasons why the process falls behind, moves ahead, speeds up, slows down, etc. These details will always provide great insights for Kaizen opportunities.

Another proven technique is to visit the work site and spend time identifying all the forms of waste that exist in the area. The seven waste categories are an excellent starting point and exist in every operation in some fashion or other. Take these points and list all the examples of them that you find, and that should lead to many areas of Kaizen opportunity.

The final avenue that I will mention in this discovery-related step is to practice the concept of 5S. In Japanese the words Seiri, Seiton, Seiso, Seiketsu, and Shitsukei relate to a disciplined method of organizing and cleaning an area. In English they roughly mean to put, sort and arrange things into proper positions. Once items are properly stored, then properly clean the items, label them, etc., and ensure they remain in a state of cleanliness. Finally, the last S refers to the Japanese word for discipline. Practice discipline to ensure that the gains you have made in terms of organization are sustained.

Any of these methods should work in terms of identifying improvement opportunities. Often you might know right away what you need to improve due to demands from the customer or senior management. When that is not the case, simply looking to improve any of these methods should help you identify multiple areas for improvement.

STEP 2: ANALYZE THE CURRENT METHOD

The second basic step of Kaizen is to analyze the current methods in place for the process or processes you are observing. There is no one magical way to analyze processes. Your goals should drive what you look at in detail and how you study the process. I will list some of the more common types of analysis that have been of use over the years at Toyota. You will have to use other methods as well, depending on the nature of your situation.

The most elemental form of analysis is something called "work element analysis." This is a fancy way of saying that you should write out all the steps of an operation in sufficient detail and then begin the step-by-step process of questioning each step. First ask exactly what this step is and what its fundamental purpose is. Then ask why that step is necessary. Look for steps that you can eliminate. Additionally ask, "where" the step is done, "when" it is done, "who" is doing it, and, of course, "how" it is being done. This method is referred to as the 5W 1H technique for investigation. Repeat it over and over as needed until all the steps in the process are covered and sufficiently examined.

In an ideal case, you are looking for steps to eliminate; however, that is not always possible for every step. Because we are looking for improvement, be sure to also consider what can be combined, what can be rearranged, or finally, what can be simplified. This step-by-step process is referred to as ECRS, the acronym for *eliminate, combine, rearrange,* and *simplify.* Each of these letters represents a different analysis and improvement angle for consideration. Often, this simple technique is all you need to generate valuable improvement opportunities.

A second common technique inside Toyota for analyzing processes is time study. Many critical elements of Toyota's system are founded upon time-based concepts. Takt time, Just-In-Time, and cycle times are just a few well-known examples. Time studies have their associated strengths and weaknesses but almost always the time required to complete a task is one aspect of productivity. Measuring times for an operation on a step-by-step basis is a valuable way to analyze processes and factually find out how long different tasks are taking to complete. Steps that take a long time to complete or vary considerably are often excellent candidates for Kaizen.

A technique that is similar to time study is that of motion study. Normally we use the phrase "time and motion study" as if it was a single technique, but the roots and methods are quite different. Time studies, as mentioned above, merely look at how long some step or process takes to complete. It says nothing about the fundamental motions required to complete that step. For time studies to have any meaning, however, the times must be related back to either work elements or discrete motions for identification purposes. Time merely reflects the action being taken; however, it is not the motion or action in and of itself.

There are special symbols that can be used in motion analysis when this sort of detailed observation is required. The symbols are quite old and were formed by the husband and wife team of Frank and Lillian Gilbreth. Eighteen basic symbols can be used to depict most human motions and they are quite detailed in nature (e.g., extend hand, grasp, remove, etc.). There is not enough space in this chapter to explain the symbols but they are easily found in old Industrial Engineering textbooks or on the Internet for interested parties. When motion study is combined with time study, it can become a powerful technique for generating many small improvements that can add up to something very big in the end.

If you combine work elements, time, and motion study in a particular way, you will arrive at a form of analysis known as *standardized work* at Toyota. Standardized work is a chapter or book all by itself in terms of difficulty and precision. If you are familiar with the concept, however, it can be a tremendous way to analyze certain types of operations. In a general sense, what you seek to do is establish a takt time or rate for a process and then align work elements for a given operator or set of operators up to that rate. In other words, you are attempting to balance the work to the rate of customer demand. When this analysis and activity is put into place, work rates are more closely aligned with customer demand and the practice of overbuilding is usually stopped. In addition to stopping this overbuilding, there is normally a large gain in terms of productivity and quality as well.

When machines are the focus of improvement of work instead of human operations, then a different lens is normally needed to spot improvement angles. For machines in most production shops, the areas of mechanical breakdown, changeover time, minor stops, speed losses, scrap, and rework, for example, represent excellent areas for improvement. Normally, one or two of these areas predominate in terms of impact on production. It is good practice to measure the extent of these losses and then pick the largest one or two for deeper study and analysis.

One more uniquely Toyota style of analysis is that of Material and Information Flow Analysis (MIFA). In the world outside Toyota, this practice is known as *value stream mapping* due to the success of a well-known workbook published on this topic. The basic concept of the analysis is to measure the lead-time throughout the facility for a given product or component. Normally, the actual value-added time for any item is measured in minutes, whereas the lead-time is measured in days. Analyzing scheduling patterns, process flow, inventory amounts, and other angles often highlights many areas of improvement.

As I cautioned at the beginning of this step, there is no single way to analyze a process. Your goal will determine what you will look at in reality. For example, if you are strictly looking to improve quality, then none of the items alone mentioned above will likely be sufficient. Other techniques related to improving process capability then make more sense to employ. Normally, however, some form of work element analysis, time and/or motion study, standardized work, machine loss analysis, or material and information flow analysis is a great way to look more deeply into a process and generate ideas for improvement.

STEP 3: GENERATE ORIGINAL IDEAS

The third step in Toyota's Kaizen method is to generate original ideas for improvement. Just as there is no one magical way to analyze a process, there is no one magical way to generate ideas. We can, however, provide some basic advice regarding the idea generation process and highlight some methods that have been used in the past to help spur thinking.

Often there are roadblocks that stifle our creative thinking process and we need to be mindful of these pitfalls. Otherwise, even the best of teams can become sidetracked and fail to generate improvement ideas. One common problem is simply force of habit. We repeat something over and over again until it becomes second nature. That habit is healthy in many respects but it does not always help in implementing Kaizen. Be prepared to always challenge the current status quo and be open to experimenting with new methods in Kaizen.

As set of related roadblocks are those of preconceptions or common sense. Often we unintentionally have mental roadblocks that hinder our thinking. For example, in the area of machine setups, it was common sense to run large batch sizes on equipment that ran multiple part numbers and were difficult to change over. Common sense said to run fewer changeovers because they took away from valuable production time. Uncommon sense challenged the assumption behind this idea that changeover time was fixed and set out to reduce that time component until it was negligible.

Emotion can also be a powerful force that limits our creative thinking power. We need both logic and emotion to form opinions and drive actions. However, the emotion of fear of failure, for example, can force us to become hesitant or overly cautious. In Kaizen we need to remind ourselves from time to time that it is okay to fail as long as no one is injured and the damage is not irreversible. Some of our best learning comes from failing and learning why something does not work. Often it requires a second or third time to get things right, and we need the patience and persistence to follow through on these sorts of items. Be careful so that you don't allow emotions to stifle trial and error and the associated learning process.

In terms of practical advice, there are several things I suggest that you attempt when generating ideas. One very important rule is to separate idea generation from that of judgment. Often we are quick to judge and dismiss ideas that are new or different. In generating original ideas, I suggest that you strive for quantity of improvement ideas first and then whittle those down later to select the most promising few. If you apply the lens of judgment too often or too early, you will inadvertently stifle the creative thinking process as idea generation and judgment utilize different parts of the brain.

Other points of practical advice include thinking from different angles and combining ideas with others. For example, if a task like fastening a bolt takes too long or is difficult, the right approach might not be to do this task faster or make it easier using the same mechanism. The best idea might be to eliminate the need for the fastener in the first place and secure it via another method. This alternative way might link in with someone else's idea about how to apply a new method for fastening the items in question.

Over the years there have been a variety of documents created to help people generate ideas, and I suggest that you research and apply these techniques as needed. Some of the methods are simple, such as mental checklists. Alex Osborn was regarded as the "father of classical brainstorming." He created several checklists that asked a series of questions pertaining to reusing, borrowing, changing, enlarging, reducing, substituting, rearranging, reversing, and combining items. Often, these thought-provoking questions can be used to stimulate idea generation.

Industrial engineers also have created various rules for motion economy. These rules can apply to use of the human body, arrangement of the workplace, or the design of tools and equipment. Reviewing these checklists and—more importantly—creating your own for your respective situation is a great way to encourage the thinking process and to make sure you are considering multiple angles.

Another fundamental piece of advice is to encourage the practice of asking questions and clarifying the purpose of various items. The fundamental 5W 1H technique for asking Why, What, Where, When, Who, and How is very useful for analysis as well as idea generation. After asking the 5W 1H questions, review everything in the context of can we eliminate it, can we combine it, can we rearrange it, or can we simplify it for improvement? This questioning process is always useful for generating new ideas.

The final and most famous method for idea generation is that of brainstorming. Almost everyone is familiar with this process and it needs no introduction. When applied correctly, it is a very useful technique for idea generation. Be sure to keep the group to a reasonable size so that participation is manageable. The four basic rules for brainstorming are to suspend criticizing during the idea generation phase, encourage speaking freely, seek quantity, and encourage thinking collaboratively. Employing an assigned facilitator and scribe are also useful techniques for running an effective meeting.

STEP 4: MAKE A KAIZEN PLAN

In Kaizen we normally try to implement improvement ideas as soon as possible. Sometimes that ideal can be done right away but at other times it takes a while to implement some items. In either case, it is important to have a plan in place to guide the actions that need to be carried out. The plan does not need to be elaborate or overly complicated. However, it does need to contain several key elements for it to be a viable plan.

First, the plan must make clear *what* is going to be done in terms of either corrective actions or altered methods to improve the current state. The action items should be as specific as possible and detailed enough to be clear. If the *what* part of the plan is not clear, then people are left to their own interpretations of the task and confusion might be the result. Take time to draft what is going to be done in a clear fashion and review it with all necessary parties.

Second, the plan should also contain *who* is going to do the task and by *when*. Plans that do not assign either responsible parties or a due date are rarely completed. In order to get things done, a person or someone representing a group of people needs to own action items for clarity. This person may in reality coordinate the completion of the work but there needs to be a single point of ownership for clarity and accountability. Likewise, without a due date, tasks will drag on for an extended period of time and not ever be completed. In Kaizen we have to make clear who is responsible for action items, along with a due date.

Additionally, in some plans it is also useful to include *how* the action item will be done if that is not self-evident. In other cases, the *what* and *how* are often mixed into one statement regarding the purpose of the proposed action items. In either case, it is also useful to make it clear *where* the work will be done and *what the expected result is* for the item in question. For example, if changing the assembly technique at station six is implemented in hopes of reducing difficulty and saving time, what is expected? Just expecting "better" is not always a clear indication of what to expect. If you expect to cut the cycle time in half, then include in the plan that the expected result is to reduce the time required from sixty seconds to less than thirty seconds, for example. This will give you something more specific to check later on when you are evaluating the success of your action items.

STEP 5: IMPLEMENT THE PLAN

Implementing your Kaizen plan is essentially the "Do" phase of the Plan-Do-Check-Act (PDCA) management cycle. Creating a good plan as outlined in Step 4 is a healthy step toward implementing your plan. Implementation normally involves a mix of short-, medium-, and longer-term items to complete. Here are a few things to keep in mind.

During implementation it is very important to communicate with all affected parties about what is being done. Often, Kaizen breaks down due to failures to explain and coordinate with affected parties. Part of being a good Kaizen leader is skill in both leadership and communication. Be sure to conduct updates and review the plan as needed during implementation phases.

Second, do not forget to provide proper training and instruction as needed. The act of Kaizen implies change, and therefore various standards and ways of doing things in the process are altered. Take the time during implementation to make sure that training, when required, is adequately conducted for anyone affected by the change. Having a good job instruction training plan in place as part of the Kaizen implementation is always a good idea to increase the chances of success.

Another key point during implementation is to remain positive and enthusiastic about the change. It is always likely that you will run into unforeseen problems during implementation. Take the time to address those items, revise plans, and alter methods as needed. Success is often a matter of sticking to the Kaizen process and repeating it as needed. If at first you don't succeed, try and try again.

STEP 6: VERIFY THE RESULTS

The final important step of Kaizen it to check and verify your results. Unless you produce results that generate measured improvement, you have not done true Kaizen. In other words, activity alone does not ensure achievement. There are several key points in this step to keep in mind. One key point is the importance of using standards as a method for measurement. Another is honestly assessing if you have met your goal. If you did meet the goal, then measure by "how much?" Was it as in the amount as expected? If not, then by how much did you miss and why not? These are critical actions to complete during the final step of Kaizen.

The other unstated part of this final phase is deciding what to do next. If you are satisfied with your results, can you replicate this elsewhere? What needs to be done in order to sustain the gains you have made? These questions and others should be considered during the completion of your Kaizen implementation. One useful way to help facilitate this discussion is by holding a brief Kaizen presentation report at the conclusion of the activity. Have the team explain their task and identify the improvement opportunity they were seeking. In addition, have the team explain the analysis methods they used and what improvement ideas they identified. Also, have them explain the implementation sequence and the results obtained from the project. As part of the closing discussion, review what was learned, how this can be shared and sustained, and what else might be done.

SUMMARY

This chapter attempted to explain some of the history, concepts, and basic steps associated with Toyota's Kaizen method. I always remind people to think of Kaizen as a process and not an event or activity. The process of Kaizen can be practiced by individuals, teams, or special groups brought together for a particular purpose. The goal of Kaizen is to generate improvement results for the organization and to develop the skill of the participants involved in the activity. The opportunity for Kaizen is endless, and the process is always rewarding for those willing to undertake the journey.

Note: For further details on this topic, including specific worksheets, examples, and more in-depth explanations, please refer to the book titled *Toyota Kaizen Methods: Six Steps to Improvement* authored by Art Smalley and Isao Kato, and published by Productivity Press in 2010.

7

Kaizen Culture: The Continuous Improvement Engine

Stephen J. Ansuini

A Kaizen Culture is evident when all levels of the organization take ownership for continuous improvement. If the Lean principles make up the bricks of a Lean organization, then the Kaizen Culture is the mortar that binds them together. Team members engaging in continuous improvement is an outward expression of the company's internal commitment to placing the customer first and giving creativity the respect it deserves.

As we begin the Lean journey, we must support continuous improvement at all levels of the organization because it is the engine that drives so many aspects of Lean and certainly drives team member engagement.

Organizations must empower their employees so they take it upon themselves to resolve the problems that occur within their area of responsibility. Through employee involvement a company progresses along the Lean journey more easily and more efficiently than they ever thought possible. In an empowered workforce, daily work is accomplished

- With higher quality
- At a lower cost
- With greater safety
- In a more timely manner

The Kaizen Culture must be seen as a way of doing business and not as another thing "we have to do." It is clearly illustrated time and again within Toyota organizations that involving all levels of employees yields far more success than those companies that do not encourage their workers to improve their work area and process. To be competitive in today's global market, organizations need the collective creative power of all employees. Collaboration is the way we do things!

The value of collaborative intelligence yields a Gestalt effect; that is, the sum of the improvement efforts is greater than its individual parts. This is often used to describe a Lean environment. Lean can be compared to a complete ecosystem. You can take bits and pieces of it and use them to better an organization and become more competitive; but to truly be Lean, each component must be working in harmony with all the others. Removing one will cause the overall system to be less than its potential.

THE KEY ELEMENTS OF A KAIZEN CULTURE

To build a Lean workplace, a Kaizen Culture must also be part of the journey so that the progression toward an empowered workforce is permanent. So what are the key elements of a Kaizen Culture? Kaizen Cultures are encouraged and developed over time through

- Visible sponsorship and support by management
- Clear purpose and aligned goals
- Evolving continuous improvement system

Visible Sponsorship and Support by Management

Visible management support has many characteristics that provide ample opportunities for the Lean leader to successfully nurture a Kaizen Culture. Some of these will likely fit the current culture and thereby provide a segue for a more empowered Lean culture. Here are four specific characteristics Lean leaders can follow that will develop a Lean culture:

1. Continuous Improvement system support
2. Employee recognition (formally and informally)
3. Promotional activities
4. Mutually established goals

Leadership Support

Nothing is more important to a team member's sense of success than to know that what he or she does is appreciated, is important, and makes a difference. Team members feel successful when leaders take notice of what they are doing. Leaders must show sincere interest in their efforts. Leaders who walk the shop floor and show interest in team members and their activities will keep their workforce engaged in actively seeking another opportunity to improve their work. This means that the leaders must be willing to speak with team members and sometimes hear things that they wish were not so. Keeping this open communication will foster effective job relations and strengthen the workplace.

The cost to the company to have this "face time" with team members is the leader's time. This time is not lost but is an investment in the Kaizen Culture. This was demonstrated to me by my plant president, Mr. Fujio Cho. Mr. Cho was the president of TMMK (Toyota Motor Manufacturing Kentucky, Inc.) from December 1988 until October 1994. Mr. Cho shared with me on numerous occasions that the quarterly tour was one of his favorite activities because he got to Gemba Genbutsu. Go to the actual place where the work is done. Spending time with the team members at their place of work and talking with them about their improvement brought smiles to Mr. Cho and the team members. I would accompany Mr. Cho on a tour through the plant to visit specific improvement initiatives. The improvements were selected through a series of elimination activities until each department leader had one representing his area. Even this elimination process brought recognition to even more team members. Managers would nominate one or two from their areas. The department leaders and their direct reports would discuss these and do their own Go-and-See activity with the nominated team members. The department leader would select the one to represent that department. This typically meant we would do our Gemba walk to no less than eight specific work areas scattered through the 1.2 million-square-foot facility. The team members valued their time with the president and were very proud to have the opportunity to show their accomplishments. Other team members were motivated to try to get an improvement activity that would get them on the list. A week after the tour, all the team members nominated would be invited to a luncheon with the president. Mr. Cho would recognize each team member and would present plaques and a special pin that could only be received by those on the president's list of quarterly recognition improvements. Each team member would also tell a little about their improvement activity. Mr. Cho identified the improvement he selected and shared why it was number-one on his list. We also had other executives present and alternated seating so every team member was next to an executive. We enjoyed a good meal and fellowship.

The quarterly recognition gifts were sought after as a visible representation of the pride they had in their work. As these team members proudly displayed their recognition items, other team members would ask them how they got it and the team member would get to tell his story again and get a little more recognition. Not only were the desired behaviors reinforced, but oftentimes the other team members were inspired to get involved as well.

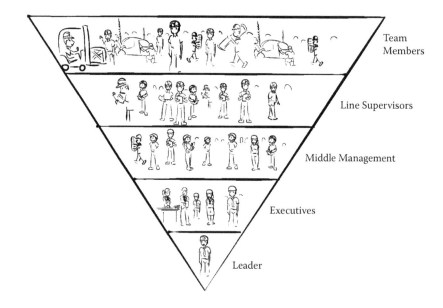

The improvement activities recognized contributed to achieving business goals so that everyone was a winner. Department leaders would seek implemented improvements for recommendation for this quarterly recognition activity. Team members would seek the prestigious recognition of the quarterly reviews. And others would be encouraged and inspired to improve their work areas.

Clear Purpose and Aligned Goals

Lean is all about alignment of business goals and clearly cascading them through the organization. The process is referred to as Hoshin Kanri. This is cascaded from the top corporate levels indicating goals and insight about future and developmental goals. As it goes to the regional level, the country level, the state level, the plant level, etc., each subsequent annual plan supports the goals on the annual plan directly above. The effectiveness of this process can only be realized when the plans are clearly communicated. This process should also be applied in the annual planning for the suggestion system.

The Hoshin can have a significant impact on how you plan and execute your continuous improvement system. All that is done would ultimately be supporting the highest-level corporate goals. There are many items that should be considered when developing your suggestion system and its annual strategy. This is one thing that can have the greatest impact on developing a Kaizen Culture. To grow your Kaizen Culture, consider the following points:

- Publish goals and progress monthly
- Success measurement criteria
- Simple administration
- Short cycle time
- Automated monthly reporting
- Continuous improvement (CI) advocates
- Local administration
- High implementation rate
- Focus on immediate work area
- Emphasize employee participation
- Participation recognition and awards
- Recognition of employees
- System integrity
- Categories of improvements (include both tangible and intangible)

Clear goals will drive clear behaviors. So, clearly identifying the goals and targets of the suggestion system will encourage the right behaviors. We needed to get team members in the habit of looking at things with "Kaizen eyes," so we initially set our goals at participation rate and the quantity of suggestions. The Steering Committee was in place for the first year and a half of the suggestions system and was instrumental in driving the right behaviors in their direct reports, meeting monthly for the first six months and then going to quarterly meetings for the remaining year. After that, an annual report to the company board provided enough information that the suggestion system was developing the desired effect.

The suggestion system had a significant impact on guiding the organization to a Kaizen Culture. The suggestion program also reflected the organization's mission and values so the company would remain on the proper course. Thus, we needed to ensure that the targets and administration of the suggestion system did not contradict our values or the long-term direction. For example, if one of our values is to get all team members engaged and empowered to make improvements in their immediate area of responsibility and I publish a goal that encourages only large savings improvements, then I am not aligning the goal with our values. Many small improvements by many team members are aligned with and power the continuous improvement engine.

I recall the two primary measures of success when we launched our improvement program and how simple they were. Sometimes we try to make things more complicated than they need to be; so in your organization, keep it simple. It is beneficial for the team member, the administration, and the company to follow that path. Savings was not and cannot be the focus of a successful long-term continuous improvement program that desires to develop a Kaizen Culture. Discussion later of the phases of an involvement program will clarify this target as just one of the stages in the life of a continuous improvement initiative.

I witnessed each department take on the challenge of getting team members actively engaged in the improvement process. Friendly competition between leaders was evident. Monthly statistics were posted on the boards located at all employee entrances and near all six cafeterias. Team members would go out of their way to see the latest information, and increased activity was evident in the areas falling below the number-one position.

With this spiraling increase in formal improvement submissions, it was necessary to ensure that the process was as efficient as possible. The last year I had responsibility for the involvement program, we had in excess of 150,000 suggestions from 5,050 employees of a total workforce of 7,300. That represents an average of thirty-plus implemented improvements from each participating team member. Across the total company employment level (7,300), this would yield an average of twenty suggestions per team member (= 150,000/7,300). Now granted, only approximately 15% of the suggestions had tangible savings but that was not the primary focus of the suggestion system. Even taking this into consideration, there were documented hard-dollar savings that were consistently between two- to fourfold that of the total cost of the suggestion system. So if the total cost of the administration of the suggestion system as $100,000, then the total savings as between $200,000 and $400,000. Any accountant would love a program that yields twice the investment, or more, to run it.

Evolving Continuous Improvement System

Like all major systems, the TMMK suggestion system went through three distinct phases. There are at least three phases that should be considered to develop a kaizen culture:

Phase 1: Introduction – Participation emphasis 1 to 3 years
Phase 2: Transition – Participant and development 1 to 2 years
Phase 3: Process maturation – System evolves as the Lean culture grows and matures

Phase 1: Introduction—Participation Emphasis

Planning the launch of an employee involvement system goes beyond the first year, the next ten years, and even generations. We must consider the activities and account for the evolution of the involvement program if we seek long-term success. To accomplish great things, we must enable our team members to begin where they are comfortable and grow from there. To announce the new suggestion system, a letter from the president was mailed to every team member's home. Included in this envelope was a nominal gift. If the team member was hired more than six months prior, he or she received a $25 gift certificate and those with less time received a $15 gift certificate. The letter thanked the team members for their contributions and said that if they had a substantial improvement that they would like to submit for additional award recognition under the new suggestion system to

do so within ninety days. Although there were thousands of improvements, no team member took advantage of that offer. And so, the TMMK team members began their continuous improvement journey toward becoming a Kaizen Culture. We had less than 200 suggestions that first month. Six years later, the highest month was greater than 17,000 suggestions. Clearly, the team members were on the track toward a true Kaizen Culture.

In the United States, our culture has a tendency to recognize the "heavy-hitters" and allow the small improvements to occur. Our team members are most comfortable with small improvements at first, so we must recognize and encourage many small improvements. The large improvements will continue to come; but to get the culture to develop into a Kaizen Culture, everyone must be engaged on a daily basis looking for improvement opportunities. To get everyone engaged, we must focus on the many small improvements that surround every team member. We must help them develop the "Kaizen Eye." In a business context, some would argue that we must track and report the costs and savings associated with the effort. Perhaps there are those who would argue that we should function as a profit center. This route will only lead to short-term success and not achieve the desired Kaizen Culture mentality in the workplace. Certainly we must take fiduciary responsibility and track costs and savings but that does not mean that we emphasize them. I formally reported quarterly to the executive board the improvement statistics. I would provide a hard copy of the number of suggestions and the number of team members participating. This information was broken down from the company level to the department level. I would also *verbally* share the following:

- Cost of administration
- Number and percent of intangible improvements
- Number and percent of tangible improvements
- Savings confirmed by accounting

At every opportunity, I would encourage the leadership to focus on the number of improvements and participation rate when they discussed this with their direct reports and cascaded the information down to the shop floor. I would see Mr. Cho do the same with those he interacted with when we had our recognition Gemba Walks and Luncheons. He would always emphasize the person and their abilities. I recall several specific instances of this. When Mr. Cho asked, "How did you discover the improvement?" One team member answered that he knew that the temperature of the fluid was too low because he kept a tropical fish tank and its set temperature was approximately that of the fluid. Another responded that when she was fastening the feedbag onto her horse one evening, she thought that the clip would be the perfect solution to a problem of parts coming loose in the dip tank of paint. And another used a bass boat seat to improve the ergonomics of a job. The examples seemed endless. Team members would see an improvement based on their hobbies or some recreational activity.

Savings was not a secret, and we published them annually on the information boards I mentioned earlier. But that was not the focus! This initial phase could last from one to three years. In some organizations it may take even longer. Culture change is a slow process if we want the change to be permanent. And this continuous improvement process is just one of the many facets needed to drive the culture change.

There is an expectation that leadership is responsible for properly administering the suggestion system process, ensuring consistency, and minimizing abuse. Whenever we provide incentives for a particular behavior, people quickly rise to the challenge. Some may try to abuse the system. To reduce abuse, it is important that a central monitoring point be established to ensure consistent adherence to the rules and guidelines of the system. Regular reviews and feedback to those not in compliance will help drive the understanding that the rules should be followed.

Phase 2: Transition—Participant Development

Team member development is necessary if the improvement process is to grow and evolve. Some development is accomplished from participating in the improvement process itself. However, we are seeking to increase the team members' effectiveness in addressing improvements that require problem-solving and investigative abilities. If the organization has a specific problem-solving process, such as Six Sigma (DMAIC), each team member should be educated in this process and be given opportunities to apply these new skills. This will require that we first develop the leadership so they can coach and mentor their direct reports in this problem-solving process. Formal training should be augmented with panel reviews and coaching sessions with leaders. So the problem-solving training would begin with the leadership long before it is deployed to the floor. "Leaders as teachers" is a very effective way of increasing the company's ability to deal with ever-increasing challenges and thrive in a global market.

Mr. Cho was a leader and very much a teacher. He used everyday occurrences to share situational learning to all who worked with him. The time I got to spend with Mr. Cho was enjoyable. It was often challenging and would require honing my skills, but he knew that to continue to raise the bar is the challenge that drives so many of us to greater things.

Leadership must walk the talk by modeling the company's problem-solving process and adhering to its values and principles. To this end, it is critical that the company values be published and made visible to all. Reinforcement of the values should be evident in the daily business routine.

The Lean principles should be enumerated and published as well as woven throughout training so that team members learn to integrate them into their daily routines. The Toyota Production System (TPS) has five precepts and fourteen principles. The five precepts are not as well-known or published but nonetheless date back to 1935. The five precepts were originally published by Sakichi Toyoda on October 30, 1935. They are

Precept 1: Always be faithful to your duties, thereby contributing to the company and to the overall good.

Precept 2: Always be studious and creative, striving to stay ahead of the times.

Precept 3: Always be practical and avoid frivolousness.

Precept 4: Always strive to build a homelike atmosphere at work that is warm and friendly.

Precept 5: Always have respect for God, and remember to be grateful at all times.

Organizations that take the Lean journey seriously should consider developing their precepts and their principles. It does not matter how many you identify, it is just important that they are identified and woven throughout daily work and evident in business decisions. In this way, all team members will begin to better understand and embrace the direction of the company.

I would also like to point out that missing from Toyota's list of principles is something that most organizations need to include in their list of Lean principles. Have you any thoughts? Well, there is nothing addressing team member engagement and empowerment. This is not an oversight by Toyota. The reason it is not called out in Toyota's principles is that the engagement and empowerment of team members is so engrained in the Toyota culture. It is a clear expectation from the first moment a team member enters the work group that they will look at how they can improve things within their area of responsibility. Continuous improvement by all is part of their daily routine. Opportunities abound to take the initiative to shine by engaging in continuous improvement. Many leaders include this aspect as one of the many items reviewed when it comes time to promote someone.

Phase 3: Process Maturation

This is probably the most elusive phase of the continuous improvement journey. The fundamentals of the Kaizen Culture do NOT change. It becomes clearly evident that the level of problem solving the team members demonstrate is much higher. Additionally, the level of the problems resolved is increasingly more difficult. This yields greater benefit to the company by improving the team member's work satisfaction and lowers the operating costs of the company.

We have a tendency to leave some of the foundational pieces behind because we feel we have outgrown them. In reality, all aspects of Lean should remain but yet grow and evolve as the organization continues down the Lean journey path. I like to say, "You cannot take a jet plane to the Lean destination. You must take the journey step by step." Patience in the beginning will yield a lasting and thriving Lean culture in the organization that will take the company to the next level and beyond. If the "culture change" is rushed, it will not be long-lived. Early efforts to force culture change usually meet with a strong passive-aggressive response. Be cautious!

Promotion Activities

There are an endless number of things that can be done in this space. Our Quarterly Recognition process discussed earlier was a huge favorite of our team members. Not just the workers, but also the leadership. I can recall on several occasions over the course of three years that Mr. Cho would say how much he looked forward to the quarterly tours where he could get out and meet the team members and celebrate their accomplishments with them. It was clear that he was a leader with great concern for his team members and their development. This was made very personal for me when we had the dedication ceremony of the NAPSC in Georgetown, Kentucky. After Mr. Cho was gone for more than seven years, he still greeted me by name. What a great leader! He inspired greatness in all who worked with him.

Promotion activities included

- Monthly recognition by the immediate supervisor and leadership within the team member's section in front of their peers

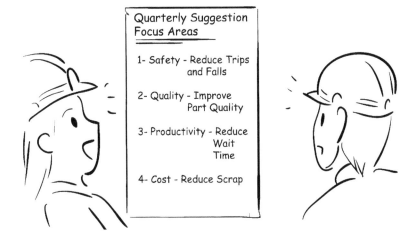

Quarterly Suggestion
Focus Areas

1- Safety - Reduce Trips
and Falls

2- Quality - Improve
Part Quality

3- Productivity - Reduce
Wait
Time

4- Cost - Reduce Scrap

- Quarterly recognition (discussed earlier)
- Annual participation awards

In addition to these company-wide efforts, each department would have activities within their sections that were structured as a result of what the team members wanted as recognition. Some liked T-shirts, others hats. Trinkets and pins were appreciated, and many would wear these pins on their hats and uniforms.

Special promotion themes were also done when we wanted to reduce problems of a specific type. For example, we would have a "Reduce Slips, Trips, and Falls" promotion for three months in areas experiencing higher than average incidents. Department heads could also establish a focus theme for their areas. When new processes were established, we would have a very short "blackout" period. "Blackout" periods typically lasted between thirty and ninety days while the equipment and processes were stabilized. Once stable, team members could make improvement suggestions and benefit from the change, the award, and the recognition. What better thing than to improve your working environment and get recognition and an award or gift for doing so!

Another aspect of our improvement system that team members really liked was the ability to accumulate award points ($1 = 1 point) up to one year and receive a cash award for their many small contributions. We had a $500 minimum required to get a cash award. The reason for this was that this amount would be more likely to be memorable. So every time they used the new appliance that was paid for with their suggestion awards, they would be encouraged to participate even more. Our award points were based on approximately 3% to 8% of the first year's savings. The larger the savings realized, the smaller the percentage of the savings would be awarded.

Cost of Operating a Continuous Improvement System

A company is in business to make a profit but a continuous improvement program should not be operated like a profit center. If the company breaks even on a process that improves morale and team member engagement, it is far ahead of where it once was.

SUMMARY

There are several lessons I learned during the evolution of our continuous improvement process. Team members frequently said that the *turn-around time* was an excellent indicator of how important a Kaizen Culture mindset was to the leadership team. We had an average cycle time of forty-five days from submission to payment. The way the system was structured allowed for such a short processing time. The line supervisor was responsible for working with the team members and supporting their improvement ideas. It was not until the improvement was implemented and proved itself that the suggestion would be submitted. Implementation was required. It was the expectation. We had in excess of 97% implementation rate during the six years I was responsible for the improvement process.

I recall an improvement initiative that the team members decided would take a year plus before they could submit it. They were proposing an improvement of a plastics process that was sensitive to both temperature and humidity. So the team said they needed to pilot the change for one year so they could confirm that the quality was not adversely affected.

Another "hot button" for team members was that the *evaluation process* was not only quick, but reflected the trust in the team members' ability to make wise choices. The improvement needed to be real, and the team members would confirm its effectiveness before they would consider the improvement implemented. Management frequently asks the question, "What about all the 'junk' suggestions? Don't we need to 'police' them and not pay for improvements that have little or no measurable savings?" Statistically, policing a healthy improvement process is often cost prohibitive so the system design and guidelines are critical to minimize this type of abuse. Training and easy-to-follow objective guidelines are used by the line supervisors. Questions and concerns raised by participants can be discussed with the administrative staff of the improvement process. Improvements submitted by the line supervisor as implemented were processed and paid with rare exceptions. In one year we had an average of thirty implemented and paid improvements per team member. Only about 8% of these had large savings that were verified during the reviewing and payment process—and that 8% yielded a 4:1 payback to the company when the total cost of all suggestion payments was compared to the measured and verified savings of the 8% group of suggestions. If we were to ignore or disallow intangible suggestions, it is very likely that we would not have received all the large savings suggestions.

Visible commitment by the leadership team was important in getting the Kaizen Culture growing and evolving. It is not enough for leaders to say, "I support the continuous improvement process." They must be visible in that support or it will not mean anything. We had eight departments that each had its own approach to support the continuous improvement process.

Another lesson learned was that the credibility of the involvement program will often be identified with the administrator and influenced by the level of visible leadership support. So it is imperative to take this into consideration when planning your system.

Training will vary with the phase of the program. The initial phase training is nothing more than explaining the rules and guidelines of the involvement system and getting team members interested in participating. As the system progresses into Phase 2, a more structured training process that includes QC tools, problem solving, and PDCA training will prove effective in moving the culture in the right direction. I would also suggest meeting facilitation training as many members will want to work as a team in solving the tougher problems. The progression to Phase 3 is much the same except a deeper dive into problem solving and statistical process control is beneficial. All of this will raise the company's effectiveness in its particular niche.

8

Elimination of Waste in Product Design

Patrick Muller

During a Lean transformation we tend to concentrate a lot on elimination of waste in our *process designs*. But how do we tackle waste in our *product designs*?

VALUE ENGINEERING/VALUE ANALYSIS

Waste in Process Design

When I started working for Toyota in the early 1990s, little literature was available on the Toyota Production System (TPS) or what we know commonly today as Lean manufacturing. Most of what we learned we obtained from our Japanese Senseis.

We learned by being challenged, questioned, and by a hands-on approach. We did not know that we were applying "Lean" methodologies. "Lean" became better-known terminology after Jim Womack, Daniel T. Jones, and Daniel Roos wrote their great best seller *The Machine That Changed the World*. It described Toyota's manufacturing process as "Lean": a constant striving to put the value to the customer first, to eliminate the waste along the value stream.

In the meantime, many books have been written on "Lean" topics—from Lean tools to Lean culture—and I am sure many more will be written (you are reading one right now!).

When we look at the Lean methodologies, the focus is mainly on how we can identify and eliminate/reduce waste in our processes, whether they are manufacturing processes or administrative processes. What started in a manufacturing world is now applied to numerous industries. Most of us are familiar with the seven types of waste (Muda), which are defined as overproduction, inventory, transport, waiting, motion, over-processing, and defects/rework. We also know that Mura and Muri (variation and overburden, respectively) have a negative effect on our processes. We have all studied several methodologies to help us identify these wastes from just simple observation at the Gemba, so profoundly taught by Taiichi Ohno, to more sophisticated approaches such as Value Stream Mapping.

Once we identify the waste, we can eliminate or reduce it by means of Kaizen or problem-solving techniques or other methodologies. But it always amazed me that not so much attention has been paid to the identification and elimination of waste in the actual design of a product (not the development process).

Waste in Product Design

Despite some ups and downs, Toyota is and has been overall a successful organization. It is one of the most studied companies in the world. Many are eager to imitate Toyota by copying techniques. One of my Senseis told our suppliers they should not just copy what they see on the surface but, rather, understand the purpose and the concepts behind what they see. Only then we can understand the true meaning behind a lot of the Lean principles. I urge you to do the same. See if these principles can apply with or without modification to your circumstances.

At Toyota it is also common practice to pay careful attention to the waste in product design.

So how can we define waste in the design of a product? Similar to the waste in processes, here waste is also defined as "non-value-added for the customer." However, here we do not define activities as non-value-added (seven wastes) but, rather, value is seen as "function" in relation to "cost" (Value = Function/Cost).

Each product design has a primary function but it can have additional functions as well that might not necessarily be required or desired by the customer, yet they add cost to the product.

On the other hand, we might also have an expensive design (e.g., material choice) that does not necessarily increase the value to the customer.

Increasing the value by looking at the functions and the cost of the product design is known as Value Engineering/Value Analysis.

Value Engineering/Value Analysis is a methodology that is commonly used in Toyota's purchasing practices. These practices follow a defined Toyota Purchasing Philosophy. This philosophy is what makes the relationship between Toyota and its suppliers quite unique.

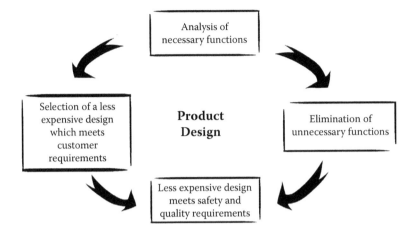

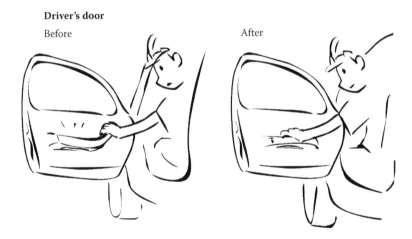

Toyota's Purchasing Philosophy

My senior coordinator, Saka-san (name changed) introduced me to Toyota's purchasing philosophy, which is based on the following three core elements:

1. Fair competition based on an open-door policy
2. Mutual prosperity based on mutual trust
3. Abidance by the law

Fair Competition Based on an Open-Door Policy

This principle means that a potential supplier can always request to become a Toyota supplier. But it also immediately outlines the fundamental principle of an open-door policy. An *open-door policy* means that Toyota is welcome at any time at their suppliers. It also, practically, means that Toyota demands an open cost breakdown approach from its suppliers. This implies that raw material, purchased material, labor and processing, and overhead cost as well as margins, which in the end define the price of the product, are disclosed in detail.

I have seen many potential suppliers that are eager to start working with Toyota but some do have a problem with this "open door" = "open book" principle and back out. This open-door policy requires mutual trust.

Single sourcing is avoided; healthy competition among a few select suppliers is encouraged.

All selected suppliers are evaluated regularly on their performance and competitiveness. Those that perform better usually will receive the larger volume share. And those that perform less will get a smaller volume share but will also get the opportunity to improve on their weaknesses. This approach stimulates fair competition within the supplier base for similar commodities.

Mutual Prosperity Based on Mutual Trust

Proper due diligence in supplier selection can take a long time. Toyota sees the relationship with its suppliers as a crucial long-term partnership for their common success. Toyota invests considerable time and resources to assist its suppliers when they need it. However, it does remain the supplier's responsibility to deliver the results.

Toyota Supplier Technical Support usually takes this role. Their engineers usually have a strong TPS background to assist their suppliers. But in addition to assistance, Toyota will also continuously challenge its suppliers to improve on all levels.

Toyota Purchasing and Toyota Supplier Technical Support will seek ways to improve suppliers' quality, reduce cost, and improve delivery times. Many Toyota suppliers will tell you that it can be quite stressful to be a Toyota supplier due to the continuous challenge to do better. However, they will also say that they feel respected, challenged, and valued by Toyota. In the end, both parties are in a win-win partnership.

Abide by the Law

All business should be conducted in full compliance with the law by all parties. This principle is applicable to Toyota as well as its suppliers. Prior to engaging in a customer-supplier relationship, Toyota performs a due diligence to make sure business can be conducted in a legal way.

Toyota's Purchasing Practices

Cost Breakdown

Toyota suppliers must submit a complete cost breakdown for the parts they will supply to Toyota. This means that the supplier must provide detailed cost information regarding the following: raw material (how much used, unit price, and supplier information), purchased components (quantity, unit price, and supplier information), processing and labor costs (man hour costs, machine hour costs, manual cycle time, machine time, and yield…), overhead costs, and margin.

The Toyota buyers will verify the accuracy of this information in detail in order to determine if the price quotation is acceptable. They will use this information in their price negotiations as well as to establish cost tables. Cost tables contain historic cost information of parts related to their physical characteristics and allow the buyers to do cost estimations for future products.

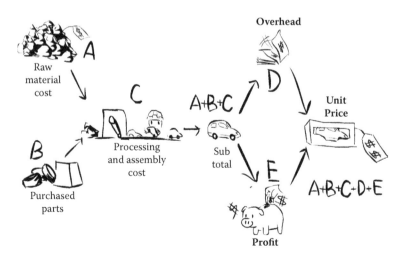

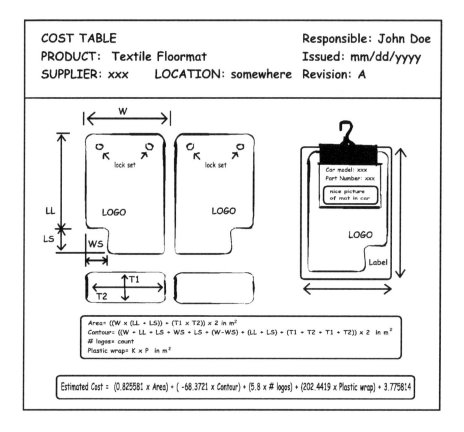

Target Costing, VE/VA, Kaizen

Toyota follows the principle of target costing when designing new products. The market price of the new planned product as well as the margin is basically being set in advance (in view of competitive pricing and required profit margin), resulting in a maximum target cost that must be achieved after the development of the new product.

This target cost is translated to target costs for every component that will need to be supplied/manufactured. Toyota as well as its suppliers are required to achieve this target cost. In order to achieve this, they will challenge the design aspect as well as the processing aspect. In other words, "How can we add the most value at the cheapest cost?" This brings us to value engineering/value analysis and Kaizen.

Kaizen, which tackles waste in processes, is explained in more detail in Chapters 6 and 7 of this book.

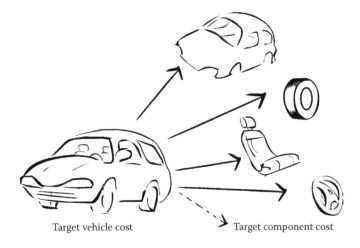

Target vehicle cost   Target component cost

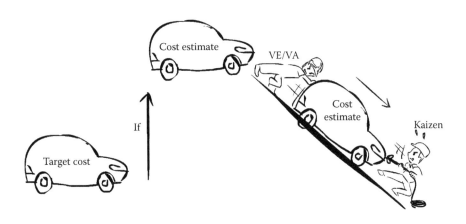

Below is an extract from a public annual report issued by Toyota Motor Corporation to the U.S. Government that gives an idea of the impact of these cost reduction efforts.

Cost Reduction Efforts (Extract)

During fiscal 2011, continued cost reduction efforts reduced operating costs and expenses by ¥180.0 billion (approximately $2.2 billion).

The effects of cost reduction efforts include the impact of fluctuation in the price of steel, precious metals, nonferrous alloys including aluminum, plastic parts, and other production materials and parts. In fiscal 2011, raw material prices were on an increasing trend; however, continued cost reduction efforts, by working closely with suppliers, contributed to the improvement in earnings by offsetting the effects from price increases. These cost-reduction efforts relate to ongoing value engineering and value analysis activities, the use of common parts resulting in a reduction of part types and other manufacturing initiatives designed to reduce the costs of vehicle production.

Note that the negative impact of raw material price increases in the fiscal year was completely offset per the cost reduction efforts by working with their suppliers. Only a successful partnership and a continuing strive to get waste out of design and processes can make this happen.

Value Engineering/Value Analysis

History

The concept of VE/VA was first practiced by General Electric during World War II. Due to the lack of raw materials and supply, the company was forced to redesign products with other available materials. In doing so they were able to make products with the same function at a cheaper cost.

VE/VA grew into a discipline of defining value as function in relation to cost, a methodology to obtain cheaper design cost.

What is the difference between VE and VA? *Value engineering* is applying this practice prior to the production stage. *Value analysis* is applying this practice after the production stage, or in other words, on existing products. Needless to say, value engineering is more cost-effective than value analysis.

At Toyota, Suppliers Challenges

Toyota adapted the VE/VA concept in its design process and purchasing practices. Suppliers are challenged to present VE/VA ideas to the Toyota Purchasing Division. Presenting VE/VA and Kaizen is part of the supplier evaluation. Each idea is evaluated in detail: What will be the impact on value to the customer? What will be the impact on safety? (It should never be compromised!) What is the impact on quality, part cost, tooling cost, etc.?

Many ideas are presented but not all ideas are implemented due to the rigorous evaluation. Some ideas might not seem to have a high impact on the unit cost but the volume of sold parts can make the cost impact considerable.

VE/VA Proposal Form						Supplier:	
	VE	Part Number:		Model:		Author:	
Proposal N°:	VA	Part Name:				Issue Date:	

Present Design		Cost Reduction Proposal	

Estimated Reduction:						Weight effect	
Per piece	Number per assembly	Estimated per year	Estimated tooling cost	Tooling lifetime		Before	After
Unit Cost	Units	Units	Unit Cost	Units			
Lead Time:							

VE/VA and FMEA

A good practice to introduce VE/VA is in conjunction with preparing the Design FMEA (failure mode and effect analysis). While performing a Design FMEA, each function and component of the product concept is evaluated in detail to verify potential failures, to determine what the current risks are with the current controls in place, and how we can improve. This is a good time to also ask the following questions for a VE/VA: Is the function needed? Can we make it at a lower cost with, for example, a different material without jeopardizing safety and quality?

VE/VA and Marketing

When we perform VE/VA on a product design, we need to make sure we include an evaluation from a marketing point of view. Theoretically, we can make a product cheaper by elements, what some would consider "marketing" value.

A good example of can be found in the packaging of a product: We can take an existing product with great colorful pictures, and add high-quality packaging to make it very attractive to the customer. We could redesign it and keep just the bare essential value (the content of the product). However, by doing so we might impact our customer base profile. So, we need to partner with our marketing division with a common goal: Give the best value-added product to our customer at the most competitive price.

Practical Example

You are a manufacturer of ink cartridges for printers. Competition is fierce so we task a team to perform a benchmarking study and a value analysis on our product.

We put a cross-functional team together with the following representation: design, manufacturing, purchasing, quality, and sales and marketing. We evaluate the total package: product and packaging. We decide to analyze the packaging first.

The first step is to define the primary function of the packaging. Protect the ink cartridge from damage from point of manufacturing to point of use (put it in the printer). What could be some secondary functions (easy to transport, attractive, informative, etc.)?

In order to perform the value analysis, we need to apply "Go and See" (sounds familiar?). So be the customer and evaluate how you would "use" this packaging. What are the unnecessary functions? Could you redesign this packaging and be more cost-effective?

9

Adapting Lean for Made-to-Order/High-Mix, Low-Volume Organizations

Greg Lane

With North America and Europe losing a large share of traditional "high-volume manufacturing" to offshore competition and low-cost country sourcing, the West is left with predominately either: short lead-time products, engineered products, high-variation/low-volume items, or made-to-order products and services. While most Lean "tools" are centered around and have proliferated based instead on higher-volume and lower-variation products, the "principles" behind these tools as well as Lean management techniques can be profitably adapted to low-volume, high-mix, and even job-shop organizations. Those who think "we don't make cars" and therefore Lean will not work, need to take a step back and understand the underlying concepts, not the highly publicized tools.

The Toyota training and mentoring I received helped prepare me for transitioning these principles into the world of lower volume and higher variation as my Sensei was continuously asking, "What is the root cause?" and "What principle are you going to use in your Kaizen?" This coaching stuck with me through the years and helped me to always reflect on what underlying "principle"—not on the specific methodology—I needed to utilize and then in adapting that principle concept to the problem at hand.

My story in practically adapting Lean principles into a job-shop environment began with my desire to be responsible for my own profit and loss statement. As an engineer who had predominantly been involved in manufacturing, although financially limited as to the size of company my personal assets (as well as some leveraged financing) would permit me to own, I ended up purchasing a profitable high-variation, low-volume manufacturing organization. We built mostly metal and plastic parts and small subassemblies predominately for semiconductor equipment manufacturers (mostly OEMs). Knowing nothing about this business or the market, I only had my Toyota experience and common sense to contribute, although the "Lean" concepts required a bit of massaging to be profitable in this made-to-order environment.

My Lean journey began at Toyota, in the higher-volume, lower-variation automotive industry, although I had to learn that the true flexibility is realized in the underlying concepts. Though during the six years in which I owned my job-shop, as well as a long period of specialized support in the transformation to "Lean" management of other high-variation companies, I have learned a few additional tricks based on my Toyota experience and share a few of those key learnings in this chapter.

Never during my tenure as a business owner did I propose that we "implement Lean"; instead, I used the concepts adapted from Lean thinking to manage, grow, and increase profitability. I followed how I had witnessed the Toyota Production System being utilized within Toyota; it was just the underlying way they operated the business, instead of trying to "implement" their production system. I did not introduce improvements with Japanese names, as this held no value for my team. Instead, everything was done in a systematic way to better the business and ensure job security in this unstable and cyclical high-technology market. By always sharing the bigger picture and relating every targeted improvement to the overall strategy, the necessity for continuous improvement was justified throughout my tenure with the team.

Clarifying our strategy (our organization's version of Hoshin Kanri), and deploying it throughout each level within my small organization, promoted successful and profitable improvement ideas. I would not call this "policy deployment" as I have heard others do, as such infers deploying "policies"; instead, this was deploying the strategy to each level, allowing input and clarity as to how each person's indicators and related actions supported the overall profitability and growth of the company (just as important to my team was how this profitability translated into job security and some form of personal reward). With this structure in place, each level in the organization was able to better propose actions that resolved real problems in meeting the organization's overall objectives.

Not only did this strategy deployment ensure our success and prioritize our improvements (i.e., which Lean concepts I could adapt to support our objectives), but it has also always been fundamental in the successful transformations I have supported in both high-mix/low-volume as well as high-volume organizations. Without this link, I have witnessed companies "implementing Lean" with mixed success, as it is often viewed as additional work with only short-term gains and rarely has any longevity in the form of management support.

OSKKK TO LEARN AND TRANSFORM

As the basis for both learning and transforming the business, I utilized a lesser-known Toyota methodology called OSKKK. I began learning this practical technique during my key person training at Toyota's plants in Japan during 1992, and became further acquainted while supporting Delphi Automotive during a period in which Toyota production control manager Yoshinobu Yamada was introducing OSKKK throughout many of Delphi's operational divisions.

The acronym OSKKK has nothing to do with the Ku Klux Klan, but instead is a form of the PDCA (Plan-Do-Check-Act) cycle. The steps in this process are: **O**bserve Deeply, **S**tandardize (in some cases, you might first need to **S**tabilize), then **K**aizen of the flow and process, **K**aizen of equipment, and finally **K**aizen of layout. It should be viewed as a never-ending loop; once the Kaizen's (meaning continuous improvement) first cycle is completed, then observation and standardization will again be required. The first steps appear as common sense, which they are, although often after only short observation periods, we "impatient problem solvers" already know the root cause and jump directly to solutions. The "Kaizen" (continuous improvement) steps are in the order of effectiveness and sorted from least to most costly to implement. The conflict with this Kaizen sequence (improve process and flow, then improve equipment, and finally improve the layout) is that it works against human nature. It is often more tangible and exciting to either work on layout issues or address equipment improvements (including investments in new or higher technology equipment) than to tackle process and flow issues that are normally dominated by years of using the same method, conflicting opinions, mediocre buy-in, or a general sense comfort with the way it has always been performed. It is frequently after "confrontational" or uncomfortable questioning that the effectiveness of the existing processes can be improved; remember that all of the existing processes have a bit of personal ownership. Many of our processes are not standardized and continuously improved, but instead have evolved with the people filling those roles and are based on their talents and backgrounds (this is especially true for indirect and administrative processes).

LEARNING THE PROCESSES BEFORE MANAGING THEM

Following my positive and profitable experience from Toyota's guidelines that new employees typically begin with a hands-on learning period regardless of their position, my first months at my new company were spent working my way up, beginning as a machine operator. Difficult as this is to imagine for the modern, educated manager, this is a valuable utilization of his or her talents, prior to jumping into "high-level" decisions and reviews. For me it is beyond a doubt the difference between a manager's misguided direction of improvement ideas and the successful evolution of supported and profitable improvements. OSKKK was my methodology to learn as I progressively worked through the various jobs and tasks (just as I had done when I started at Toyota). Not being a naturally patient person, this period of humbly learning without jumping in and quickly introducing change (in other words, not performing "machine-gun" improvement) required discipline and restraint, but its necessity was reinforced by the lack of standardization I found. I knew from my former TPS training that trying to remove waste where standardization was nonexistent, was itself a wasted effort. In my business, "tribal knowledge" was king, so instead of just losing sleep imagining the hardships we would experience by the departure of any single employee with critical tribal knowledge (undocumented processes) in his or her head, I learned by day and documented by night. Later, these standards would be the basis of structured improvements based on constraints in meeting our strategy deployment. *(Note: At this time, the "strategy" had not been developed; it only came after gaining a much deeper and better understanding of the shop and office processes as well as gaining the "voice of the customer" through customer visits. I had hired the former manager to stay on-board during this period until I had learned enough that I could begin to lead.)* This hands-on learning was also necessary preceding my introductions to the customers (to gain an understanding of what was important to them), as sharp customers are able to quickly identify those leaders who cannot relate to the realities of the business.

CONSTRAINTS REQUIRE MORE THAN QUICK FIXES

Understanding and linking constraints to our business objectives requires that we have both robust strategy deployment and an understanding of our constraints (or bottlenecks) prioritized in relation to our strategy.

It is easiest to first think of bottlenecks on the shop floor. Most would agree that in high-variation businesses the bottlenecks are more difficult to locate because they are constantly moving, depending on many factors, including changes in customer demand, changes in model mix, etc. We need ways to visualize these bottlenecks in real-time, so that we can work to also minimize them in real-time. In other books[*] I have demonstrated examples of how these visualizations can help identify and elevate bottlenecks in the shop and indirect processes in real-time, but here I would like to move on to where the bigger constraints traditionally reside in high-variation or made-to-order businesses.

In high-variation organizations it is likely that the majority of high-impact improvements lie waiting within our flow of information (our indirect processes). Remember that in high variation, proportionally more of our resources are dedicated to managing the flow of information that is associated with more complicated products and services as well as smaller quantities and highly technical orders. Typically, 50% or more of our payroll goes for our indirect costs. Planning within these organizations is one specific area of general weakness often observed. However, if you have "proper metrics" and indicators, they should help to identify issues within this "flow of information," and many of these will be related to lead-time. When working with Toyota, it appeared that there was always an awareness and often a measurement versus a standard for lead-time, although I find that many other organizations do not have that as their focus.

Planning was not only a key constraint within my business, but it is a primary area of opportunity within the organizations I support. There are various levels of planning that involve different stakeholders and have different functions within an organization. Figure 9.1 is an outline of the typical levels and planning functions, starting with the "Master" plan. All organizations should have similar clarity when visualizing and improving their planning processes. Each of the three levels should have a tool that is

[*] Made to Order Lean-Excelling in a High-Mix, Low-Volume Envirnoment (Productivity Press, New York: 2007) and Mr. Lean Buys and Transforms a Manufacturing Company—The True Story of Profitability Growing an Organization with Lean Principles (CRC Press, New York: 2010).

Levels	Who	PDCA - Improve
Rolling monthly forecast *Move into MRP planning (as applicable)*	Marketing/sales/ bus. develop/ops/ supply chain	Monthly review of actual vs. forecast & reasons for difference
Weekly schedule (fixed & rolling)	Prod. control/ops/ sales/supply chain	Weekly review of actual vs. schedule & isolate: Ops, supply chain issues
Fixed daily schedule day-by-hour min. 24 hour firm Cross training matrix	Ops/team leader	Daily tracking: Pareto reasons, i.e. OEE, std. hours, quality mtls, improved cross training, etc.

FIGURE 9.1
Levels within production planning.

used to visually gather and communicate the information, and this "tool" should be the basis of a PDCA (Plan-Do-Check-Act) cycle for improving your planning. This can often be a good starting point when a company realizes a problem or bottleneck within its delivery or profitability. Within Toyota, production control was considered absolutely a critical function; in other enterprises it is only viewed in a supporting role.

Returning to my company's Lean journey, after I completed learning the shop and office processes and had met my customers to better understand their needs and opinions of how well we were solving their problems, I was ready to develop my strategy deployment (to avoid "machine-gun" improvements). As I disseminated my profit and growth objectives through my relatively flat organizational structure, I realized that a key constraint was my ability to forecast and plan, and the estimating process was crucial to both. Essentially, a made-to-order (job shop) business can do very little forecasting; in my case we rarely had more than a two-week customer lead-time, so that was our basic forward-looking horizon. Although based on various factors in our current estimates (type of part, customer relationship, part specifications, etc.), we could forecast a little longer term. However, a critical shortcoming was that we lacked any sort of feedback or improvement loop in the estimating process, so we were unsure of our estimating accuracy and this accuracy directly affects sales, profitability, and our ability to plan operations by their cycle times. In this type of business, your estimate really replaces or becomes your takt time (Takt Time = time available/customer demand). Once the customer confirms his order based on your estimate, this is your link to what the customer needs and what is commercially acceptable; if you maintain the material costs, estimated cycle times, and your G&A (General and Administrative) costs are absorbed as expected in your estimate, you will earn the anticipated margin. So if the estimating process is so critical, why was there no improvement cycle built in? And why did it lack basic performance indicators? This was a critical starting point for me, as improving this process would likely affect both profitability and growth targets.

PROCESS FOCUSED, NOT PRODUCT FOCUSED

To improve an indirect process such as estimating, I needed the team to first visualize the process in the same way. This requires that you basically follow a standard and have some process stability, although like most of our processes we did not utilize a standard method. Although as with most high-variation businesses, those likely to have hundreds to thousands of part numbers, we needed to focus on a standard "process" instead of how we handled individual parts (as we had many types). What I call "process mapping" is a method to reach a common visualized understanding of the current status of an indirect process (involving flow of information, whereas flow of material utilizes Value Stream Mapping) as a basis for discussing and identifying improvements. Process mapping is also a method that supports OSKKK, as you must first Observe, then agree on a Standard, followed by identifying areas requiring Kaizen (improvement). Our first map to visualize our estimating process was done with Post-It° pads on the wall but has been redrawn and shown in Figure 9.2. In reality, this "current state" map represented approximately what we did more often than not, but our process was not stable or well-standardized to begin with, so "current state" was actually closer to "best case."

Indirect processes essentially represent a flow of information and although harder to grasp and map than the flow of material (as done in value stream mapping), it is vital to reach a consensus on where the information flows, and where it stops and waits. We want to keep the information flowing just like when using Lean methods to improve material flow; any time the flow stops, there is an opportunity to improve. When information flow is stopped, it is more difficult to see as this often resides in computers or in-baskets, and some of these might be well outside your organization or control; but just as with material, lead-time is critical and therefore we always show a timeline at the bottom of the process map. Remember that

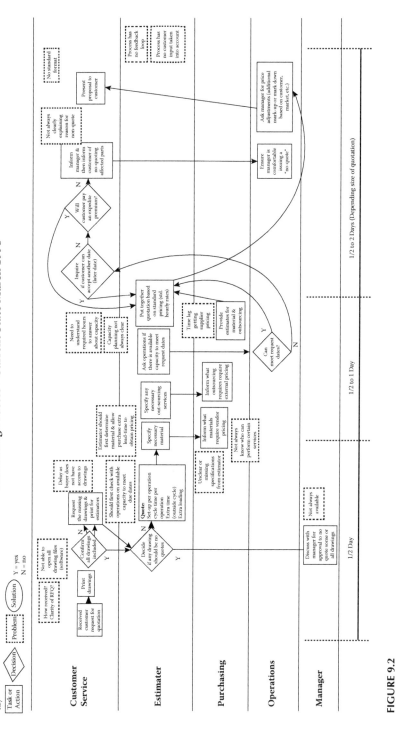

FIGURE 9.2

Process mapping with swim lanes and lead times.

something you might initially think is outside your "control" likely remains in your "influence" (normally if you gather the facts demonstrating what the problems cost the organization, you can influence change).

After finally getting the current state drawn (I use the word "finally" because this involves more time and discussion from the cross-functional group than you would imagine), you need to note the problems encountered at each step; those are shown in the broken lines in Figure 9.2. Even if someone immediately jumps to suggesting an improvement, I always ask them to write it as a problem; if someone is unable to articulate what problem their idea is likely to resolve, it might be a "nice-to-have" but not as high a priority as some other solutions. Once the problems are identified, then you can brainstorm for solutions (usually displayed on green Post-Its, but not shown in Figure 9.2).

When you start identifying problems on the map, you are likely to find the team justifying unstable processes based on factors being outside their control (i.e., customer demands, changes to orders, etc.); they see themselves as victims and try to get others to commiserate. The conversation instead needs to demonstrate where we have "influence" on these areas although we may not have "control." Often you must first work on "stability" even before "standardization"; sometimes firefighters cannot even imagine standardization because they are busy justifying all the reasons they cannot establish stability.

Using similar methods to visualize your bottleneck processes (prioritized from your strategy deployment) avoids isolated "machine-gun" improvements and can directly help in prioritizing improvements by focusing only on those that have a correlation to the measurements you want to improve. In my example of our estimating process, one objective was to improve lead-time (as shown in the timeline at the bottom of Figure 9.2); but we also wanted to focus on quotation accuracy, and this map clearly shows that there is no feedback loop to improve the process or gain input from the customer. I needed to base our planning, pricing, cost allocations, and profit margins on accurate quotations, so that any solutions in this area were profitable for the business.

We utilized similar maps for other process as dictated by our strategy deployment and OSKKK. Keep in mind the criticalness of the documentation and improvement of these indirect processes. A 2002 study[*] look-

---

[*] Rasmus D.W. (2002). Collaboration, Content and Communities: An update, Giga Information Group, Inc. May 31, 2002, Malabar, FL: Gigatel.

ing at how an organization's knowledge is maintained found that 80% of this knowledge is stored in people's heads, while 16% is stored in unstructured databases (i.e., people's hard drives, spreadsheets, etc.) and only 4% is stored in structured databases. While that figure might have changed in recent years, it still represents an alarming situation; this is exasperated by nonstandardized processes that were apparent in my company and many other organizations I have supported. Perhaps more timely is the nearing retirement of many baby boomers, which will siphon off considerable experience and should prioritize better knowledge management.

SEGREGATING PARTS TO MANAGE DIFFERENTLY

If you produce a commodity and build to a constant demand, or manufacture to maintain a warehouse full of finished goods, the subsequent discussion is likely not applicable. However, if you build a product with high variation, then you will find this useful.

While not all businesses have sales distributions that follow the 80/20 rule of Pareto's Principle (20% of something is responsible for 80% of the results), many do. This is true for high variation and even made-to-order organizations. First let me clarify the type of sales distribution to which I am referring and then how it affects the management. Many organizations have 80% of their sales (based on sales price) coming from 20% or less of their total part numbers sold during that period. Analyzing this is typically referred to as ABC part analysis, and usually a simple spreadsheet will prove how applicable this is. Normally, the last six months of sales data (one year or more of data for seasonal businesses) is sorted by descending sales order and those products accounting for 80% of sales are considered "A" parts while the next 15% of sales value makes the "B" parts and all remaining are the "C" parts. This requires some additional filter based on volumes, exceptions, and marketing intelligence of what is really representative of "A," "B," and "C" parts, respectively; but for our purposes, this explanation should be sufficient. The reason for undertaking this exercise is that these categories of parts might benefit from different management systems assuming they cannot all be economically made "just in time"; in other words, you are not able to quickly adjust your capacity to the customer's varying demands. Remember that ideally we want to build the part only when the client needs it and then keep it flowing through our processes, although typically because of lead-time expectations, capacity

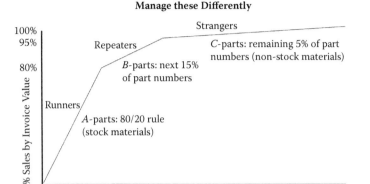

FIGURE 9.3

Pareto's Principle (80/20 Rule) applied to high variation manufacturing.

issues, and supplier and manufacturing problems we might have to utilize other options. This ABC distribution is visualized in Figure 9.3.

One option is that some or all "A" parts can be put onto a pull system (typically a "Kanban" replenishment system) with relatively low risk of obsolescence and minimal inventory carrying cost. This type of pull system would not involve finished goods inventory; instead, it might entail work-in-process inventory of "A" parts directly in front on the process in which the majority of variation is introduced. This helps to improve lead-time and better balance our less-flexible capacity with the variations in customer demand. How to qualify particular parts for replenishment, how to calculate these levels (Kanban levels), and how the planning works are discussed in detail inside my book *Made to Order Lean*[*]. Figure 9.4 helps visualize the first advantage of how this small amount of inventory of "A" parts improves the balance of capacity and demand variation.

Some "B" parts might be managed by a two-box (or pallet) exchange system. This means that you would have one box or pallet in inventory from which you are currently shipping parts to customers, while the other box or pallet is waiting to be replenished. Very likely, many "B" parts would be left as a "make to order" only when there is demand from the client. Finally, "C" parts, your "strangers," are entirely too risky to manage with a replenishment system; therefore they would only be manufactured when there is an order. Managing with this segregation of your parts into "A," "B," and "C" categories allows more options in planning (including many

---

[*] Productivity Press, New York: 2007.

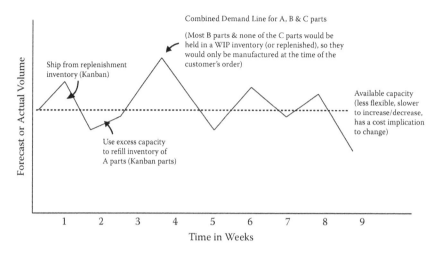

FIGURE 9.4

WIP inventory (Kanban) utilized to improve balance of capacity and demand.

simplified visual planning options instead of trying to plan these parts with traditional Material Requirements Planning (MRP) logic.

These optional ways to manage parts differently link back to both the planning discussed earlier and the importance of a feedback system for your estimates. Managing your parts by segregating them into "A," "B," and "C" allows you to use some visual planning techniques for your daily operations planning (this is the lower level of planning displayed in Figure 9.1, the "fixed daily schedule"). Because the basis of this planning is likely to begin by utilizing your estimated times, it also creates the feedback loop that helps to evaluate the accuracy of your estimating process; if you plan based on this time and do not achieve the plan (assuming no outside problems), it is likely that the estimated time was not correct. This should also lead to a better understanding of your specific profit margin on a part-by-part basis. The connection between managing by "A," "B," "C," and using visuals to plan demonstrates how Lean principles are connected and only cherry-picking a few principles can be dangerous.

On the contrary, my job-shop really did not allow me to identify "A" parts; we had no ability to know whether a part was likely to receive a repeat order; and although we asked our customers for forecasts, nothing of substance ever materialized. Our market intelligence allowed a bit of guessing based on the type of part, revision level, and past history with the customer, but beyond this it was pure gambling with very poor odds. Although we did evolve to using our quotations as the basis for planning our machines, Figure 9.5 shows our first attempt at an hourly scheduling

FIGURE 9.5
My first "day by hour" board for one CNC machine.

board for a particular machine. Other than creating a feedback system for our estimating process and allowing us to better plan and utilize our capacity, this board was linked to capturing our problems in real-time, which helped not only in prioritizing the issues, but also in determining other Lean principles that we needed to incorporate.

MANAGING IN REAL-TIME NECESSITATES OTHER LEAN PRINCIPLES

As our boards began to quantify which were our reoccurring problems and their corresponding costs to the organization, like most organizations we were overwhelmed with problems and had few resources to resolve them. Toyota had its team leaders as its first real line of defense, and I needed a similar solution. I was lucky in that I did not suffer the typical business school mentality of direct-versus-indirect employees, thinking direct employees added the significant value. Therefore, I was able to look at a position in terms of the quantifiable value it brought to resolving our customers' problems. My shop foreman was partial supervisor, partial problem solver but had always been challenged to operate a machine as often as he could, which typically amounted to more than 50% of the day. Instead, I proposed to transform him into a full-time team leader. New responsibilities were to include everything from minimizing set-up times, to eliminating material shortages, root-cause problem solving, and a host of other duties that translated into more responsibility. I proved this to be of great benefit by comparing a few previous months of the machine's OEEs (Overall Equipment Effectiveness) to the OEEs after he had been functioning in his team leader role for a few months. What this proved was the following: I was seeing an average of 7% to 8% OEE improvement on our critical machines after the first few months. A rough translation of the savings based on our five main machines (which at the time were averaging over thirty hours of scheduled production per week) was 30 hours per week × 5 machines 8% improvement = 13 additional hours of production per week. If you now multiply the additional 13 hours per week that I gained (you have to assume that I was able to sell most of that capacity, which was realistic for us) and multiply by the average of $60 per hour for which we sold our machining time, that was a total of an additional $780 per week of machine time, which almost covered Tom's total wages (without benefits); but you must remember that Tom also still ran a machine when covering for absenteeism and performed many other value-added activities such as functioning as the supervisor. This was only the beginning, as we made further OEE improvements and expanded the team leader role to resolve other types of problems. It proves the correct decision was made and implies you should not get hung up on the number of direct and indirect employees but instead on the value each position is adding.

Most managers unknowingly accept 70% to 80% effectiveness of their entire workforce as they randomly struggle to resolve their own problems. Instead, providing a team leader (Toyota had approximately a 1-to-5 ratio of team leaders to members during my tenure) can increase the entire team's effectiveness to more than 90%. Other than overcoming the mind-set of direct versus indirect, problems in transitioning to team leaders reside in the selection process, the job description, developing management support, and mentoring this person. Even if you feel you have an existing position similar to a "team leader" in your organization, get a hold of a copy of Toyota's team leader responsibilities (available in my other books) and compare your current job description to Toyota's. You are likely to discover that you have a vastly different concept and are missing out on some profitable benefits.

Our daily planning boards also identified the opportunity for more cross-training to minimize lost time. This was not only apparent on the shop floor, but just as critical in the office. Again, visualization was the key; when I took over the company, the status of cross-training was also being done in the supervisor's head based on tribal knowledge. We were always too busy to train but somehow always found the time to make up for the shortfalls this caused. The first step was to get some form of agreement on our current status; this was done through visualization. Figure 9.6 is an example of a chart similar to the one we used for our indirect tasks in the front office.

The format to display this information is not important, but for high-variation companies it is the underlying principle being demonstrated that is critical. For example, in the shaded-circular quadrants, you see the current status (normally this is first completed by the manager or supervisor and then publicly displayed, which draws in various and often unsolicited opinions from the team); naturally, the distinction between the four levels of training is subjective, but it is a far cry better than only that envisioned in the supervisor's head. Next, you can add your future training plans (show shaded squares in Figure 9.6); you might also display the status of any standardized documentation that exists that are displayed at the top of Figure 9.6 with R = red (no documentation), Y = yellow (partial documentation), G = Green (complete documentation). Having this visualized is likely the first step toward improving your cross-training, thereby creating more standardized operations, reducing downtime, minimizing ergonomic issues, and improving process effectiveness as more people contribute their ideas for improvement. The principal importance of this technique is to increase flexibility, thus allowing you to better balance your capacity with your fluctuating demand; this is even referenced in Figure 9.1 as critical when making the daily plan. Again, this demonstrates how many Lean principles are connected as a system to make improvements.

Skills Matix-Purchasing Department

Status of the Standardized Operations (Documentation)		G	G	R	R	Y	R	R	R	R	Date for Training/Notes
		Prioritize Purchasing Requisitions	Input Purchase Requisitions into System	Place Purchase Orders for Stock Items	Place Purchase Orders for Non-Stock Items	Set-up New Stock Item on the System	Negotiate Prices and Terms for New Stock Item	Configure Weekly Purchasing Status Report	Configure Monthly Purchasing Status Report	Approve 1X Purchases in Excess of $5,000	
Employee	1 Beverly Jones										Training completed Feb 06
	2 Frank Callahan										Training completed Feb 07
	3 Brenda Fisher										
	4 Roger Moore										Training completed Feb 07
	5 Derek Ford										
	6 Jessica Shipmen										
Status of Cross Training		G	G	G	R	G	R	R	R	R	

Key:

- Trainee, requires assistance to perform this task
- Able to perform task alone
- Able to perform task and update system
- Able to train others and modify standardized procedures

Planning to train to this level in the future

G - Low risk
Y - Medium risk
R - High risk

FIGURE 9.6
Skills matrix with current status and training plan.

PROPORTIONALLY MORE INDIRECT COSTS NECESSITATE LEAN ACCOUNTING

One of the more interesting parts of my journey was how I pulled us out of our worst sales slump caused by a cyclical downturn in the semiconductor equipment industry. I used an extremely basic adaptation of activity-based costing (considered a method of Lean accounting). This increased our revenues (and margins), bringing us back to profitability. Activity-based costing more accurately allocates overhead, indirect and fixed costs (including G&A costs), to the type or family of parts that consumes these various levels of activities and their related costs. The downturn exasperated our sales problems because customers now had more time to shop around on the reduced level of quotations they were soliciting. Our hit rate on transforming quotations into orders previously ranged between 65% and 70%; it had fallen below 50%, and this was on a significantly reduced volume of quotations.

I figured that our fixed costs were equal to or lower in many cases than those of our competitors. I also knew that our labor and material estimates were very accurate based on our weekly review of quoted versus actual costs and working time on each order. Therefore, I speculated that the only reason we could be losing orders to our competitors (other than their own quoting errors) was that my allocations of fixed costs were being incorrectly assigned, or I was demanding too much profit. I had reduced the margin to the minimum acceptable; consequently, I was determined to more accurately allocate fixed costs. My assumption was that my basic quotation method did not truly allocate the indirect costs appropriately to the parts consuming these costs.

Remember that in high-variation/low-volume businesses, often half or more of your payroll covers the indirect positions. In the worst case, these large amounts of indirect costs combined with the other fixed and overhead costs are all lumped together and allocated (to a product or service) based only on direct labor hours; compounding this inaccuracy would be basing these generalized allocations on imprecise direct labor hours. Because I knew that my direct labor hours were accurate and it was too difficult utilize another basis, I decided direct labor hours should remain my reference in distributing my indirect costs.

After reading a few books on activity-based costing, I realized I did not have the time or resources to implement the core concepts to the level of detail described, but the concept was sound and would likely improve the accuracy of my costing so I simplified how I allocated my activities to the parts and customers consuming them. I decided to work on two general levels: the shop and the office. I created an arbitrary point system in the form of a matrix (one for the shop and another for the office); the more points assigned, the more "activity" or time that was proportionally consumed. Then I would only need to relate these points to a cost factor. I had to first determine the characteristics that most directly affected my overhead. I will quickly discuss the first matrix I built for the office so that you can conceptualize what I was doing.

I began by listing both the characteristics of our parts, the types of services we provided, and how our customers affected the activity levels of the various indirects who worked in the "office." Then I put these in a two-dimensional matrix in ascending order from left to right and top to bottom based on the increasing level of activity they consumed. Then, by looking at proportionally how much more of the person's time they would normally consume, I started assigning them points. Figure 9.7 shows the first matrix I drew up for the office indirect functions.

In the matrix, additional points are equated to additional indirect activity being consumed by that product or customer; this opened up the opportunity to reassign these overhead costs more accurately instead of utilizing only various rates for work centers, often leaving the majority of costs applied like spreading butter on bread. I also developed a similar but

Office Activity Rating

		(+1) Easy customer (on time pay, good terms, etc.)		(+2) Difficult customer (not on time pay, poor terms, etc.)	
		(+1) Easy ship & pack requirements	(+2) Difficult ship & pack requirements	(+1) Easy ship & pack requirements	(+2) Difficult ship & pack requirements
(+1) Minimal or standard customer support requirements (few changes, easy sales support, std. specifications, qty., etc.)	(+1) Short bill of material (1–5 items) and no outsourcing	1+1+1+1= 4	1+1+1+2= 5	1+1+2+1= 5	1+1+2+2= 6
	(+2) Medium bill of material(6–15 items) and outsourcing 1–2 services	5	6	6	7
	(+3) Long bill of material (16 + items) and outsourcing 3 or more services	6	7	7	8
(+2) Increased customer support requirements (freq. changes, extra sales support, additional specifications, qty., etc.)	(+1) Short bill of material (1–5 items) and on outsourcing	5	6	6	7
	(+2) Medium bill of material (6–15 items) and outsourcing 1–2 services	6	7	7	8
	(+3) Long bill of material(16+ items) and outsourcing 3 or more services	7	8	8	9

FIGURE 9.7
Assigning arbitrary points to influences resulting in heightened activity levels.

Conversion of Office Activity Rating to an Hourly Cost

Office activity rating	4	5	6	7	8	9
Hourly office cost	$12	$14	$16	$18	$20	$22

FIGURE 9.8
Simplified "activity-based costing" for estimating office indirect costs.

more detailed matrix for the overhead costs in the shop (not shown). Now I had to connect these with a dollar value to more accurately distribute these points. Although I had various rates for my work centers, I predominately utilized computer numeric controlled (CNC) mills and during the late 1990s these had a shop rate of $60 per hour. On average, my fully burdened labor for the direct operators in the shop averaged about $20 per hour; therefore, the other $40 per hour was successfully covering all the overhead, fixed, and indirect costs. The only shortfall was likely the accuracy of how these costs were being allocated. I knew from my financial statements that about 60% of my costs after removing direct labor were being consumed in the shop and the other 40% were supporting the office (people, equipment, and miscellaneous fixed costs). Therefore, one could calculate that $24 per hour ($40 per hour × 60%) was associated with the shop and $16 per hour ($40 per hour × 40%) was linked to the office. Now all I needed to do was connect this to my matrices.

I played with some different theories, but I finally settled on linking this hourly cost to the midpoint of this arbitrary scale in each matrix, Figure 9.8 demonstrates this for the office matrix.

The $16 per hour that I knew the office was costing was plugged into the midpoint of "6." I then examined quite a few actual cases of time spent on various orders in the office and felt that if I increased or decreased $2 in my labor cost, respectively, for each point, that I would have covered my actual costs. When both matrices were taken into account, my CNC mill work centers would then have a rate that varied from $48 per hour (utilizing the least indirect effort in the office and shop) to a maximum of $74 per hour, instead of $60 per hour covering all levels of activity that the part or customer demanded. Now for each quotation I had the extra steps of qualifying a point level in the shop and office matrices, but it was usually only a matter of a few seconds. I do not want to mislead you that this was always the only basis for the actual price the customer was quoted. I consider this portion the technical quotation; then this was almost always adjusted up or down depending on the "strategic" pricing factor. In other words, depending on our current workload, the particular customer, the likelihood it would lead to further work, etc., we would adjust the price we presented to our customer, but at least we knew more accurately the true cost and could make better decisions.

In the end, unless this leads to increased profitability, it is only additional effort. In my case, over the next few months the hit rate on quotes climbed from the low 50% to the low 60% with the average earnings-before-interest-and-tax (EBIT) increasing from the low 40% to just over 47%. I slowly refined this concept and although it would not likely be considered true activity-based costing, it dramatically increased my profitability.

FAILURES

I had my share of failures from the "school of hard knocks." One example is that I never designed a very effective bonus system. I wanted to motivate and share profits with my employees when we worked together to increase profitability, and although any accountant can define how profitability is calculated, I had significant financing to repay and varying salary levels for myself and other indirects that left it hard to define true profitability and put it into any profit-sharing plan. Ideally, I would have connected a bonus system to the goals defined in my strategy deployment. In the end, my only bonus system was based on attendance; and although better than no bonus, it did not always drive home the points that I felt were important.

Another area where we often deviated was in following the order established by OSKKK. For example, we were by no means far enough through our journey of improvements to begin Kaizening our layout; but because of some external factors, it became prudent to move the business. Naturally, we used this opportunity to improve our layout in both the office and shop with a "Lean layout." It also happened on other occasions that changes in our business environment offered us an opportunity to introduce improvement, and OSKKK was never intended to be so rigid as not to take advantage of an opportunity to introduce improvements.

SUMMARY

By sharing a few of the Lean concepts I successfully adapted to a high-mix job-shop, I hope you see more clearly how you often have to return to the Lean "principles" instead of a specific Lean "tool" (often being described for a higher-volume or lower-variation application). Frequently, the principle will lend itself to a profitability improvement if correctly supported by management. This is a critical reason for failure with many of the Lean journeys that begin at the "tool" level; you need to cultivate and develop the right culture. I did not discuss in this chapter since my journey was made easier and likely was more successful because I had the continuous improvement characteristics engrained into my character; actually, this was the strong characteristic and advantage I brought to the business. Although there are many schools of thought and publications to help with this, it will likely require the most effort. Strategy Deployment, OSKKK, Plan-Do-Check-Act, A3 (complete problem resolution contained on A3 size paper), and other Lean principles will all help to shape and reinforce this. In the type of business environment discussed in this chapter, you will need to focus on improving your office and shop processes instead of trying to focus on individual product improvements. This will be strongly linked to the people within those processes as the procedures are rarely planned and standardized; instead, they have developed over time based on the people working within them, the knowledge and skill they bring, along with many other factors in the ongoing development of your business. Methodologies such as value stream mapping and process mapping discussed in this chapter will help in understanding and improving them. No matter your goals or the plan for your Lean journey, you need to take advantage of all problems and changes your business environment throws at you as opportunities to introduce improvements through Lean principles. I hope this helps to expand the paradigm that Lean can be adapted to profitably support all types of businesses.

10

Lean Logistics

Robert Martichenko

"When the student is ready, the teacher will appear"

—Buddhist Proverb

PART 1: PURPOSE + PEOPLE

Introduction

It is amazing how fast time flies when one is having fun helping organizations implement Lean thinking. It seems like only yesterday that I graduated from university with a degree in mathematics. What was most startling upon graduation was how few companies were looking for graduates of mathematics! Fortunately, I was given an opportunity to learn at a very progressive, entrepreneurial trucking/logistics company in Cambridge, Ontario, Canada. After several years of working in the Canadian trucking industry, I was offered a position with a third-party logistics company that was responsible for supporting portions of the inbound logistics processes for Toyota Motor Manufacturing. My role would be to lead the efforts for my organization on site at a Green Field Toyota Facility in the United States. For a young professional in the logistics industry, I was aware that this was a great opportunity. In hindsight, what I did not realize was that this experience would be a catalyst to define who I am today, both personally and professionally. Although this experience is now over a decade in the past, I continue to learn from the memories of conversations, tactical experiences, and strategic principles that were taught to me along the way. In fact, the experience of supporting Toyota Motor Manufacturing provided the foundation for my own third-party logistics firm, the LeanCor Supply Chain Group.

As a young professional who was born in northern Ontario, moving to the Midwest of the United States was quite a big deal. When I arrived at the factory (Toyota's Green Field Plant) for the first time, it was literally a huge steel building set in the middle of nothing but cornfield. I was immediately given a tour of the "will-be factory" in process, including the strategy deployment room (Hoshin) where the timeline for the entire factory construction and implementation was being managed on one wall. This was my first experience with "red" and "green" conditions, outlining plan, do, check, act (PDCA) relative to the entire project. From that day it would be another ten months of work before we had the first vehicle come off the new line. I can sincerely say that my learning started that first day.

The factory and all construction sites were clean, and a safety culture was clear and evident. People took their time to introduce themselves to me and they made sure I knew how to contact them if I needed assistance. The "open-office" concept for desks and workstations was startling, with a sea of desks in one room seeming as large as a football field. A busy hub of collaboration and teamwork hummed and moved with what looked like planned chaos and great purpose. I was surprised to see the plant president's desk right in the mix with all other leadership and team members. On that first day, I saw (but did not yet understand) the essence of 5S (Safety), Hoshin Planning (Strategy Deployment), Teamwork, Waste Elimination, Visual Management, and other principles of the Toyota Production System (TPS).

My role was to support the implementation of the logistics processes between the supply base and the factory, so it did not take long to start getting into the purpose of our work.

Note: For purposes of my essay, I will use the terms "TPS" and "Lean" interchangeably. While supporting Toyota we did not use the term "Lean" but rather "TPS." Since my Toyota experience, I use the term "Lean" to describe principles and techniques from the thinking of many historical people and companies, including influences from Henry Ford, William Deming, and Toyota Motor Manufacturing.

Purpose

The core purpose of the factory was to meet customer expectations by building the highest-quality vehicle at the lowest possible total cost, all while respecting all team members and the community and world at large.

My (and my team's) purpose was to play our part in this greater vision by connecting the supply base to the new factory using principles based on the Toyota Production System (TPS). The core principles of our work were to design and implement an inbound logistics system based on pull replenishment, velocity, leveled flow, and lead-time reduction. While these are the TPS logistics principles, the tactical elements to successfully implement these principles would quickly take us into transportation management, cross-docking, and process management systems to support the higher-level TPS principles of stability, standardization, quality at the source, flow, and waste elimination.

What I remember most about the first part of my work was the steadfast focus on TPS principles. Not once did I hear "our job is minimizing transportation cost" or "we need to only buy parts from a supplier in truckload quantities." The focus was always on the core purpose of our work, which was to connect the supply base to the factory using TPS principles of *pull, velocity, leveled flow, and lead-time reduction.* That is not to say that we ignored transportation cost. Quite the contrary, managing transportation costs became an obsession; however, it was not the guiding principle or the primary driver of our work.

I define a guiding principle as something "that you just believe, no data required to support your belief; you just know it's the right thing to do." This was my first lesson supporting Toyota Motor Manufacturing. You absolutely must have guiding principles to guide your supply chain and logistics efforts. In this work it was pull, velocity, leveled flow, and lead-time reduction. In subsequent years I have learned that the absence of guiding principles only serves to create a business environment where senior leaders continuously tamper with the business by changing strategies and directions as frequently as business conditions change. This in my opinion serves only to confuse customers, team members, and all other stakeholders in the supply chain.

Lesson 1: You must have guiding principles in place to support supply-chain and logistics strategy.

Customer and 3PL Collaboration

I worked for a third-party logistics (3PL) company to whom Toyota outsourced portions of its logistics operations. At first I was surprised to learn that Toyota outsourced portions of its logistics processes, namely transportation and cross-docking management. Is Toyota not the best of the best in logistics, after all? I quickly learned that Toyota's idea of outsourcing is very different from that in other organizations. What I have seen all too often is that a company wants to outsource a function because it does not understand the process and just wants to avoid it. Nothing is further from the truth with Toyota. They strategically outsource processes they feel other companies can operate successfully; however, they never leave the process from a thought leadership point of view. It may not be a Toyota truck going down the road; however, Toyota and TPS thinking have been a part of where the truck is coming from, where it is going, and what is on it. This is true collaboration. While it may not always be fun for the 3PL company, the successful relationships are those where the 3PL company embraces what it can learn from its customer. I personally tried to learn as much as I could from Toyota—on the job, through reading, and through asking questions. I learned quickly that an environment where people focus on problem solving is an environment where if the student is ready, teachers will appear in all corners of the building.

> **Lesson 2: Supply-chain collaboration is about understanding the strengths and weaknesses of all supply-chain partners and working with and teaching all partners in the supply chain.**

People and Planning

When I arrived at the factory I was the second employee on site representing my company. The first was a talented young logistics engineer who was laying the groundwork. He helped me immensely to start to understand our task and the Toyota culture. Between the two of us, combined with excellent support from our corporate offices in Canada and the United States, we had to go from a team of two to a team of over fifty people within six months. Those fifty people would need to have experience in logistics engineering, transportation, fleet management, and the most important role on the team, the actual truck driver who will be responsible to pick up and deliver parts from the supply base.

Building the team was the most important part of our work. It was my first lesson in understanding the principle of "quality at the source." In other words, get it right the first time. We were in a hurry, but we tried not to be hurried. We interviewed people several times before we made a decision. Leaders from corporate came to the factory to support interviews.

We reached out to universities and asked for their "star" players. We knew that if we hire the right people up front then we will be successful with our operations and processes. Processes do not run themselves. People are required to implement and sustain brilliant processes.

Over the first few months, Toyota expected us to hire and train the team that we would need in place for the Start of Production (SOP). We brought people in, including truck drivers, when there were no actual routes to run and no freight yet to pick up. Why? Because teaching and educating our team members on TPS, planning, and more planning was part of the culture. Many would criticize that there may have been too much planning, however I never saw it that way. I have been involved with many projects since my Toyota experience where the people and planning side was not taken seriously. The results (or lack of results) were obvious very quickly.

Lesson 3: People development and process planning are critical to the initial and sustained success of any operational undertaking.

PART 2: PROCESS

Logistics Route Design

With people getting in place and processes being developed, our first real "logistics" task was to create a route design to connect the supply base with the factory. This was set up as a week-long focused initiative in a conference room with a cross-functional team from Toyota and my organization.

We started by outlining our purpose and plan for the week, and then set up tollgates for each day of the week. The below are the high-level steps of the process we used (note that much of the process was manual, with only limited aid of computer programs):

1. We plotted each supplier on a map of North America (it was nice to see that Toyota embraced sourcing domestically).
2. We identified the projected volumes per day and week for each supplier.
3. We ran the projected volumes through our packaging file (PFEP) to get "cubic" volumes from each supplier. This allowed us to understand how much space each supplier would require on a trailer.

4. We regionalized the suppliers into geographical clusters for multi-stop milk run route development, direct routes to the plants, or routes to be picked up to run through a cross-dock with parts ultimately heading to other Toyota factories.
5. We targeted the number of pickup and delivery frequencies we wanted for each supplier.
6. We finalized the routes, named them, and began the work of running miles and developing route specs (standard work for our truck drivers) to ensure a driver or team of drivers could safely run the route and adhere to all rules under the Department of Transportation regulations.

While the above list of steps may seem simple, it was far from trivial. During that week, we routed hundreds of suppliers supplying thousands of part numbers combined. The task did not only include getting parts to the plants, but also getting returnable containers back to the suppliers using the same TPS principles of pull, velocity, leveled flow, and lead-time reduction. To say the task was complex and daunting would be an understatement.

Although my entire career at the time was in logistics, I had never participated in a route design this large in scale. I remember feeling that "there must be a software package that can do all this for us." However, that was not the point of the exercise. Manually plotting the suppliers ensured that we understood the names of the suppliers; manually plotting supplier volumes ensured that we understood the volumes and part complexities for each supplier; and manually building routes ensured that we understood each route implicitly. I learned later that forcing a process to be completed manually is known as putting a "fingerprint" on the process. Simply allowing a computer to do the work for you does not allow you to understand the work. That is not to say that over time we did not automate some processes that could be automated; however, when you do something the first time, there is no greater lesson than to perform the process manually.

Lesson 4: For any big initiative, develop a cross-functional team and perform the process manually the first time.

Pull Replenishment

Pull replenishment (or Just-In-Time) is defined "replenishing in the exact quantity as was consumed in the previous period and having the replenishment arrive only when the parts are required." I think *pull* has been oversimplified by many companies; and because of that, many people feel it is easy. Nothing could be further from the truth. The essence of pull is that "if I used it today, then I need to replenish it in the same quantities for tomorrow." The fundamental premise is that "if I used it today, then I will need it again tomorrow." This works for Toyota yet it seems to elude other organizations. The fact that it works for Toyota is the brilliance of the TPS. The heart of TPS is stability. The heart of stability is "how can we make every day look the same." If every day looks the same (that is, our production schedule each day can mirror the day before), then pure pull will work. In other words, if today is the same as tomorrow, and I used parts today, then I will need those same parts in the same quantity tomorrow. Under these circumstances, there are no complicated algorithms (or MRP) required to determine part requirements. Simply order what you used today from the supply base for tomorrow.

It would be naive to say that Toyota or any other organization achieves this utopian state of every day looking exactly the same; however, this was the goal of production planning and the materials function during my Toyota experience. It was yet another nonnegotiable guiding principle of Lean supply-chain management.

Our job of logisticians was to take the work of the production planners (who focused on stability) and to connect the production plan to the supply base. At no point did the plan start with the supplier simply shipping parts. It always started with the production schedule, which downstream was connected to actual customer demand, and upstream was connected to supplier replenishment.

Lesson 5: Pull starts with customer demand and then dovetails into the production schedule and then upstream to the supplier.

Velocity and Understanding the Importance of Lead-Time Reduction

Velocity is an ambiguous word in logistics. When we say velocity, we are talking about increasing the speed of flow of material and information in the supply chain. This is about reducing lead-time, a core principle of Lean thinking. I often tell people that as a student of Lean, I became a thinker of "economies of time" as opposed to "economies of scale." The theory of lead-time reduction may seem simple but is far from intuitive. The theory of *economies of time* is fundamental to our understanding of Lean.

The worst waste of all is overproduction. Overproduction is defined as building more than you need to service customer demand or building earlier than you need to meet customer demand. From an inbound logistics point of view, overproduction can be defined as ordering more parts than you need or ordering parts earlier than you need them. Overproduction is considered the worst waste of all because it creates all other wastes. As soon as you have material or finished goods that are not required by the customer, you are forced to store, transport, rework, and wait on those goods to be required by the customer.

So, if overproduction is the worst waste, why overproduce? Because of lead-time dynamics.

Let's review a few definitions of lead-time:

- *Outbound-logistics lead-time:* The amount of time it takes to stage, ship, and transport an order to the customer upon receiving a customer order.
- *Manufacturing-replenishment lead-time:* The amount of time it takes to manufacture your product after you receive a customer order.
- *Inbound-logistics lead-time:* The amount of time it takes to order and receive material from your supply base in order to manufacture your product.

With these definitions in mind, we can define total lead-time as the amount of time it takes for us to order material from our supply base through to when we deliver the product to our customer. (A more rigorous definition of lead-time would include the time it takes to get paid from the customer after receiving a customer order.)

If you could design the ideal supply chain, it would be a process where you build to customer order (Build to Order or BTO) only. You would carry no inventories and only initiate your inbound supply chain and manufacturing processes after receiving a customer order. The brilliance of BTO is that you eliminate overproduction because you do not order material from your suppliers or manufacture finished goods until you have a firm customer order. As well, there is no need for warehousing or storage of any kind as you simply flow product to the customer upon completion of the manufacturing process. In essence, this is the definition of a pull system, where the customer order triggers all supply-chain activities to fulfill the order, resulting in no overproduction. Supply-chain professionals need to focus on eliminating overproduction because it creates other serious wastes such as excess inventory, excess warehousing, and excess transportation. BTO also eliminates the need for forecasting, which in turn results in the elimination of excess inventories due to inevitable forecasting errors. Eliminating the need for forecasting is another key area that the Lean supply-chain professional needs to focus on.

BTO is the perfect solution to a waste-free supply chain, but it requires a specific dynamic to be in place to succeed:

- *Total lead-time must be less than customer-order-to-delivery lead-time expectations.*

For instance, if a competitive environment states that customers expect to receive a product in ten days after placing an order, a BTO process would require you to be able to order and receive material from your suppliers, and then manufacture and ship the product to the customer in less than ten days. Although many of us never will reach the state of perfect BTO, this needs to be the stretch goal for the Lean supply chain.

When we are not faster than our customer, we are forced to guess (forecast) what they may need, and when we guess we will guess wrong. If we can reduce the lead-time, we will get closer to our customer demand and will therefore reduce the horizon of guessing, and this will result in less waste of overproduction.

This was the guiding principle of our work on Toyota's inbound supply chain.

Lead Time & BTO
The Ultimate Business Model

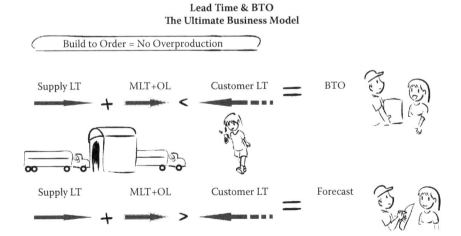

Driving Velocity

Velocity is a powerful method to reduce lead-time. From a tactical point of view, the only way to create velocity is to move smaller shipments (lot sizes) more frequently. This was our goal during our initial work at Toyota.

We started with a minimum factory delivery frequency of four deliveries per day for any and all part numbers. High-volume suppliers (part numbers) may deliver as many as sixteen times per day. Once again, these guiding principles of velocity guided our work in logistics engineering and transportation management. At no time did we simply try to fill up a truck to minimize transportation costs. The goal was to create velocity in order to connect to the factory and reduce overall lead-time. Interestingly, a huge benefit of velocity is a substantial reduction in inventory and all related inventory-carrying costs.

Sadly, I have to admit that I was not a believer in velocity in the beginning.

"How could this make sense?" was a question I asked myself many times. In fact, I pressed the point to extremes with a senior Toyota coordinator who mentored me during my tenure.

"Show me the math, show me the numbers; this will cost too much in transportation" was a sentiment I asked many times.

"No numbers needed Robert, just believe it is right," was the answer I continuously received.

I did not relent and one day my coordinator finally got frustrated with me and said, "You want numbers… look at Toyota's global performance in cost, quality, and delivery!"

"What does that have to do with anything?" was my initial reaction.

I suspect it took two years for me to truly learn the lesson. My head was in the weeds, trying to minimize inbound transportation costs only. My coordinator saw the big picture. This big picture started with customer demand, then went to the leveled production schedule and then continued upstream to the supplier. The goal was never to minimize inbound transportation costs, but rather to create velocity in order to connect to the factory and the customer, ultimately to reduce the overall supply-chain lead-time and total cost of the entire system. Ultimately, this also leads to a reduction in overproduction, the grandfather of all waste.

It is important to stress again that I am in no way saying that we ignored transportation costs; it simply was not the main driver of our work.

Therefore, our job was to create velocity and "manage" transportation costs. We had a plan to accomplish this.

> **Lesson 6: Reduction in lead-time must be the goal of the logistician. We must believe in "economies of time."**

Manufacturing Plant Integration

Volume is the Lean logistician's best friend. The more volume we have, the more flexibility we have to consolidate material to drive velocity. While this may sound like "economies of scale" thinking, it is a harsh reality to driving velocity (increased delivery frequency) and managing transportation costs at the same time. In order to accomplish our velocity goals at Toyota, we needed to consolidate all freight that was available in the entire Toyota North American network. This meant collaboration with all factories in order to look at the entire network and not simply each factory in isolation. Once an organization combines all volumes, velocity goals can be met and transportation costs can even be reduced in totality. We call this the "triple crown" in Lean Logistics where we increase delivery frequency, reduce inventories, and even reduce transportation costs. In seems completely counter-intuitive, yet I can tell you that it is possible. What it requires is commitment to the hard work of standardizing processes across an entire organization.

The transportation aspects of the factory integration of supplier volumes include milk run deliveries and cross-docks to consolidate and redirect material from suppliers to specific factories. The goal is send one truck into a supplier and pick up all material for all factories that the supplier services on the one truck. The truck picks up at the supplier and delivers to a predetermined cross-dock where material is unloaded and consolidated with other suppliers going to a specific factory. In doing so, pick-up routes are optimized and line hauls to the factories are optimized as well. We achieve our frequency goals and have full trucks in the supply chain at the same time. Yet, this logistics technique of milk runs and cross-docks is the relatively easy part of the work.

The challenging part of the work is not the physical flow of material but rather is in the information flow! Factory supplier codes must be harmonized, part numbers must be standardized, and suppliers must be

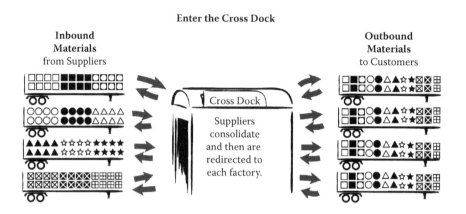

educated on how to pick and pack parts destined for multiple factories. A high-frequency cross-dock-based transportation network will live and die on information flow. This is where the real work begins; recognizing the benefits of this important work are immense.

> **Lesson 7: Consolidate all volumes in the entire network and complete the hard work relative to information flow.**

Leveled Flow

There is no point in creating velocity if you do not level the flow of material. For example, what is the point of going from one delivery per week to five per week if all deliveries arrive Monday morning? Velocity will accomplish its goal of lead-time reduction and inventory reduction when we level the increased frequencies over available working time. This gets to the heart of "takt" where we design the inbound network to connect to the factory in rhythm (or cadence) to factory needs.

A simple and powerful technique to accomplish this is the inbound factory receiving schedule. The receiving schedule is a simple way to level part number deliveries over available working time. If we are unloading fifty trucks per week, we should service ten trucks per day. If we are working ten hours per day, we should service one truck per hour. Once this receiving schedule is built, we design the transportation system and parts to flow from suppliers to the factory using this receiving schedule.

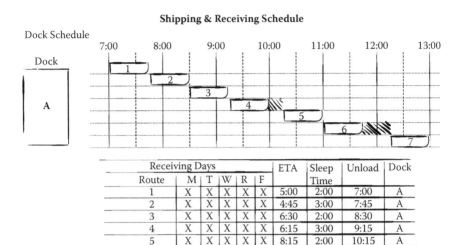

Shipping & Receiving Schedule

	Receiving Days					ETA	Sleep Time	Unload	Dock
Route	M	T	W	R	F				
1	X	X	X	X	X	5:00	2:00	7:00	A
2	X	X	X	X	X	4:45	3:00	7:45	A
3	X	X	X	X	X	6:30	2:00	8:30	A
4	X	X	X	X	X	6:15	3:00	9:15	A
5	X	X	X	X	X	8:15	2:00	10:15	A
6	X	X	X	X	X	8:00	3:00	11:00	A
7	X	X	X	X	X	10:15	2:00	12:15	A

Implementing a receiving schedule is an example of *standard work* in logistics. The point is that all flow of material is planned and coordinated. Plan versus actual condition can be measured, and problems can be highlighted immediately. In many respects, the receiving schedule is the true logistics bridge to connect the external supply base to the internal factory. It is a fundamental technique that is required for Lean Logistics to be successfully implemented.

In my experience at Toyota, the receiving schedule was a fundamental technique to be used. It was nonnegotiable and its use was a given. Therefore, I assumed it was basic in all organizations. History has now proven my thoughts wrong. In working with other organizations, implementing a disciplined receiving schedule can prove to be challenging. The main reason is that many receiving departments feel that truck arrival and flow of material is a chaotic process that cannot be managed. Disciplined material receiving requires trucks to arrive only during their scheduled arrival times (windows times). In the event that trucks do not run on time, then the entire schedule will collapse. While I do not deny this is true, it should not stop us from driving the implementation of the receiving schedule in order to level the flow of material. At Toyota we recognized this challenge and used the trailer yard to mitigate the disturbances and variances inherent in common cause variation in the external transportation network.

Lesson 8: Level the flow of materials and implement a disciplined receiving schedule.

Trailer Yard Layout and Visual Management

Of all the lessons I learned while supporting Toyota, one of the most important was relative to the trailer yard. The trailer yard is simply the space allocated for inbound trailers to be placed while waiting to be unloaded as per their window of time in the receiving schedule. I will never forget when our Toyota coordinators asked us how many trailer spots we needed, as we were required to asphalt and pave these spots to get ready for the factory "Start of Production" date. As logistics engineers, we did what we do and we concluded that we needed more than 200 spots. The answer we received from our coordinators was that we would get only 100 spots—not even 50% of our request! We were dumfounded and confused. "How will we ever make this work?" was our immediate response. So we went to work to attempt to make it work.

With our requested 200 trailer spots we would not require any discipline of process. A trailer would simply show up and find an empty spot in the yard. With the approved 100 spots we would need an extreme amount of discipline. Each trailer spot would need to be named, each inbound route would need to be allocated to a certain spot when it arrived at the factory, and it could only stay in that spot for its allocated time, as we would need that spot for another planned route when it arrived at the factory. In

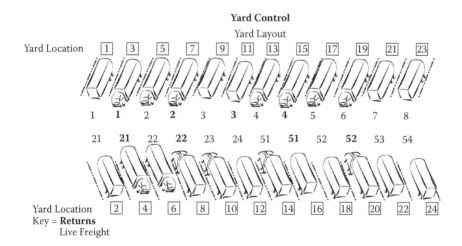

other words, we had to "turn" the trailer yard in the same way you turn inventory in a warehouse. While this may seem ludicrous considering all the space we could have paved in the mass of cornfield, by having the minimum amount of trailer spots, we were forced to plan to the smallest level of detail in order for the system to operate. In addition to this, visual management was naturally created. For example, if a route arrived and the preplanned trailer spot was not open, that meant that a trailer had not been shuttled to the factory unloading dock as per our plan. Therefore, the trailer yard itself highlighted abnormalities with the receiving schedule, which highlighted potential problems with the material receiving function inside the plant. This was truly a system of visual management cascading into several aspects of the operation. This was my first fundamental lesson in visual management. That is, that true visual management connects people to processes and processes to processes.

Lesson 9: Use asset and resource minimization to force process discipline and visual management.

Quality at the Source and Discipline of Process

Quality at the source is defined as "getting it right the first time." In logistics, this manifests itself in "getting it right as far up in the supply chain as possible." In most inbound logistics networks, suppliers get an order, they ship, and then when the parts arrive at the factory the factory hopes they receive what they ordered. If they don't, then an expedite process will ensue and the factory may shut down. This is not quality at the source. Getting it right the first time means that we have a way to ensure that suppliers are shipping the right parts at the right time prior to the supplier loading the parts on a truck. This process is known as "driver pick-up verification."

This verification process is completed by the truck driver who is responsible for picking up the parts. Acting as an agent for the manufacturer, the driver is trained to verify all perfect order components of the supplier order. To accomplish this, the driver is armed with a manifest that outlines in detail what the supplier is to ship that day. Prior to the freight being loaded on the truck, the driver verifies that the order staged for shipping has the right parts in the right quantity in the right packaging with the proper labeling and any other variables critical to quality of the process. By doing this, the driver recognizes any issues with the process. For example, if the supplier is supposed to ship twenty steering wheels and there are only eighteen on the rack, then the process is stopped immediately by the driver. Called Jidoka in the Lean lexicon, this is the act of stopping the process immediately when an abnormality is detected. Hence, we uncover an error and avoid a defect. In this case, the driver would inform the supplier of the parts shortage and a solution would be developed right there on the spot in real-time.

Compare this process to one that has no mistake-proofing mechanism in place. The driver would arrive at the supplier and have the truck loaded with whatever the supplier had ready to ship at the time. The trailer would arrive at the manufacturing facility and upon inspection they would realize that there are two steering wheels missing (if it is detected at all!). However, at this point it is too late, and a parts shortage will likely result, possibly shutting down the manufacturing line and at the very least resulting in an expensive expedite.

Quality at the source teaches us to detect errors as quickly as possible. In logistics, this means we need to have mistake-proofing tools in place for all critical processes. In practice, this means we should look at processes as far up the supply chain as possible. The goal is to detect and resolve issues prior to their becoming a burden on the organization.

We must develop processes and train our drivers to verify parts on the suppliers shipping dock before the parts are allowed to be loaded onto the truck. While this may seem simple in concept, it can be very difficult in application.

For driver verification to take place, we need to collaborate with suppliers, have stability with training and keeping trained drivers on the team, and we need a support structure of logistics coordinators to perform the track-and-trace function of managing the routes.

Lesson 10: A Lean Logistics system focuses on quality at the source and error-proofing all critical processes as far up the supply chain as possible.

LESSONS LEARNED AND CONCLUSION

It would be a gross understatement to say that my Toyota experience was good for my career. It literally defined who I am today as a supply chain professional and businessperson. Today, the LeanCor Supply Chain Group helps companies drive Lean thinking in their logistics processes and supply chains. While it is impossible (and not advisable) to attempt to turn other organizations into Toyota, many of the principles I learned in those days are the guiding principles we use with other organizations. In other words, processes and techniques can be different to meet the needs of a particular organization; however, the *guiding principles* should be consistent in Lean Logistics. These are pull replenishment, velocity, leveled flow, and lead-time reduction. From a tactical point of view, the lessons I learned and the lessons I urge all organizations to embrace are

Lesson 1: You must have guiding principles in place to support supply chain and logistics strategy.

Lesson 2: Supply-chain collaboration is about understanding the strengths and weaknesses of all supply-chain partners and working with and teaching all partners in the supply chain.

Lesson 3: People development and process planning are critical to the initial and sustained success of any operational undertaking.

Lesson 4: For any big initiative, develop a cross-functional team and perform the process manually the first time.

Lesson 5: Pull starts with customer demand and then dovetails into the production schedule and then upstream to the supplier.

Lesson 6: Reduction of lead-time must be the goal of the logistician. We must believe in "economies of time."

Lesson 7: Consolidate all volumes in the entire network and complete the hard work relative to information flow.

Lesson 8: Level flow of materials and implement a disciplined receiving schedule.

Lesson 9: Use asset and resource minimization to force process discipline and visual management.

Lesson 10: A Lean Logistics system focuses on quality at the source and error-proofing all critical processes as far up the supply chain as possible.

11

Leading a Kaizen Culture

Bob Plummer

Kai' zen: (noun) change for the better

I arrived in Fremont, California, in February 1993, nervously excited and greatly anticipating the learning experience that lay ahead. I had been selected to receive one of the two dozen coveted two-year GM Coordinator positions at New United Motor Manufacturing Inc. (NUMMI), the GM/Toyota joint venture managed by Toyota. Although I had no way of knowing, walking out of my career-long stint with what would become Delphi, the GM components division, and into the GM Coordinator position would prove itself as one of the most profound learning experiences of my career.

NUMMI was conceived nine years earlier to provide a learning laboratory for its joint venture partners—each partner with its own objectives. GM wanted to learn how Toyota manufactured vehicles of vastly superior quality and lower cost, while Toyota wanted to learn about GM operations with an American workforce, in this case, workers represented by the United Auto Workers (UAW).

When the venture was formed in 1984, GM significantly trailed Toyota in assembly labor hours per vehicle and in the J.D. Power annual new car survey, which ranked car models by defects per vehicle. At the same time, Toyota did not yet have a vehicle assembly plant in North America.

At the point of my arrival at NUMMI, GM had sent thousands of mid-level managers to visit NUMMI and receive tours of the facility. More than a hundred GM Coordinators before me completed assignments like mine: learning and teaching Toyota Production System (TPS) methods to GM visitors and then returning to implement TPS methods back at GM facilities after their assignments had concluded.

After nine years in the learning laboratory, GM had been largely unsuccessful in transferring TPS methods to its own factories. Recognizing that

GM had not yet found the right formula for successful execution—and not wanting to personally labor in vain to meet the same fate—I established two personal goals for my experience at NUMMI. First, learn about the TPS methods. Second, determine why GM failed in applying the TPS in order to develop methods that allowed successful implementation of the TPS in a non-Toyota factory.

A TPS SYMPHONY

My assignment as GM Coordinator of Assembly at NUMMI provided full access to the plant, all training classes available to team members, as well as participation in the 285T truck launch project. While working on the truck launch, I spent three weeks in Japan at Toyota facilities: the 4 Runner and Lexus plants in Tahara, a machining plant in Motomachi, and two assembly plants in Toyota City.

My first goal remained to learn the TPS methods themselves. As such, I quickly discovered how fundamental these methods were to the Lean lexicon used today: standard work, 5S, PDCA (Plan-Do-Check-Act) problem solving, Heijunka (leveling and smoothing), Muri (overburden), Mura (unevenness), Muda (waste), Kanban (Just-In-Time), material conveyance and production control, Jidoka (error proofing), building quality in station, SMED, takt time, Andon (visual management), balance boards, team structure (group leader, team leader, team member), the model change process, A3 report writing, and perhaps most importantly to my goals, Kaizen (a change for the better).

Learning the TPS methods and their effects on the plant was fascinating. Each individual method as a part of the system enabled the plant to operate smoothly, efficiently, and in unique harmony. The combination of all the methods in use reminded me of one of Beethoven's pieces resounding in a symphony's performance hall (Figure 11.1). I could see many different instruments, with different purposes and functions, blending together as if under the leading and tempo provided by a conductor. My manufacturing experiences within GM up to that point were typified by pressure and varying degrees of chaos, conflict, and management/union disharmony. Now I saw a factory designed and operating as intricately as the intertwined notes of an orchestral piece.

The harmony I saw so clearly at NUMMI and other Toyota plants left me to ponder the question: What was producing the excellent productivity,

FIGURE 11.1
The harmony of TPS.

quality, and output on a day-in and day-out basis at NUMMI and at the plants in Japan? Was it the TPS methods? Or was it something else?

That question led me to reflect on the discouraging fact that for nine years GM's top manufacturing leaders observed, studied, learned, and reworked these methods in their own factories with poor results. These were smart, experienced leaders and their failure was not due to incompetence or a lack of effort and motivation. There had to be something else that made TPS work in harmony. I needed to figure out what it was.

DISCOVERING THE KAIZEN CULTURE

As I dug further, I came to the realization that many elements of successful TPS implementation required the involvement of top company leadership—leadership, in particular, beyond the plant level. Perhaps the conductor of this symphonic interrelated system was the CEO himself.

Then, discovery. I toured two plants in Toyota City in the same industrial complex and operated by the same company, and making similar sized passenger cars. What I expected—to see two sets of identical production processes—was not what I found. Of course, both plants had a body shop, paint shop, and assembly area. But when I looked at the individual operations, I began to notice slight differences. Then it hit me: Kaizens. Different individuals implemented Kaizens on each line over time based on the individual's ideas as a result of assessing the needs of the situation, which also had a varied layout, process equipment, and production model mix. There were literally thousands of Kaizens.

Everywhere I turned I saw small improvements. On the assembly line with a very high model mix, I noticed light screens and Andon lights indicating which item to select line side corresponding to the Katishiki (manifest) for the vehicle in station, as there were many potential part choices. On the other line, I discovered that the parts presentation line side was already sequenced in the line-side storage container. Toyota had chosen to test the idea of off-line sequencing on this particular line. In another example, on the high-mix assembly line, a team leader built a unique electronic/pneumatic device that selected the correct owner's manual for a vehicle, based on information stored in the radio frequency identification tag of the vehicle coming into station. The device selected from among more than two dozen different manuals—written in several languages— and dropped the correct manual on the top of a small ramp that looked like a mini ski jump. From there, the manual slid down the ramp and landed on the floor of the front passenger seat. A team leader, not a factory engineer, constructed this device.

The Kaizens in the five plants in Japan far outnumbered those at NUMMI, and the realization left me awestruck (Figure 11.2). A vast majority of the

FIGURE 11.2
Kaizen team members create competitive advantage.

Kaizens were quite simple and not as complicated as the ski-jump or the lightscreen processes. The genius of TPS struck me and presented a key question: How can a competitor keep up with a company that is continually and frequently using significant quantities of ideas of all its employees to implement improvements that eliminate waste of time and energy? The answer is: They can't. They can't unless they improve just as rapidly. In my opinion, the Kaizen Culture is the reason Toyota is the leading car manufacturer in the world and will remain so as long as it sustains that culture.

Recently, I read Alan Weiss' book, *Million Dollar Consulting*. One of Weiss' recurring concepts in the book is "The One Percent Solution," a phrase he coined and a concept that Toyota implements precisely. The One Percent Solution describes the transformational benefit of continuous improvement. Weiss explains that if every day a person implements a change (a Kaizen, in Japanese) that improves a business process by 1%, then in 70 days the process will have been improved by 100%. Looking at this concept mathematically, the transformational effect of compound continuous improvement is clear: $1 \times 1.01^{70} = 2$, or 100% improvement. Toyota leadership executes TPS in such a way that it produces the same transformational effect.

What, then, is the key to generating the transformational effect of thousands of Kaizens within a single organization? I sat in on a presentation for NUMMI managers and GM Coordinators on TPS by a team member from Toyota's Operations and Management Development Division (OMDD), considered within Toyota to be the elite group of TPS masters, and I discovered the answer. The speaker described TPS in very simple, fundamental terms: Create an environment where team members implement Kaizen. Frankly, I did not think he would provide such a simple, straightforward, no-nonsense answer. I expected, and had prepared myself for, an elaborate explanation with charts and graphs and complicated implementation methodologies. Strikingly though, when quizzed about the time frame of implementation in an American factory, he responded, "More than ten years." Perhaps his benchmark was NUMMI. At nine years old, it continued to lag behind its Japanese counterparts in strategic TPS implementation. Leadership is responsible for initiating, fostering, and implementing an environment conducive to team-member Kaizen. If American factories did not follow suit, our more than ten-year time frame until seamless implementation would not be too far-fetched.

The picture—and the symphony of moving parts—was slowly becoming clearer. TPS is more than just methods alone. The objective is for team members to implement Kaizen and to use the methods to support and sustain their individual Kaizen efforts. There is a harmony between leadership, team members, and TPS methods. The symphony moves as individual players, and as a collective group.

CREATING AND SUSTAINING THE KAIZEN CULTURE IN AMERICAN FACTORIES

The leaders at Toyota and the philosophies they modeled and taught demonstrated the dramatic role that a TPS leader plays in the change-accepting culture that exists in a Toyota facility. In my observations of this unique culture, I concluded that Toyota leaders implemented eight philosophies that have a profoundly positive effect on creating and sustaining a successful Kaizen Culture:

1. *Customer first:* It is a simple truth that a company would not exist without customers. Not surprisingly then, the needs of the customer are of primary importance at Toyota. A philosophy of "customer first" embodies several elements that are not to be compromised, including quality, delivery, features, performance, and excellence. It is every team member's job to put the customer first. For example, if I was a line operator and I realized that I had misassembled a part, I would pull the Andon cord to alert my team leader that I have a problem and stop the line if necessary so the defect is not passed to the next operation. In this example, the external customer is highlighted, but the needs of internal customers are also a crucial aspect of this philosophy. There were numerous examples of the needs of internal customers being met with extraordinary priority and importance. Of course, leadership oversight also played a role in assuring that commitments were met when personal performance in this area was lacking.

2. *Team member safety and security:* The physical safety of every team member is of primary importance at Toyota. Leadership backs up this point with weekly safety meetings among team members, measurement of safety incidents, and safety slogans shown on signs distributed throughout plant facilities. Leadership communicates openly and regularly that they care about the safety of team members, which then proved it a genuine concern. In Japan, the commitment to the

team, and a renowned commitment to low turnover, are well known to Toyota team members. This philosophical commitment satisfied team member security concerns and removed a significant barrier to team member Kaizen. Without the trust in each member's safety and security, team members would be disinclined to participate in Kaizen that improved productivity and resulted in fewer workers required in production.

3. *Mutual trust and respect:* Mutual trust and respect both among peers and between managers and team members is a foundational element of this revolutionary culture. In order for the ideas of all team members to be heard and used to Kaizen operations throughout the company, each team member needs to be heard and to hear what others have to say. If their thoughts and opinions are ignored, valuable input and the future participation of the individual in the Kaizen are lost because of the denied efficacy of the individual. If their thoughts and opinions are instead highly valued, not only can team members contribute, but they want to contribute. When team members feel valued, important, and significant because they are trusted and respected, the organization can then tap into the creative power and potential to implement Kaizen that exists within the individual. Team members are energized, excited, and proud of their work and can transform an organization by contributing to successful change in their work processes. They are uniquely qualified to execute improvements in their work because they know more about it than anyone else in the organization. When their effort to Kaizen is combined with support, direction, training, and resources provided by their team leader or group leader, all the team members in the organization can become a powerful transformational source of thousands of Kaizens.

4. *Teamwork:* Companies vary with extreme degree in the culture of the workplace and how it treats its worker—including the nomenclature for the worker himself. Some are "employees." Some are "associates." For Toyota, they are "team members." Every time this phrase is spoken, which is often dozens of times in a single day, the company reinforces an important philosophical point: Everyone in the organization is a member of a team, working together with others to achieve a common objective. The team method includes many aspects of activity that Toyota wants to promote: working together, supporting one another, making decisions together, solving problems together,

trusting and respecting one another, helping one another, and suc-
ceeding together. Additionally, I observed that individual character
traits of personal discipline and honor are personal traits that played
a significant role in meeting commitments to other team members,
and promoting this team culture.

5. *Communication:* The culture in these plants demonstrated a philosophical value that almost over-emphasized communication. There
were daily team meetings, a daily plant newsletter, company-wide
meetings, visual and audio tools that allow knowledge of the status
of an operation at a cursory glance possible, performance feedback
tools, quality and productivity feedback tools, planning meetings,
the Nemawashi process, and A3 reports. A culture that so values
communication to its team members allows access to a massive array
of information in multiple mediums, at multiple levels, in order
to equip the team member with the latest knowledge and skills to
improve his or her contribution to the team and to the company.

6. *Direction and establishing improvement goals:* Toyota leadership
provides coordinated direction of the company using the Hoshin
Kanri (policy deployment) process. Using this trickle-down process,
company strategies, initiatives, objectives, and goals flow from the
top of the company down to the department and finally to the individual team member. The flow of this process creates a coordinated
improvement effort and harmony between functions and team members within functions that results in the corporate-wide achievement
of improvement goals.

7. *Knowledge, teaching, and modeling:* Over the course of my own career,
I have found that no organization can rise above the level of its leader.
If the leader of an organization does not understand Heijunka, for
example, the organization cannot be expected to maintain smooth
and level production. As such, the existence of knowledgeable leadership is vital to the success of TPS in both foreign and American
plants. Particularly in organizations where TPS is not practiced or
understood, it is critical for leaders to have sufficient knowledge of
a Kaizen Culture and to be able to both teach and model the desired
behavior and methods associated with Kaizen and TPS.

8. *Support and resources:* The organization structure used in Toyota
includes support resources, both human and capital, for Kaizen.
The Group Leader-Team Leader-Team Member structure itself
provides for team member support and Kaizen activity. Toyota

plants have Kaizen areas equipped with materials and tools that team members can utilize to implement Kaizen in their work areas. For larger Kaizen projects, I repeatedly observed where leaders supported the projects with people and capital. For example, Toyota approved a $1.5-million project that I developed to replace the seat assembly robot and relocate it further upstream in the final assembly line. The justification for the investment was increased line space available for final inspection and reduced final line downtime.

9. *Genchi Genbutsu:* The practice of Genchi Genbutsu means going to see on your own in order to personally grasp the situation and make the best decision. Genchi Genbutsu is a foundational method that enables leaders to sustain TPS and the Kaizen Culture because problems are not solved in the conference room. Problems are solved out on the shop floor or office at the point of cause, where the problem is occurring. The quality of decision making using this method is several times more effective than the conference-room method. I personally learned the value of this method during my training at NUMMI and numerous times since then. I discovered that in the conference room, accurate facts required to solve a problem or make a decision are generally not available. Also, because there is inadequate access to the amount of data required to make a good decision, there is a tendency to make assumptions that are incorrect. The result is usually ineffective decision making. Conversely, when practicing Genchi Genbutsu and seeing for yourself at the point of cause, the access to more accurate and more complete data can be achieved, which improves the quality of the decision being made.

IMPLEMENTING TPS METHODS

Successful TPS implementation requires leaders to evaluate the value streams within their company and identify opportunities to eliminate waste through the application of TPS methods. Knowledge of customer requirements, market responsiveness, the current value streams, and the TPS methods is required for a successful implementation.

Having implemented TPS methods in non-Toyota facilities, I have learned that there are interactions between the methods and there is an implementation order that should be followed when using these methods. Some methods have prerequisites that should already be in place in order to function properly. In my own experience implementing these methods in non-Toyota facilities, I found that the prerequisites for an effective Kanban system are Heijunka and takt time (standard rate of production), and the prerequisites for Heijunka and takt time are small lot production, and even further, the prerequisites for small lot production are setup time reduction, one-piece flow, and process stability. Leaders of TPS implementation, therefore, need to orchestrate the implementation of methods in their correct sequence.

However, the effective application of some methods is not within the control of manufacturing alone. Achieving a smooth and level Heijunka, or workload, requires the involvement and cooperation of senior business leaders in general, and the sales and marketing function in particular. Without this apparent cooperation, it is impossible for the plant to operate at a constant output rate and workload for months at a time.

My observations at the Toyota plant pointed to significant cost-benefits that a workload, implemented in such a way, allowed (Figure 11.3). Heijunka enables manufacturing to optimize its manpower and production cost. As a hypothetical illustration, a Toyota assembly plant knows that during every hour of every day for the next three months that fifty-eight vehicles per hour will be produced and they will have the following option content: 60% of the vehicles will have automatic transmission, 30% with sunroofs, 35% with high-trim content, and 40% with side curtain airbags (and the list continues). The plant can then optimize manpower loading throughout the plant to provide only the minimum amount of manpower required to support this option mix. Maintaining this smooth workload for such an extended period requires a coordinated corporate-wide effort.

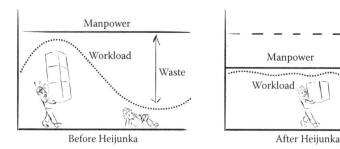

FIGURE 11.3
Heijunka eliminates waste corporate-wide.

It requires well-organized Heijunka. And it takes leadership to recognize the role that each function plays in supporting TPS.

The standardized model-change process is another TPS method that has successful application beyond the control of manufacturing. In my experience and observations, an extraordinary amount of plant-wide focus and resources is required to complete a model-change smoothly. Manufacturing is the recipient arm of the process, which is usually managed by other functions in the company. In Toyota, model-changes are done frequently and regularly, every four years for many models. When this regular cadence exists, manufacturing resources (manufacturing engineering, supplier quality control engineering, production control and planning, and manufacturing management) maintain a more level workload of changeover activity at all times. Resources outside manufacturing, such as product design and engineering, also maintain a regular cadence and workload.

These observations have led me to conclude that TPS leaders should identify functional interactions between sales, marketing, finance, engineering, human resources, and manufacturing. Effective implementation of TPS methods can be achieved when leaders implement them from an organization-wide perspective. TPS methods are not just for manufacturing and, even more importantly, the full benefits of TPS cannot be realized if only manufacturing implements them.

BACK TO THE BEGINNING

When I stood observing the plant at the start of my work with NUMMI, my eyes were opened to a symphony of parts and players in TPS methods. But what I came to discover throughout my time there was that the harmony I experienced was not just created by the TPS methods themselves. The conductor is leadership and the harmony exists when leadership sustains a Kaizen Culture where the Kaizen potential of team members is unleashed throughout the entire organization. TPS methods support the Kaizen Culture; they are not the reason for the culture.

Once I had learned about the harmony of the TPS methods, leadership, and the Kaizen Culture, it became clear to me why TPS had not been transferred successfully to GM. In most GM facilities there exists an acrimonious relationship between workers and management, which is typified by staunch resistance by workers and the UAW to participate in conceiving and implementing productivity improvements. Undeniably so, I had discovered the core reason GM had made such little progress implementing TPS during the previous nine years. GM and UAW leadership had not only failed to establish a Kaizen Culture, where all team members implement Kaizen, but had instead fostered acrimony between workers and management.

Unfortunately, the culture of disunity in the relationship between the UAW and GM management was so entrenched that a culture of change could not possibly be implemented by anyone other than the top leadership of GM and the UAW. Until those key leaders decided to and worked for change, GM would have to settle for implementing as many methods as possible but stopping short of unleashing the potential that exists within team members to embrace successful change—to Kaizen—and to then transform the company.

LEAVING GM

As a determined pupil of the successful Toyota Kaizen Culture, and understanding what lay between GM and that goal, I made the difficult decision to leave GM. GM's ability to remain competitive with Toyota and other similar organizations concerned me. Instead, I went on to implement TPS first in a growing non-union global packaging company whose leadership was very supportive of TPS methods and creating this revolutionary Kaizen Culture. That experience, which was followed by others, became the first of several additional stories of TPS observation, learning, strategy, and change that are for other chapters, in another book, another day.

12

Hoshin Kanri

Alistair Norval, with Darril Wilburn

Hoshin Kanri is known by many other names—Hoshin Planning, Policy Deployment, Strategy Deployment—but all refer to the same thing.

It's all about "Getting the Right Things Done versus just getting things done." Too often we put a lot of hard work into getting things done but fail to ask the question: Are they really the right things that will move the organization forward? In football terms, are we running back and forth between the sidelines, or are we moving the ball down the field? We've seen, in many organizations, a disconnect between individual activity and the higher-level strategy. Hoshin Kanri helps connect all levels of the organization so that everyone is aligned with the strategy. The result is that we can answer the question with facts and not "I think so."

This chapter discusses how Lean is applied to management processes and how the use of Hoshin Kanri reduces the waste in those processes and the waste in the entire organization.

As I began my own personal Lean journey in the mid-1990s, I was amazed at the Japanese terms and all the new techniques and wanted to learn as much about them as I could. Like many people, I became enraptured by the techniques. I chuckle to myself as I think back on those times. Fortunately, I was lucky enough to have a Sensei who would guide me and steer me in the right direction. Pascal Dennis, who worked at Toyota Motor Manufacturing Canada (TMMC) and later went on to author several Shingo prize-winning books on Lean including *Lean Production Simplified* and *The Remedy,* coached and shaped my thinking around Lean. Specifically, that Lean is not just about techniques; in fact, techniques are the small part, rather, Lean is about people. Pascal taught me that because Lean was about people, there were a few key concepts that I needed to learn:

- Engaging people
- Problem solving
- The role of management

If we can do these things, we can turn a Lean transformation into something special. That is, the achievement of successful business results in a way that is consistent with the TPS principle of "Respect for Humanity," which is part of the foundation of the Toyota Production System (TPS):

- Continuous improvement
- Elimination of waste
- Respect for humanity

To do this, we need a systematic way of driving improvement throughout the organization, one that allows us to make improvements in a way that is consistent with the values of the organization and one that does not sacrifice the fabric of the organization to meet short-term business results. I have seen companies achieve targeted earnings by eliminating spending on maintenance or by laying off experienced people and replacing them with cheaper, less-experienced labor, or by overworking people in broken processes, or by neglecting quality and customer service. Eventually, these tactics erode our working relationships and destroy our ability to plan for the future.

All systems need a purpose. The business processes we use within the system must be organized to achieve that purpose. The purpose of Hoshin Kanri is to crystallize the strategy of the organization and to engage the power of the people to pull the organization into the future.

WHAT IS HOSHIN KANRI?

Hoshin Kanri is a Japanese term that can be broken down into four kanji or thoughts, as illustrated in Figure 12.1.

Japanese is a very visual language. I remember being on a trip to Japan around the millennium and being very impressed with the visual displays of food, train schedules, and directions. Although I did not speak or understand Japanese, the visuals made it easy to get around. For example, plastic food in window displays of restaurants made ordering food easy. In the case of Hoshin Kanri, we can picture the Kanji or thoughts as the following:

方針 管理

HO SHIN　　KAN　RI

FIGURE 12.1
Hoshin Kanri.

Management, Direction, Logic, Control

Together they give us

A system for developing strategic goals and bringing them to reality.

WHY WE NEED A STRATEGIC PLANNING SYSTEM

Many organizations suffer from problems in their strategic planning systems. As I observe organizations, several problems become visible:

- No strategic planning system and so default to financial planning and the budget becomes the strategic plan.
- Command and control systems that do not engage people doing the work in the development of plans to achieve the organizational goals; often, these result in plans that are impractical and do not address the larger issues.
- Great strategies that are never transmitted to the rest of the organization and thus remain in the domain of the "ivory tower."
- Lack of a complete PDCA loop; they plan over and over again and get caught in Plan, Plan, Plan; or alternate between Plan, Do, Plan, Do; or worst of all just Do, Do, Do; and in most cases they never have a complete PDCA cycle.
- Planning by the numbers without a sense of what is actually happening gained by "Going to Gemba," talking to customers, suppliers, and employees.

WHAT DOES THIS RESULT IN?

Dysfunctional organizations where people

- Are pulled in many different directions
- Are pulled in the wrong direction
- Have no clear vision of what is really important

I once worked with an organization that had thirty-one different strategic objectives. I could not see how anyone could focus on thirty-one different things, and yet the organization insisted that all thirty-one things were critical and needed to be done. It is easy to see how many Strategic Planning issues lead to the cartoons we all enjoy.

COUNTERMEASURE TO STRATEGIC PLANNING PROBLEMS

Toyota's countermeasure to these common strategic planning problems is Hoshin Kanri. Toyota developed it in the mid-1950s and has been using it ever since. Hoshin Kanri is founded on the Scientific Method through PDCA. It is a blend of both data analysis and intuition based on experience gained at Gemba.

Hoshin Kanri has three purposes:

1. Focus on the vital few instead of the trivial many
2. Align the organization to these focus areas
3. Rapid response to problems

HOSHIN KANRI ENABLES ORGANIZATIONS TO DEVELOP STRATEGIC PLANS THAT ARE

- A balance of central control and local autonomy
- Neither too rigid nor too loose
- Engaging of team members by allowing PDCA to flourish
- A communication method for facilitating dialogue

This last point is worth exploring a bit more. One of the major problems organizations face in today's world is an overload of data and a lack of information that is useful. Laptops and PowerPoint have allowed people to create mammoth presentations replete with embedded files and fancy graphics that are so big that they lose the essence of the problem. I worked with a large corporation once that gave me a ninety-eight-page summary of their strategic plans. The original document was almost 900 pages long—so long, in fact, that no one could read it and therefore make either head or tails of it.

There is a great quote by Winston Churchill on this:

> "This Treasury paper, by its very length defends itself against the risk of being read"
>
> **—Winston Churchill**

Hoshin Kanri is a way of boiling down the strategy into its bare essence so that it is understandable and thus enables people to engage in dialogue on it.

TRUE NORTH

Sounds great, but as we align the organization, what do we align the organization with?

We align the organization with achieving *True North,* which is the strategic and philosophical direction the organization is heading toward. I always thought *True North* was a great image for the direction organizations wanted to take. Picture *True North* as the North Star, Polaris, guiding mariners across the rough and stormy sea and leading them to a safe harbor (Figure 12.2).

True North consists of two parts:

1. Hard business objectives (such as Revenue, Earnings, EDIT, and Working Capital). These appeal to the head and are the hard business targets that must be achieved.
2. Soft or broad brush goals. This is a vision or direction for the organization that appeals to the heart. It is often inspirational in nature and represents both who you are as an organization as well as what you

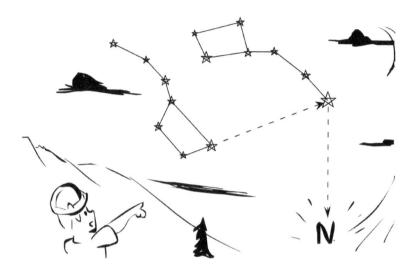

FIGURE 12.2
True North.

value. It is critical in the engagement of team members, who often have difficulty relating to high-level financial goals. It allows us to test our plans against a set of goals to ensure consistency.

One of the best broad-brush goals I have ever seen was a health-care provider who used the broad-brush goal of *"Affordable Excellence."* It represented both who they were, a health-care provider with a long-standing reputation for health-care excellence in the community, and what they needed to do to continue to succeed in the community in the future, which was to make that same level of care more affordable. It became very motivating for the front-line staff who could relate to both parts. It also allowed them to test their plans against it. Are we doing things that are not consistent with providing the community with affordable, excellent health-care services?

TREE OF FOCUSED ACTIVITY

Now that we have a *True North,* what is next? How does this help an organization to align and focus?

We start by asking the question: What is preventing us from achieving *True North*?

What boulders block our pathway? These typically are framed as problems with the countermeasures to these problems becoming the key areas of focus for us to work on.

Sounds good so far, but what is different?

The key is to split work into two basic types of work:

1. Routine work
2. Improvement work

Improvement work refers to the breakthrough things we need to do to drive the organization toward *True North* and achieve the goals we have set. *Routine work,* on the other hand, is all the day-to-day things we need to do to run the business and deliver value to our customers. It also includes daily continuous improvement work. Things we need to improve but which are not the breakthrough improvements that will make a difference in the organization achieving *True North.* Many of these items are a type of problem solving that returns us to a standard rather than driving the standards higher and higher. Routine work takes most of the time of the people in the organization.

Let's go back to the example of the organization that had thirty-one critical improvements. They had a war room with wall charts indicating the status of the thirty-one areas. Red and green were highlighted. There was a perfunctory review, but usually dates were adjusted on most items and the comments on progress were weak. To the people doing the work, there was no clear focus. They worked on whatever was pushed or was the current hotspot.

Even worse are organizations that try to solve this problem by tying in the thirty-one key focus areas to a Human Resources-sponsored annual commitment plan. With each item worth about 3% of a grand total number that defines people's contribution to the organization for the year, how does this help people know what to focus on? That is not to say that one should not set personal commitment plans; just set them to make it clear to people what you want them to focus on.

In dealing with organizations over many years, my experience would say that organizations can only focus on five or six breakthrough items at any one time. So the key becomes pruning the list and de-selecting certain items to get to the vital few focus areas that will lead to breakthrough improvement. Typically, what I observe is that people think that because things are important, they must be breakthrough. Things can be

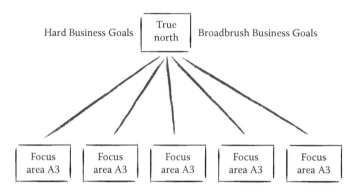

FIGURE 12.3
True North and focus areas.

important but all we need to do is stay the course or make small improvements. We still need to monitor these to ensure that we do not fall back, yet we do not need to focus our improvement activities on them. They are important but routine work.

The key is to focus our improvement efforts on those few things that will lead to breakthrough improvements. We need to align the improvement activities of the organization to do those things. We gain alignment through

- Structure: improvement teams
- Communication: dialogue leading to consensus

This leads to a tree of focused activity. The top is *True North,* and supporting *True North* are five or six key focus areas (Figure 12.3).

PLAN, DO, CHECK, ACT (PDCA)

The last thing that Hoshin Kanri does for us is to bring in a rapid response to problems. This recognizes that "No plan goes according to plan." Problems are natural. Toyota excels in its ability to make problems visible and to swarm all over them once they have surfaced. When I deal with organizations, I always ask: Has anyone ever had a plan go exactly according to the original plan? This always gets a few chuckles and smiles. Things change during the execution of the plan. There are many unknowns when the original strategic plan is put together that cause problems when they

FIGURE 12.4
PDCA.

come to light. Knowing this, the last part of Hoshin Kanri is a very rapid PDCA cycle where we do the Check/Act phases in frequent, small lot-size cycles.

PDCA (Figure 12.4) is a short form of Plan, Do, Check, Act, the cycle made famous by Dr. W. Edwards Deming, who many consider to be the "father of modern quality control," based on his study of the Shewhart cycle.

PDCA is based on the Scientific Method, which can be summarized as

- Hypothesis
- Experiment
- Evaluate

These correspond to Plan, Do, and Check; Act completes the cycle and drives us back to the beginning with changes to the Plan/Hypothesis based on what we have learned.

As I think about this and how it applies to strategy, some great examples come to mind. One that I would like to highlight is General Dwight D. Eisenhower, who was the Supreme Allied Commander at the time of the D-Day invasion of Europe on June 6, 1944, on the beaches of Normandy. He and his staff outlined an invasion plan that remains the largest amphibian invasion in history. The plan was deployed through the various units becoming more and more detailed and tactical as it got closer to the front-line troops. During this planning, they were faced with many daunting unknowns—weather conditions, the moon, tides and currents, strength and readiness of the Nazi forces; would the naval bombardment be effective?

Did they stick rigidly to the plan? Or did they have an overall plan with objectives that were to be met but minute tactics that were being changed after going through a rapid Check/Act process on the day of the battle?

Of course there were many mini, rapid Check/Act cycles as they learned more about the unknowns. The detailed plans were changed so they could meet the overall objectives.

The Plan is a hypothesis:

> If we do these actions in this time frame, we will get these results.

The key to a hypothesis is that it is testable and that is it binary. This means that we can boil the hypothesis down to a Yes/No question. We either did or did not get the results we expected. Many times these are expressed as Red and Green, which are great visuals for the binary condition. I am personally not in favor of Amber/Yellow because it is not consistent with the Scientific Method and is often misused by organizations as a way to hide the truth.

My observation of most organizations is they stick with a monthly or quarterly review of their strategic plans. The meetings often look like this:

- Most of the time is spent on Green or items that are in good shape. Long, detailed explanations are given and everyone feels good about them.
- Only a short period of time, often five minutes or less, is left toward the end of the meeting to review the items that are Red and need the most help. No detailed problem solving is done, and a few action items are hurriedly assigned.

In summary, a Check/Act process is shallow even during the infrequent times it is done.

As stated before, most companies spend the bulk of their time in the Plan and or Do phases. Check and Act get very little time and are often short-changed in the management process. Even when Check is done, it is often a check against the results and not a complete check of the hypothesis.

Now compare this to what a Toyota Check and Act process would look like.

The hypothesis remains the same:

If we execute these plans in this timeframe, we will achieve these results. The questions asked around it would be:

- Did we achieve the expected results?
- Did we execute the plans?
- Did we meet the planned time targets?
- Did the execution of the plan cause the achievement of the results?

Wow! So much richer and so much more can be explored and looked at. For this reason, most of the time (up to 90%) in the Check/Act meetings is spent dealing with Red items—but Red items are not just results; Red items are anything that deviates from the plan. This allows us to enter the Act phase, which entails

- Launching problem solving on any Red condition
- Standardizing and locking in any learning points

Often these are recorded using a Book of Knowledge to ensure that the organization continues to build its capability.

MANAGEMENT PROCESS

In either case, we need to reflect on why things are Red or why things are Green. This deep reflection leads to insights that allow us to keep strengthening our systems.

This general process develops into the Management System. The Management System for strategy centers on the annual process. It follows the following process:

- Develop the plan:
  - Reflect on last year's results and execution of last year's plan
  - Consider True North and this year's objectives and strategies
  - Determine the barriers preventing the achievement of the objectives
  - Develop countermeasures to these barriers or problems

- Deploy the plan:
  - Assign Key Thinkers
  - Catchball
  - Determine any capabilities the resources need
- Check the plan:
  - Rapid, fast cycles
  - Standardized work for management
  - Make the status visual
- Adjust the plan:
  - Reflection and learning points
  - At mid-year and year-end, a deeper reflection on the objectives and execution of the plan
  - Identify systems that need to be strengthened
- Book of Knowledge to record key learning

CATCHBALL

This same basic management process exists at all levels of the organization. To link the levels together and to deploy the Tree of Focused activity within the organization, we need to utilize a process called catchball.

Catchball is a process that links the strategies to the functional organization and allows them to be deployed throughout the organization. It is the opposite of management just setting blanket objectives such as reduce costs by 5% everywhere. It is based on the principle that the people closest to the work know the most about the work and the associated problems and so must be involved in the setting of the tactics that will allow the strategies to be met. It allows the strategies to be translated as they are deployed throughout the organization. As the strategies are deployed, they become more and more concrete as they get closer to the value stream. As they are translated, catchball forces frank, fact-based dialogue on the translation. Ideas are tossed back and forth. All parts of the plan are open for discussion. The sessions are usually short and iterate several times, with each iteration bringing the teams closer to consensus. Once consensus is achieved, the plans are signed off and locked in for the year. The key is to get many ideas tossed out and good open dialogue without rambling on and on with war stories. This creates buy-in and eliminates many traditional organizational barriers and excuses to deploying strategy.

KEY THINKER

To facilitate this process and to ensure the plan optimizes the entire value stream and not just individual units, we use a functional called a Key Thinker. The Key Thinker must be a person who can scan the entire horizon and pull various groups together to come to a consensus. A Key Thinker must also be the conscience of the group to ensure that real problems are put on the table. Generally, this is a person who is more senior in the organization and thus has the experience and political clout to make things happen even though he or she does not have a line responsibility.

Each focus area would have a Key Thinker who is responsible for

- Facilitating the overall catchball process
- Capturing the ideas arising from catchball and reworking them into the plan
- Writing the A3
- Ensuring problems get surfaced at Check/Act
- Supporting problem solving

Typical examples of a Key Thinker would be

- Chief Engineer in Development or Shusa
- Finance for Cost A3
- Supply Chain Manager for Delivery A3

In summary, the Key Thinker needs to be a senior person who can break down silos in the organization to ensure that value flows through to customers.

A3

Finally, to keep things crisp we use a methodology called the A3 to boil things down to their pure essence, which enables us to keep focused. I remember one time asking my Sensei what an A3 was and watching him smile. I thought it was another Toyota technique and was surprised to learn it referred to an A3 size of paper. Everyone in the world outside the

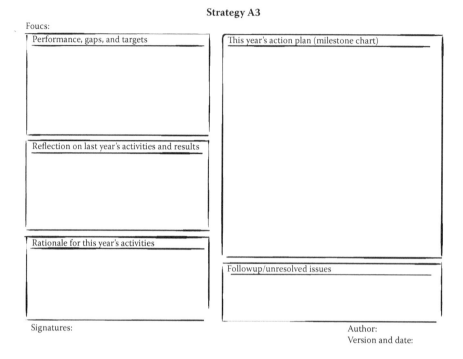

Strategy A3

Foucs:

| Performance, gaps, and targets | This year's action plan (milestone chart) |

Reflection on last year's activities and results

Rationale for this year's activities

Followup/unresolved issues

Signatures:

Author:
Version and date:

FIGURE 12.5
A3

United States knows that A2, A3, A4, etc. refer to metric sizes of paper. In this case, an A3 is about the size of an 11" × 17" piece of paper. The thing about an A3 is that it encompasses the entire management process thinking on a single piece of paper. It is laid out like this (Figure 12.5):

- The upper left-hand side consists of the background and overall problem statement.
- The middle and bottom left-hand side contains the reflection summary, causal analysis, and conclusion stated as a hypothesis.
- The right-hand side consists of the countermeasures as a plan, complete with who does what by when.
- Finally, the bottom right-hand side has any unresolved issues that need follow-up.

The catchball and iterations continue to refine the A3 until it crystallizes the strategy into a plan that is concrete. Boiling down the strategy to an A3 allows the Key Thinker to tell the strategy as a story. Hoshin

Kanri is a story-telling approach to strategy. Listening to a story that is interesting, persuasive, and compelling becomes engaging of our team members. People pay attention. People relax and feel free to engage in dialogue. They understand why and buy in so that the execution of the plan is much smoother.

The key is that the story told in an A3 must be a short story, not a full-length novel such as *War and Peace* by the great Russian novelist Leo Tolstoy.

To make it into a short story requires time. The iterations from catchball help but the A3 must be refined to its essence, which then makes it easy to communicate.

There is a famous quote from Blaise Pascal that sums up this concept behind an A3:

"I would have written a shorter letter, but I did not have the time."

Blaise Pascal

Take the time to refine the story. Use simple diagrams, bullets, and visuals—a picture is worth a thousand words. Finally, do not fall into the trap of trying to squeeze as much information onto an A3 as possible using size-6 font. Make it easy to read. Less is more!

It takes time to gather our thoughts to tell a short story. Lean is about reducing waste, and the A3 is a key methodology to help reduce waste in the management process. Once the A3 is signed off, we can use it as the basis of the Check/Act process.

THE POWER OF HOSHIN

My colleague Darril Wilburn often cites this example when explaining the power of Hoshin to focus an organization on the important things and to illustrate Toyota's discipline in seeing a plan through. In 2000, Toyota Motor Corporation in Japan established its Vision 2010. This vision was used to set mid- to long-term Hoshin items for regions around the world. It was determined that the North American region should have, as one of its themes, "Self Reliance."

I was working at the North American manufacturing headquarters at the time in Human Resources and was on one of the teams charged with understanding and deploying part of the Hoshin to address "Self

Reliance." The leadership first considered what was meant by self-reliance. It was determined that one way to measure self-reliance was the number of Japanese engineering resources needed to support a major model change. Let's say it took a hundred such resources in the year 2000. If we could reduce this number to zero by 2010, we would be considered self-reliant at least by that measure. (There were many other indicators of self-reliance.)

One of the key elements of the catchball function is for the previous level in the organization to translate the objectives for the next level in the organization so that it is meaningful to them. Our cross-functional work team was given the objective of recruiting and developing the next generation of engineers with the goal of self-reliance. We continued to break down this objective and determined that if we were to be self-reliant, we needed to boost the skill level of engineering co-ops and eventual new-hires. There were numerous activities that preceded this point but the highlights included choosing additional universities that we would target for talent and developing a program that would facilitate rapid skill development and experience with model change. We called it the "Engineers in Training Program."

As often happens, people on the team change, and this team was no exception. Soon after we developed the plan, I transferred to another Toyota location. Good planning facilitated transfer of duties and the programs were developed and the recruiting focus adjusted. The plan was rolling along without me.

In 2008, after leaving Toyota, I was asked to come back to conduct Problem-Solving coaching training for the management team and engineers at one location. During one of the classes, we were doing introductions and one of the students introduced herself as a new-hire to the location and that she was a recent graduate of the first class of the Engineers in Training Program. Now for me this was a wonderful moment for several reasons. One, it was the culmination of a project that had started several years previous. Two, I was amazed at the discipline it took for a company to keep focused on the objective for so long despite changes in leadership and team composition. I explained to her that she was a living, breathing countermeasure to a problem that was first established eight years earlier in Japan. She was probably just entering high school when she was, in a sense, "dreamed up." I was so excited to meet her that I even gave her a hug (in the least offensive, non-policy-breaking way I could). I am unclear on the success that Toyota Motor Manufacturing North America had in closing the gap of model change support needed, but I am quite sure that at least one of the plans was nurtured and implemented.

This is the power of Hoshin, clarifying the right things to do and providing the structure for the discipline needed to see it through.

SUMMARY

Hoshin Kanri—a simple, elegant system for strategic planning within an organization but not an easy one to master. My experience shows that it takes most organizations three years to learn the process, which sounds like a long time but is only three cycles of the annual process. The key is to begin by knowing where you are going and what is stopping you from getting there.

Index

A

A3 report, 90, 184, 201–203
ABC parts analysis and segregation, 146–149
Abidance by the law, 131
Activity-based costing, 152–155
Analysis paralysis, 83
Analysis step, Toyota Kaizen, 102–105
Andon boards, 14, 50, 53–54
Andon cords, 50–51
Ansuini, Stephen J., xx–xxi, 111–125
"AQD" (analytical, quantitative, and detailed), 101
Automation, Jidoka definition, 44, 49

B

Balancing the line, 25, 36
    workforce balancing, 34
Bandeirante, 58, 65
Batch size calculation, 66–67
Blackout periods, 123
Bonus system, 155
Bottlenecks, 24, 141, 145
Brainstorming, 81, 83–84, 106, 145
Breakthrough activities, 195–196
Build to order (BTO) supply chain, 166–167

C

Cash awards, 87, 123, 155
Catchball, 200, 204
Cause-effect diagram, 83
Check/Act phases, PDCA, 197–199
Check and verify results, 109
Checklists, 106
Cho, Fujio, 3, 46, 113, 119, 120, 122
Churchill, Winston, 193
Collaborative intelligence, 112
Common sense, 105
Communication philosophy, 184

Constraints, understanding and linking to business objectives, 141
Continuous flow process (one-piece flow), 62, 64
Continuous improvement, *See also* Kaizen; Kaizen Culture
    across organizational levels, 111
    compound transformational effect, 181
    cost of system operation, 124
    evolving system, 117–123
    goals, 55, 93, 115–117
    types of work, 195–196
Cost breakdown, 131
    indirect costs and Lean accounting, 152–155
Cost reduction, 98–99, 133–134
    target costing, 132
Courage, humility, and Kaizen, 4, 12–14, 15, 19
Covey, Stephen, 6
Creative thinking, 105–106
Cross-functional teams, 163–164
Cross-training, 151
Customer first philosophy, 182
Customer-supplier relationship, 128–136, *See also* Toyota purchasing philosophy and practice
Customer total satisfaction, 59–60
Cycle time, 103

D

Damiani, Gerson Valentim, xvi–xvii, 21–41
D-Day planning, 197–198
Deadlines, 81, 85–86, 107–108
Defects (scrap/rework) waste, 24, 61, 98, 128
Delphi, 177
Deming, W. Edwards, 197
Dennis, Pascal, 189
Direct supervision, Jidoka and decoupling from, 47–49

Discovering improvement potential, 100–102
DMAIC, 120
DNA of Toyota, 3
"Do" part of PDCA, 83–85
Driver pick-up verification, 173–174
Dulles, John, 74

E

Economies of time, 165, *See also* Time study
ECRS (eliminate, combine, rearrange, simplify), 103
Edjalma, Marcelino, 30
Effectiveness of workforce, 150–151
Eisenhower, Dwight D., 197
Emotion and creativity, 105–106
Employee recognition, 87–90, 114–115
  Gemba walks and luncheons, 119
  promotion activities, 122–123
  rewards, 87
  suggestion system, 117–118, 123–124
Employees as king of the factory, 26–27
Employee suggestion system (Kaizen Teian), 51, 52, 115–125
  implementation issues and lessons learned, 124–125
  planning and participation emphasis, 117–119
  profit-sharing, 155
  promotion activities, 122–124
  team member development phase, 120–122
Empowered workforce, 111
Engineers in Training Program, 204
External customer, 182
External setup, 66

F

Factory layout, 35–38
Failed attempts, 13, 106, 155–156
Failure mode and effect analysis (FMEA), 135
Fear of failure, 106
Fear of problems, 72–74
Fingerprint on a process, 164
First-In-First-Out (FIFO), 62

Five precepts, Toyota Production system, 121
Five S (Seiri, Seiton, Seiso, Seiketsu, Shitsuke), 31, 52, 70, 102
Five W 1H, 25, 103, 107
Five Why problem solving, 7, 81, 83
Flow visibility, 38
FMEA, 135
Ford's Production system, 57
Forging process, 66
Fukamizu, Carlos Yukio, xviii, 55–70
Furuta, Nate, 72

G

Gemba, 2, 113–114, 128, *See also* Genchi Genbutsu
  employee recognition, 119
Genchi Genbutsu, 3–4, 25, 77–78, 81, 88, 101, 185
Gilbreth, Frank and Lillian, 93, 104
GM/Toyota joint venture (NUMMI), 177–182, 187–188
Goal dissemination (Hoshin Kanri), 115, 138, 184, 193–194
Goal statement, 81
Goshi, 30–31
Green Field Toyota facility, Lean logistics development, 159–175, *See also* Lean logistics
Guiding principles, Lean logistics, 161, 175

H

Habit, 105
Hands-on learning, 140, *See also* Genchi Genbutsu
Heijunka, 184, 186–187
High-mix, low-volume organizations, *See* Made-to-order manufacturers, adapting Lean for
Honor traits, 184
Hoshin Kanri, 115, 138, 184
  A3 report, 201–203
  catchball, 200, 204
  kanji and definition, 190–191
  Key Thinker, 201
  management process, 199–200

PDCA and problem solving,
  196–199
power of, 203–205
purposes, 192
strategic planning system issues,
  191–193
Toyota's Vision 2010, 203–204
tree of focused activity, 196
True North organizational alignment,
  193–194, 196
House of TPS, 46, 51
Human factor in TPS, 38, 190
Humility and Kaizen, 4, 12–14, 15
Hypothesis, 198–199

I

Idea generation, 105–106
  brainstorming, 81, 83–84, 106
Improvement potential, discovering,
  100–102
Improvement work, 195–196
Inbound-logistics lead-time, 166
Incidental waste, 97
Indirect processes, 143–146
Information flow, 141
  indirect processes, 143
  Lean logistics, 169–170
  strategic planning issues, 193
Informative inspections, 52
In-source inspections, 52
Inspections and problem identification,
  51–52
Internal customer, 182
Internal setup, 66
Inventory reduction, velocity and, 168
Inventory waste, 24, 61, 98, 127
Ishida, Taizo, 98
Ishikawa diagram, 83

J

Jidoka, 43
  "automation" definition, 44, 49
  bringing problems to the surface,
    51–53
  built-in quality, 48, 54
  decoupling quality and flow from
    direct supervision, 47–49, 53

implementation stages, 51–53
Just-In-Time and, 59
Kanban and, 49
Lean logistics, 174
origin, 43–44, 56–57
TPS pillar, 43, 44–48
training and, 47–48
Job-shop environments, adapting
    Lean for, *See* Made-to-order
    manufacturers, adapting Lean
    for
Judgment inspections, 52
Junk words, 79–80
Just-In-Time (JIT), 56, 103
  concept, 58–59
  continuous flow process (one-piece
    flow), 62, 64
  Jidoka and, 59
  Kanban, 49–50, 56, 58, 64–70
  origin, 57–58
  pull system, 58, 62, 64
  total customer satisfaction, 59–60
  TPS pillar, 46, 56
  training issues, 28
  waste elimination, 60–62

K

Kaizen, 56, 63–64, 178, *See also* Problem
    solving
  "AQD" (analytical, quantitative, and
    detailed), 101
  conceptual development inside Toyota,
    94–100
  cost reduction principles, 98–99
  courage and humility, 4, 12–14, 15, 19
  creativity, using cardboard and tape,
    12–13
  definition, 93, 177
  failed attempts, 13
  origins, 93–94
  OSKKK, 139, 143, 156
  problem solving versus, 100
  as process, not activity, 110
  quality improvement, 94
  standard work instructions and, 40
  teaching outside Toyota, 14–19
  team member development, 120–121,
    125

Toyota purchasing philosophy and
practice, 132
tryout and Goshi, 30–31
waste principles, 97–98, *See also* Waste
Kaizen, main steps inside Toyota, 99
analyze current method, 102–105
discover improvement potential,
100–102
generate original ideas, 105–107
make Kaizen plan, 107–108
plan implementation, 108–109
verify results, 109
Kaizen Culture, 44, 179–182, *See also*
Toyota Production System
clear purpose and aligned goals,
115–117
continuous improvement system costs,
124
creating/sustaining in American
factories, 182–185, *See also*
Kaizen Culture, philosophies for
creating and sustaining
employee involvement, 111
Hoshin Kanri, 115
implementation issues and lessons
learned, 124–125
management support, 112–115, 125
participation emphasis phase,
117–119
phases, 117–123
points to consider, 115
process maturation phase, 122–124
suggestion system, 115–125, *See also*
Employee suggestion system
Toyota do Brasil, 55, 60
transition phase, 120–122
turn-around time and, 124
worker-manager relationship issues,
187–188
Kaizen Culture, philosophies for creating
and sustaining, 182
communication, 184
customer first, 182
Genchi Genbutsu, 185
goals and leadership, 184
knowledge, teaching, and modeling,
184
mutual trust, 183
safety and security, 182–183

support and resources, 184
teamwork, 183–184
Kaizen implementation
GM problems, 177–179, 187–188
Heijunka, 184, 186–187
leadership issues, 179
team member support, 184–185
Kaizen plan, 107–108
implementation, 108–109
Kaizen presentation report, 109
Kaizen Teian (suggestion system), 51, 52,
See also Employee suggestion
system
Kanban, 49–50, 56, 58, 64–70
ABC part analysis, 147
batch size calculation, 66–67
Order Point (OP) calculation, 67
prerequisites for implementing, 186
required information, 69
rules, 68–69
Kato, Isao, 110
Key Thinker, 201
King in a factory, 26–27
Kitazuka, Renato Eiji, xvii–xviii, 43–54
Knowledge, teaching, and modeling, 184

L

Lane, Greg, xxii, 137–157
Layout of the factory, 35–38
Leadership
assisting operators for greater
productivity, 31
commitment to safety, 182–183
Gemba approach, 2, 113–114, *See also*
Genchi Genbutsu
Kaizen Culture and management
support, 112–115, 125, 184
Kaizen implementation, 108
managing in real-time, 149–151
policy deployment, 75–76, 138, 184
team member development, 120–121
team member recognition, *See*
Employee recognition
TPS/Kaizen implementation issues, 179
Lead-time, 33–34, 104–105, 141, 165–169
definitions, 166
Lean accounting, indirect costs and,
152–155

Lean culture, 46
Lean environment, 112, *See also* Kaizen
    Culture
Lean implementation
    job-shop environment, 138, *See also*
        Made-to-order manufacturers,
        adapting Lean for
    standardized work, 39–41
Lean is about people, 189–190
Lean logistics, 159
    build to order supply chain, 166–167
    core principles, 161, 175
    driver pick-up verification, 173–174
    Green Field Toyota facility, 159–161
    Jidoka, 174
    lessons learned, 174–175
    leveled flow and receiving schedules,
        170–172
    manufacturing plant integration,
        169–170
    pull replenishment, 164–165
    route design, 163–164
    supply-chain collaboration, 162
    team building and development,
        162–163
    Toyota outsourcing, 161–162
    transportation cost issues, 161,
        168–169
    "triple crown" in, 169
    velocity and lead-time reduction,
        165–169
    volume consolidation, 169
    yard layout and visual management,
        172–173
Lean methods and concepts, 159, 178,
        189, *See also* Toyota Production
        System
    adapting for made-to-order
        manufacturers, 137–157, *See also*
        Made-to-order manufacturers,
        adapting Lean for
    early TPS-related literature, 127
    economies of time, 165
    foundation of courage, humility, and
        Kaizen, 19
    importance of problem solving,
        71–74
    managing in real-time, 149–151
    team member development, 121
toolbox approach, 46, 54
TPS versus non-Toyota systems, 46–47
waste elimination, 63
Lean specialists, 47
Learning processes before managing, 140
Leveled flow and Lean logistics, 170–172
Logistics, Lean methods, *See* Lean
        logistics

M

"Machine-gun" improvement, 140
Machining process, 62
Made-to-order manufacturers, adapting
        Lean for, 137–139
    ABC parts analysis and segregation,
        146–148
    cross-training, 151
    indirect costs and Lean accounting,
        152–155
    learning before managing, 140
    managing in real-time, 149–151
    OSKKK, 139–140, 143, 156
    planning and forecasting issues,
        141–143
    process focus, 143–146
    strategy deployment, 138–139, 142
    understanding constraints, 141
Management process, Hoshin Kanri,
        199–200
Management support and Kaizen Culture,
        112–115
Manager training, 140
Managing in real-time, 149–151
Manufacturing-replenishment lead-time,
        166
Martichenko, Robert, xxiii, 159–175
Material and Information Flow Analysis
        (MIFA), 104–105
Measurement standards, 109
"Mistake proofing" (poka yoke), 48, 52,
        See also Jidoka
Model-change process, 187, 204
Moretti, Carlos, 43
Mortgage banking company, 14
Mosquito problem solving case, 76–91
Motion study, 103–104
Motion waste, 24, 61, 98, 127
Muda, 6, 97, 127–128, *See also* Waste

Muller, Patrick, xxi–xxii, 127–136
Mura, 6, 10, 97, 128
Muri, 6–10, 97, 128
Mutual trust, 1, 130, 183

N

Nemawashi process, 184
New United Motor Manufacturing, Inc.
　　(NUMMI), 177–182, 187–188
Nike, 80
Non-value-added times, 33
Non-value-added waste definition, 128
Non-value-adding activities, 63
Norval, Alistair, xxiv–xxv, 189–205

O

Obara, Sammy, xviii–xix, 71–91
Ohno, Taiichi, 11, 17, 32, 51, 57–58, 63,
　　64–65, 98, 128
One Percent Solution, 181
One-piece flow, 62
Open-door policy, 130
Operational procedures and standard
　　work, 29, *See also* Standardized
　　work
Operations Management Development
　　Division (OMDD), 1, 5, 181
"Opportunities," problems as, 72–73
Opportunities for improvement, Kaizen
　　approach for discovering,
　　100–102
Order Point (OP) calculation, 67
Osborn, Alex, 106
OSKKK, 139–140, 143, 156
Outbound-logistics lead-time, 166
Outsourcing, 161–162
Overburden, *See* Muri
Overprocessing, 24, 51, 61, 98, 127
Overproduction, 24, 62, 98, 104, 127,
　　166–167

P

Packaging, 135–136
Pareto law, 82, 146
Pascal, Blaise, 203
P-courses, 94

PDCA, *See* Plan-Do-Check-Act cycle
Personal commitment plans, 195
Personal discipline traits, 184
Photos in standard work procedures,
　　39–40
Plan-Do-Check-Act cycle (PDCA), 21, 71,
　　74, 160
　　Check/Act phases, 197–199
　　Hoshin Kanri, 196–199
　　implementation ("Do"), 83–85
　　Kaizen plan, 107–109
　　Kaizen steps inside Toyota, 99, *See
　　　also* Kaizen, main steps inside
　　　Toyota
　　mosquitoes complaints case, 76–91
　　need for problem solving method,
　　　74–75
　　OSKKK, 139
　　PDCA team, 76–77
　　plan as hypothesis, 198–199
　　point of cause, 77–78
　　rewards and recognition, 87–90
　　standardization ("Act"), 86–87
　　strategic planning system issues,
　　　191
　　visualizing planning process, 142
　　Yokoten and sharing the learning,
　　　90–91
Planning and forecasting constraints,
　　141–143
Plummer, Bob, xxiii–xxiv, 177–188
Point of cause, 77–78
Poka yoke, 48, 52
Policy deployment, 75–76, 138, 184, 189,
　　See also Hoshin Kanri
Precepts and principles, TPS, 121
Problems, fear of, 72–74
Problems as opportunities, 72–73
Problem solving, *See also* Kaizen
　　5 Whys, 7, 81, 83
　　common mistakes in, 71
　　creativity, *See also* Kaizen
　　Genchi Genbutsu, 3–4, 25, 77–78
　　Hoshin Kanri, 196–199
　　how to find problems, 75–76
　　importance along Lean
　　　transformation, 71–74
　　improper use of Andon boards,
　　　53–54

Jidoka implementation and, 51–53
Kaizen versus, 100
leaders and team member
    development, 120–121
managing in real-time, 149–151
mosquitoes complaints case, 76–91
need for a method, 74–75
PDCA, *See* Plan-Do-Check-Act cycle
policy deployment and, 75–76
process observation and problem
    identification, 5–9, 22–23
root cause, 9, 45, 51, 54, 72, 74, 81–84,
    100, 137
scientific method, 72, 80, 192, 197, *See*
    also Plan-Do-Check-Act cycle
types of inspections, 52
types of work, 195–196
visualization methods, 82–83
Problem statement, 78–80
Process analysis and Toyota Kaizen,
    102–105
Process mapping, 143–146
Process observation and problem
    identification, 5–9, 22–23
Process stabilization, 25, 65, 145
Product design, waste elimination in,
    127–129
    FMEA, 135
    packaging, 135–136
    purchasing philosophy, *See* Toyota
        purchasing philosophy and
        practice
    value engineering/value analysis, 128,
        134–136
Production analysis board, 102
Production count boards, 14
Production planning problems,
    48–49
Productivity
    comparing planned versus actual,
        17–19
    human factor in TPS, 38
    measure development, 15–19
Profit equation, 98–99
Profit-sharing, 155
Promotion activities, Kaizen suggestion
    system, 122–124
Pull production systems, 58, 62, 64, 147,
    164–165

Purchasing practices, *See* Toyota
    purchasing philosophy and
    practice
Pure waste, 97

Q

Quality, Jidoka principles, *See* Jidoka
Quality at the source, Lean logistics
    principles, 173–174
Quality improvement, Kaizen and, 94

R

Real-time management, 149–151
Receiving schedules, 170–172
Recognition of team members, *See*
    Employee recognition
Rewards, 87, 123, *See also* Employee
    recognition
Root cause, 9, 45, 51, 54, 72, 81–84, 100,
    137
Root cause analysis, 74
Route design, 163–164
Routine work, 195

S

Safety and security philosophy, 182–183
Scientific method for problem solving, 72,
    80, 192, 197
Scrap/rework, 24, 61, 98, 128
Self-reliance, 203–204
Setup times, 62, 66
Seven types of waste (or Muda), 10–11,
    24–25, 51, 61–62, 98, 127–128
Shingo, Shigeo, 48, 94
Siam Toyota Manufacturing (STM), 76–91
Signaling Kanban, 66
Six Sigma, 120
Smalley, Art, xix–xx, 93–110
SMED, 63, 66
Stability
    heart of TPS, 165
    Kanban and, 65
    standard work and, 25, 145
Standard inventory (Temochi), 34, 36
Standardized work, 21, 63, 104
    balancing line activities, 25, 34, 36

facility layout, 35–38
implementation issues, 39–41
importance of, 21, 25, 27–28
lead-time verification, 33
learning to see waste, 10–11
line operator audit, 39
model-change process, 187
operator training, 28–31
OSKKK, 139
PDCA and, 86–87
photos in procedures, 39–40
process observation and, 23
process stability and, 25, 145
reasons for using standards, 28–30
receiving schedule implementation, 171
Toyota and use of technology, 32–33
Toyota time management before technology, 31–32
using operator's experience, 29
workforce balancing, 34
Standards for measurement, 109
Standard work diagram, 35f.
Standard work instructions, 25
where to place, 40
Strategic planning issues, 191–193
Strategy deployment, 138–139, 142, 189, *See also* Hoshin Kanri
A3, 201–203
catchball, 200, 204
Key Thinker, 201
Suggestion system, *See* Employee suggestion system
Supermarket system, 58, 64
Supplier relationships, 128–136, 162, *See also* Lean logistics; Toyota purchasing philosophy and practice
Supply-chain design, build to order, 166–167
Support and resources, 184
Surfing school, 90

T

Takt time, 23–24, 59, 103, 104
balancing line activities and, 25
facility layout issues, 36
Goshi and, 30–31

Kanban system prerequisites, 186
learning to see waste, 10
Target costing, 132
Taylor, Fredrick, 93
Team building and development, Lean logistic system design, 162–163
Team leaders and real-time management, 150–151
Team member recognition, *See* Employee recognition
Team member safety and security philosophy, 182–183
Team member support and resources, 184–185
Teamwork philosophy, 183–184
Temochi, 34, 36
The Lean Production System Manual, 46–47
The Toyota Business Practice, 1
The Toyota Way 2001, 1, 2–4
Thinking simple, 29, 36
Time and motion study, 103–104
Time study, 103, *See also* Takt time
economies of time, 165
Just-In-Time concept, 59
large effects of tiny savings, 33
setup times, 62, 66
Toyota and video technology, 32–33
Toyota before technology, 31–32
velocity and lead-time reduction, 165–169
Toolbox approaches, 46, 54
Tooling changeover times, 66
Total customer satisfaction, 59–60
Toyoda, Kiichiro, 57
Toyoda, Sakichi, 32, 43, 56–57, 121
Toyota City, 89, 178, 179
Toyota do Brasil, 49, 55, 58, 60, 65
Toyota in Thailand (Siam Toyota Manufacturing), 76–91
Toyota Kaizen methods, 93–110, *See also* Kaizen
Toyota logistics, *See* Lean logistics
Toyota Motor Manufacturing Canada (TMMC), 189
Toyota Motor Manufacturing Kentucky (TMMK), 1, 3
employee suggestion system, 115–125
Toyota Motor Manufacturing Texas, 1

Toyota outsourcing, 161–162
Toyota Production System (TPS), 27–28, 127, 160, 177, *See also* Kaizen
  behavior/culture versus technology, 50
  GM problems implementing, 177–179
  House of TPS, 46, 51
  human factor, 38, 190
  importance of standard work, 21, 27–28, *See also* Standardized work
  Jidoka pillar, 43, 44–48, *See also* Jidoka
  Just-In-Time pillar, 46, 56, *See also* Just-In-Time
  logistics system design principles, 161, *See also* Lean logistics
  model-change process, 187, 204
  non-Toyota Lean systems versus, 46–47, 179–182
  precepts and principles, 121
  stability as heart of, 165
  successful implementation in non-Toyota facilities, 185–187
  symphony metaphor, 178
  time management before technology, 31–32
Toyota purchasing philosophy and practice, 128–129, *See also* Lean logistics
  abidance by the law, 131
  cost breakdown, 131
  Kaizen, 132
  mutual trust, 130
  open-door policy, 130
  target costing, 132
  Value engineering/value analysis, 128
  value engineering/value analysis, 132, 134–136
Toyota Supplier Technical Support, 130
Toyota's Vision 2010, 203
Trailer yard layout, 172–173
Training and standard work, 28–31
Training for Kaizen implementation, 108, 120, 125
Training managers, 140
Transportation cost, 161, 168–169
Transport/conveyance waste, 24, 61, 98, 127
Transport logistics, *See* Lean logistics
Tree of focused activity, 196

Tribal knowledge, 140, 151
"Triple crown" in Lean logistics, 169
True North, 193–194, 196
Tryouts, 30
Trystorming, 84
Turn-around time, 124

U

Understanding, 6
United Auto Workers (UAW), 177, 188

V

Value-added work, 95–97
  training and, 28
Value engineering/value analysis, 128, 132, 134–136
Value stream mapping, 104, 128, 143
Velocity, 165, 168
Video applications, 32–33
Vision 2010, 203
Visualization of problems, 82–83
Visual management, 14
  ABC parts analysis and segregation, 148
  developing productivity measures, 15–19
  making flow visible, 38
  planning process, 141–142
  trailer yard layout, 172–173
  understanding constraints, 141
Voice of the customer, 140

W

Waiting-related waste, 10–11, 24, 61, 98, 127
Waste, *See also specific types*
  definition, 60, 128
  incidental and pure, 97
  Kaizen principles, 95
  opportunities for improvement, 63
  in product design, 128–129, *See also* Toyota purchasing philosophy and practice
  production planning, 48–49
  the seven wastes (or Muda), 24–25, 51, 61–62, 98, 127–128

standards and finding, 10–11, 25
  understanding and, 6
  waiting, 10–11, 24, 61
Waste elimination
  cost reduction principles, 99
  Hoshin Kanri and, 189, *See also*
    Hoshin Kanri
  Jidoka as pillar of TPS, 44–48
  Just-In-Time and, 60–62
  Lean methodologies, 63
  in product design, 127–129, *See also*
    Toyota purchasing philosophy
    and practice
  using PDCA, 21, *See also* Plan-Do-
    Check-Act cycle
Wasteful action, 11
Weiss, Alan, 181
Wilburn, Darril, xv–xvi, 1–19, 72, 189–205
Womack, James, 53, 127

Work, types of, 195
Work and labor procedures and standard
    work, 29, *See also* Standardized
    work
Work element analysis, 103
Worker-management relationship,
    TPS implementation issues,
    187–188
Workforce balancing, 34
Workforce effectiveness, 150–151
Work in process (WIP) inventory, 24, 36,
    49, 57, 147
Work instructions and standard work, 29

Y

Yamazumi chart, 25, 34, 35*f.*
Yokoten, 90–91
Yoshiki, Hiro, 3